MW01591012

Terry J Woodhi

Oct 2013

Making Marathon

A History of Early Wyncote

~~~~~~~~~~~~~

Thomas J. Wieckowski

Copyright © 2009 by Thomas J. Wieckowski

ISBN 978-0-7414-5554-3

Cover: Robinson Park, Greenwood Avenue and Bent Road, the former H. K. Walt estate. Photograph by Thomas Wieckowski.

Published by:

INFINITY
PUBLISHING

INFINITY PUBLISHING
1094 New DeHaven Street, Suite 100
West Conshohocken, PA 19428-2713
Info@buybooksontheweb.com
www.buybooksontheweb.com
Toll-free (877) BUY BOOK
Local Phone (610) 941-9999
Fax (610) 941-9959

Printed in the United States of America

Published January 2013

Marathon

Marathon is a euphemism for a wonderful place in time: it stands for the village of Wyncote at its genesis near the beginning of the twentieth century. The term was adopted by Christopher Morley, a famous and prolific author and social critic, who lived in Wyncote while writing for the Curtis publishing empire. Although an urbane citizen of the world, he occasionally turned his attention and pen to life in the little village, and found many traits and customs, some laudable and others restrictive, that merited consideration and comment. His eye caught the beauty of the landscape and the upright - or uptight - conduct of its residents. He felt it necessary to disguise the object of his ruminations as protection from recrimination from potentially irate citizens. After all, he noted, it was a place where it is a "worse sin" to have your lawn uncut than your hair.

To

Sarah, Matthew, and Kathryn

The best kids a guy could have,

And my Mom, Wanda

Acknowledgments

I have benefited from the generosity of many knowledgeable people and I am most appreciative of their assistance. Thanks are due to David Rowland, President of the Old York Road Historical Society for his general support and encouragement. Many other colleagues at the Society contributed their expertise, and I thank in particular Joyce Root, our curator, who knows where everything is in our crowded archives, Millie Wintz for discussing historical issues, Betty Smith for sharing her experience in researching deeds, and Jack and Mary Washington for sharing their knowledge of Revolutionary War matters. I would like also to thank W. Kent Haydock for his willingness to share information about the Kent family as well as discussing fine points of Wyncote history; Donna Benner for her help with the archives of the Calvary Presbyterian Church and Linda Gunn at All Hallows Church; Rodman Barker for sharing knowledge and artifacts of the Barker family; David Harrower for sharing his research. Dorothy Lester Spruill is due thanks for guiding me through the archives of the Cheltenham Township Historical Commission as well as sharing her encyclopedic knowledge of Wyncote history. I thank my wife for putting up with my endless excited reports on the all-too-often trivial facts that I uncovered after a day's research. I thank my editor, Sarah Wieckowski, for her careful manuscript review and insightful suggestions, as well as for taking on this project at a very busy time. Thanks to Dr. Edward Trayes for sharing his expertise on the mechanics and aesthetics of creating a book. As always, I salute Rev. Sydney C. Burgoyne, teacher. Any shortcomings in this work are mine of course, but I could not have achieved anything resembling a worthwhile story without so much assistance.

Contents

PREFACE

As a young fellow growing up in Wyncote, I thought I lived in a perfect location: a suburb with a small-town feel and plenty of open space with nearby friends always ready to roam and explore the streams and woods. There was a long field across the street from my house on Glenside Avenue that was perfect for hitting fly balls or the Thanksgiving football scrimmage. The Tookany creek ran parallel to the field and was a constant source of fascination and distraction. It teemed with wildlife and, in the woods on the other side of Washington Lane, it had a deep hole in a bend around the jutting hillside that formed a perfect swimming spot for hot summer days. The hole was formed by the falling water of a small rivulet, which was fed by a spring further up the hill on the old Wanamaker estate. Before emptying into the creek, the spring nourished a sizable pond that was the site of winter bonfires and ice-skating.

Carousing in the woods, the game-making included poking through the debris occasionally in the hope of finding buried treasure like a six-shooter or bows and arrows. It was not until many years later that I learned that I was not too far off from reality: that very hillside above the swimming hole was an encampment for Continental troops during the Revolutionary War. A colleague from the Historical Society, poking in the debris as I did but with knowledge aforehand and a good metal detector, had actually found artifacts from that event, which now rest in the Cheltenham Township Wall House museum.

My affection for "home" was confirmed every Sunday when we travelled the short distance into the Kensington section of Philadelphia to visit my grandparents. As much as I loved them and the treats they provided, I felt greatly relieved to travel homeward, hanging out of the back window of my father's green 1939 Buick with my popsicle dripping down the side of dad's car. The air freshened, more trees appeared, and in the summer the temperature dropped by many degrees as we approached Chelten Hills Drive and drove along the creek. The dank cool woodland air, brushing my face through the open window, with its barely-there fresh scent of the ferns along the embankment, gave instant relief from the oppressive heat of the city.

As a boy, I was not particularly concerned about what happened on these grounds before me, other than recognizing and pondering briefly that the estate across the tracks shared its name with the big downtown department store with the organ and eagle. Like most young people, my conception of the world about me was that it coincided with my introduction into it.

To this day, I remember my first tickle of excitement that historic events stimulated in me, much the same way that people say you never forget your first kiss. A couple of the guys were shagging fly balls in the field when I went to retrieve a particularly long hit that landed in the rough at the end of the field near the Washington Lane bridge. I noticed an older gentleman poking through the rubble at the edge of the creek with a long, stout stick. My first thought was to hope that he knew about the poison sumac and prickly weed that infested that area. I am not sure what motivated me to be inquisitive, maybe only because I had to look for my baseball in the same place he was poking about. He mentioned that he was a local historian and was looking for signs of the old colonial mill – the Mather Mill - that once stood near this spot. The thought piqued my interest. Imagine: a mill from the days of the revolution on this spot.

Another pastime in the neighborhood provided many hours of adventure and exercise: we called it "Heacock hide and seek" but my parents called it "trespassing." At 110 Glenside Avenue, we lived next door to the Heacock homestead and were always enticed by the orchards and vineyards that the property afforded. The gray and square eminence of the Heacock mansion sat on the hillside next to our house maintaining a brooding eye on the lawn, street, field, and then creek below and woods of the Rodman Wanamaker estate beyond.

Further up the hill, Miss Heacock's skinny farmhouse faced east overlooking a broad lawn down to the street that bore their family name. My parents, as all parents in those days, were fastidious in their insistence that children should not go on other peoples' property without invitation. But the charms of the seemingly vast estate were too much to resist and Mr. Heacock in the big house and Miss Heacock in the farmhouse, while not overtly friendly to young interlopers on the very few occasions when they were encountered, were nonetheless not prone to complain.

The driveway from the mansion to Glenside Avenue, with its steep decline and soft curves was the neighborhood center for sledding after a winter snowstorm. Many a speeding rider overshot the end of the drive and ended up in the middle of the street, much to the horror of my parents, ever concerned about a tragic accident. Often the territorial violation was innocent as when the ball from our backyard game of catch went out of bounds into the vineyard. I would sneak through the gap in the boundary hedge and find the right row to enter and retrieve the ball. Occasionally I would take the opportunity just to stop and marvel at the quiet beauty of this hidden "backyard," but in season, the ripe fruits of the raspberry or blackberry vines would prove too enticing and I would have to snap off a couple of tasty berries or grapes for a quick treat, always glancing over my shoulder to see if anyone at the mansion was watching.

We did consciously trespass, however when we went up the hill to play "mountain climber." The object of our escapade was to climb the ebony conical pile that arose at the top of the hill out of the corral behind the big red barn. The mountain was made of coal, piled there during the summer in preparation for the long winter season in which the extensive Heacock greenhouses needed to be warmed. At least two stories high, we would clamber up, feet digging for traction in the loose coal, but often initiating an avalanche of craggy anthracitic chunks that noisily tumbled to the ground. We were always busted for this gig upon returning home by sharp-eyed parents who noticed the blackness of our hands and face and Stygian appearance of our otherwise colorful play clothes, sure clues as to the nature and location of our games.

One of the worst days of my life was coming home from college in 1962, after the Heacock property had been sold to a developer, and finding not only the farmhouse gone but the mansion sliced in two, half eaten it seemed, by a yellow monster bulldozer that sat parked after work hours in the driveway as if calmly digesting its prey. The destruction had reached the library, and hundreds of books, obviously not claimed by any remaining heirs of the Heacock family, were strewn about the rubble. My trepidation about trespassing and stealing was intense, and yet I sensed that I might be forgiven for salvaging some of these abandoned treasures. I have today on my bookshelf two books dated 1897, one signed by "E. Heacock" and the other by "J Heacock." I can bring myself to tears by thinking about what treasures were consigned to scrap by the powerful jaws of that yellow bulldozer.

Even with my new awareness, many years passed before I engaged my interest in the history of the area again. As I studied more about my particular neighborhood, I was captivated by the events I discovered and the people behind them. I recognized the charms of the area that brought the first residents who came from England in 1682, successive residents who came out by train to establish fine estates after the Civil War, and, finally, more ordinary people who discovered a comfortable suburb that flourished after World War II. Some of the residents were "rich and famous," to borrow a phrase from a popular '90s television program, but we all valued, I realized, the touch of nature, quiet residential streets, involved citizenry, many trees, and varied housing stock that distinguishes Wyncote.

The area is a beautiful community in which to live, and, for the historian or the person with just casual curiosity about how the village got to be the way it is, it is a treasure trove of interesting people and events. Poised on the outskirts of what was still America's greatest metropolis at the end of the nineteenth century, the community attracted some of the most important movers and shakers of the era. If one thinks of the illustrious residents of the Church Road corridor that runs through Wyncote, it is easy to name that thoroughfare Philadelphia's "Gilded Age Millionaires' Row." Just enumerate the names and history pops out at every turn. Starting at the western reaches of Church Road in the township at Willow Grove Avenue, we have traction magnate William H. Kemble; his son, Clay (the story of the area is very much a family affair); then sugar magnate William Welsh Harrison, and publisher George. H. Lorimer; John Gribbel; the several Lippincotts; bankers Abraham Barker and son Wharton; publisher Cyrus Curtis; and financier Jay Cooke. Step a few hundred yards off of Church Road to the right or left and one can add merchant John Wanamaker; P.A.B Widener; F. Eugene Dixon; William Elkins; John I. Rogers; another sugar magnate, Joseph S. Lovering; and Civil War hero and businessman, General Ario Pardee. Their wealth and ideals could not but help impact the tenor of the area. We will meet some of these remarkable people in this book.

A brief word about the maps that lead each chapter: they are meant to illustrate the changes that occurred over each period. Locations of indicated structures are approximate and some structures may not be indicated.

This book represents my desire to pull together many of the stories about the early development of the neighborhood of early Wyncote and the residents that shaped its formation. I had two goals in mind: to present a narrative of the unfolding story of Wyncote, and to present some of the long buried details and facts surrounding that story. The audience for one may not appreciate the other, but both are important. In particular I am indebted to my colleagues at the Old York Road Historical Society for their support and assistance with this project. I hope that it will contribute to an enduring appreciation for this fine village of "neat houses" and "sparkling sheets of water."

Thomas J. Wieckowski
Wyncote, Pennsylvania
March 2008

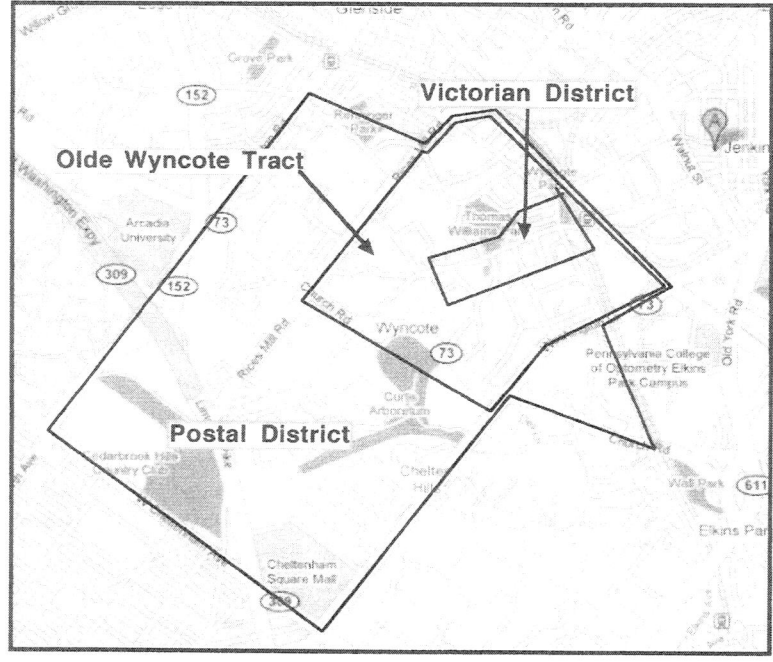

Three Definitions of Wyncote
The Olde Wyncote Tract, the Wyncote Post Office boundary, and the
Victorian Historical District.

Chapter 1

THE OLDE WYNCOTE TRACT

---

*We were whirled along with great speed along an exceedingly
beautiful country, in which cultivated farms and fields were
agreeably alternated with majestic and park-like groves, hill and
dale, and watered with sparkling brooks and streams.*
(Inquirer, 7/3/1855)

Wyncote is a small residential neighborhood in the
western part of Cheltenham Township, Pennsylvania, about
ten miles northwest of the center of the City of Philadelphia.
Gentle rolling landscape, a leafy green canopy of old trees,
and diverse housing stock define the village today much as it
did in the late 1880's when the first popular subdivisions
turned the former wooded estates of wealthy industrialists
and bankers into attractive residences for a more ordinary
population. A reporter for the *Philadelphia Inquirer* made
one of the first trips out of Philadelphia on the new railroad
through the area in 1855 and reported on the lush
countryside he found after "descending to the waters of the
Taconey [*sic*] Creek." Another Philadelphia newspaper in
1890 described the burgeoning village as containing "about
50 of the neatest and most substantial dwelling houses."

Where is Olde Wyncote? It seems presumptuous to call it
"Wyncote" in the era before it officially received its name
when there was nothing there but the thick canopy of trees,
subtle, sensuous terrain, stream and fields. To simplify, let's

call the area of our interest before 1887 "the Olde Wyncote tract." This definition recognizes the people, places, and events that defined the village before the time of its naming.

The Olde Wyncote tract is located in the western part of Cheltenham Township, northwest of Philadelphia. It is roughly a mile square and 320 feet above sea level. This area is hereby defined as follows: start at the northeast corner of the tract, Township Line Road and Washington Lane; move south on Washington Lane to Church Road; move west on Church; then north on Rices Mill Road to Glenside Avenue; east to Greenwood Avenue; east along the Township Line Road returning to the start point at Washington Lane. The properties on both sides of the boundary roads are included in this formulation of the tract. This definition, though arbitrary, was chosen for this study because it incorporates the homes and locations of most of the historic figures and events in the development of the village through the end of the 19th century. Conveniently, it has historical significance as it is also the definition proposed by the Wyncote Improvement Association for the "Borough of Wyncote" in 1893.

There are other definitions of Wyncote. The easiest definition, and most expansive, is that of the Post Office. This incorporates an area of approximately three square miles, but ignores the historical realities of the Olde Wyncote tract.

A more specific definition, "Victorian Wyncote," was created by preservationist Doreen Foust. Her research sought to identify the area of greatest historical architectural significance of the Victorian era. As a result, the Wyncote Historical District was established by Cheltenham Township in 1986. The district comprises an area of approximately 108 acres that is 80% populated by Victorian era residences and centers on the "downtown" business district below the Greenwood Avenue and Glenside Avenue intersection.

Later, we will explore the genesis of the name and the process by which the name was affixed to the village. It is a rare name. *The Old English Dictionary* parses it to mean "windy cottage." There is no other town in the United States with the name. However, there is a new golf club and housing development in rural Oxford, Chester County with the name of "Wyncote Golf Club." The developer, in response to the author's inquiry, indicated that the name was suggested to him by his wife after a visit to Great Britain. He also noted that he was unaware of the existence of the town of Wyncote in Pennsylvania when he embarked on his real estate development. (Pebble, 2003) The name is similarly rare in Great Britain with a web search turning up only a property development company in Surrey named "Wyncote Development Limited" and homes for sale on "Wyncote Way" in Surrey. There is a "Wyncote Yacht Club" in Huntington, Long Island and a "Wyncote Apartments" in Germantown, Philadelphia. There are a few streets that bear the name: "Wyncote Avenue" in Philadelphia, Rochester, New York, and Gloucester, Virginia; several named "Wyncote Road" as close as Jenkintown, PA, and as far away as Lingle, Wyoming, with samples in between in Cleveland, Ohio, Ho Ho Kus, New Jersey, Columbus, Ohio, and Bethel Park, PA; "Wyncote Lane" in Shawnee Mission, Kansas. "Wyncote Street" doesn't seem to have ever caught on. It would be an intriguing study to find out how the name migrated to these diverse locations through the years.

Wyncote itself doesn't have a thoroughfare named "Wyncote." It used to have a Wyncote Lane, but the name was changed about 1910 to honor a famous physician who built his home on that road, Dr. John B. Deaver.

The current names specified above all seem to have been appropriated after the official naming of Wyncote. However, there are two other locations by that name that are an integral part of the Wyncote story. They are the only examples of the name that pre-date the official naming of the post office. Their role in defining the town will be discussed later.

Before the original settlers started attaching prosaic English and Welsh names to these parts of the land, indeed before there was history itself, there was just a rolling landscape of fertile soil supporting an endless wilderness of thick woods where Wyncote now lies. In a practical as well as natural way, Wyncote today is the product of hundreds of millions of years of geologic history: we owe the modern appearance of the land and communities to the geologic forces that worked their slow-motion magic over the past 300 million years or so. The geologic terminology of that time frame is as daunting as the effort to comprehend the millions of years that the terms describe, but the settlement of our village as well as the state was affected by these geological realities.

During those eons, the great single continent of Pangaea split, tearing apart the neighborhood that had the whereabouts of, say, Dakar Africa as close on our east as Atlantic City perhaps is today. Wyncote found itself near the eastern edge of a new continent, on the geological line demarcating the coastal plain from the Piedmont. At the time of the Triassic period, the grand Appalachian Mountains began to age. Dinosaurs roamed what at one time was a tropical land during the Mesozoic era and left their footprints in some Triassic red mudstone deposits just north of us along route 309 on the way to Allentown. The last 24 million years, termed the Miocene Epoch, marked the sculpting of the land as we know it today. Erosion from the highlands to the lowlands continues to this day and the rivers and creeks that we see today were developed.

The modern geology of Pennsylvania divides the state into six geologic areas called physiographic provinces. Wyncote finds itself just on a line, running southeast to northwest, marking the transition between the hard rocks of the upland Piedmont province to the softer sedimentary lands of the Atlantic Coastal Plain.

The crushing forces of moving land masses that formed the mountains also formed ruptures or cracks in the earth's surface, called faults. We are more likely to associate earthquakes with the west coast with distinctive features such as the famous San Andreas fault, but we also have our own fault right here in Wyncote. The fault line lies below the bed of the Tookany creek that forms the most distinctive (though relatively minor as these things go) geological feature of Wyncote's landscape. Earthquakes have been recorded by the Indians as early as 1680 and experienced by village residents as recently as 1980 and 1994. The latter one registered 4.6 on the famous Richter scale: big enough to be noticeable and the source of water cooler conversation, though small enough to avoid the catastrophic damage of earthquakes in other regions that cause much more destruction and injury. The 1994 quake on January 7 was the biggest on record in Pennsylvania as of that date.

From earlier geologic periods, we inherited Wissahickon schist, the rock that underlies the region and provided ample building material for the substantial, hulking and gray houses that typify our village and neighboring communities throughout the Philadelphia region. Shale beds to the north provided the gray slate that distinguishes the roofs of our homes. Residents of Wyncote like to speculate on how much longer than a hundred years slate roofs will last as they gently rib owners of newer houses about their more modern – and more short lived – roofing materials.

The rich geological features of the landscape interested one visitor to the area in 1857. Bucks County namesake and historian, William J. Buck, viewed the deep railroad cut at Chelten Hills. He marveled not only at the size of the cut, but the plethora of rock samples that he was able to find.

About two hundred yards below the Chelten Hills station is one of the deepest cuts – for a number of miles distance on the road. It is fully forty feet in depth, and appears to divide the hill into two equal parts, and has required a vast amount of labor to achieve a level way through it. These excavations of which there are between Abington and York Road station some four or five, each from twenty to forty feet deep, afford to the geologist a fine study of the various strata of tocks that comprise the interior of the hills of this section. Perhaps few neighborhoods within the same distance afford a greater variety of stones, among which can be enumerated gneiss, quartz, talc, chlorite, schorl and mica. There afford also the following mixed species in abundance; micaceous gneiss, micaceous schorl, tacose and chlorite slate, serpentine, feldspar, etc. I found lumps of pure mica, of the size of an American dollar, which when split to the thickness of writing paper, was perfectly transparent. (Buck, 1857)

Another product of geological history, coal, also figures in the social history of our community. We have our position on the edge of the coastal plain to thank for the recurring periods of swamp and vegetation that covered our region through geological history and the decaying mass of which produced the coal beds that underlie most of the state. Coal is the most important mineral resource in Pennsylvania. The unique beds of the hard variety, anthracite, just to our north, fueled the industrial growth of our host city, Philadelphia, through the 19th century and provided the relatively clean, efficient heat for homes that made our village viable in the cold winter months.

In a way, the coal economy was also responsible for directly enabling the creation of the village in the late 19th century. Responding to the increasing demand in the metropolitan area for the valuable anthracite in the coal regions, investors created a railroad that would transport the coal to the factories and homes of Philadelphia. Eventually called the Reading Railroad, it passed through what would be called Wyncote in 1855 and provided a means for working in the city but living in the verdant countryside. The large Nicholson coal yard that operated on the Wyncote side of the railroad station at Jenkintown fed the local appetite for energy for almost a hundred years.

At the time of Columbus' discovery, the only occupants of the area were the local tribes of the Lenni Lenape nation whose name meant "the original people." The Indians of the North American continent were themselves immigrants about 16,000 years ago as Paleo-Indian explorers moved across the Siberian peninsula to Alaska and filtered south to people the lands of North America. One band settled in the area of the Delaware Valley, spreading from today's state of Delaware up to New York. European settlers, always bestowing their own brand of names freely on local places and peoples, renamed the Indians the "Delawares," a moniker itself derived from the name of Sir Thomas West, the Lord De La Warr, the first governor of the Virginia plantation.

The Lenni Lenape adapted to the geological features of the land by establishing their home villages in the area of the border between the coastal plain and the Piedmont. They planted vegetables in the spring – corn, squash, beans, pumpkin – then migrated to the coast – the first Jersey shore commuters – to fish and gather clams and oysters. Fall brought them back to the villages for harvest, then the migration reversed as they moved into the woods for the winter to hunt the abundant wildlife. There is little evidence of their existence today, except for the trail that early settlers found in pre-Wyncote days that would serve as a template for a colonial road. Running south to north, it would become today's Old York Road.

The Tacony creek (spelled differently earlier in this chapter: explanation later) may have been a route to the upland woods from the Delaware River where the Lenape had their major area village, Shackamaxon, in what is now the Kensington and Port Richmond sections of the city. The creek's name was derived from the Indian name, "Towacawonick," allegedly meaning "uninhabited place." Tamanend, the chief of the tribe in the late 17th century, met settler William Penn at Shackamaxon in 1682 and proclaimed that the Leni Lenape and the English "would live in peace as long as the waters run in the rivers and creeks and as long as the stars and moon endure" according to a report sent home by Penn. Early efforts to treat the indigenous people fairly included the practice of compensating the Lenape for the land obtained by the settlers and, for seven decades, the Europeans and the Indians coexisted peacefully as the Europeans slowly developed their farms. Tamanend became a folk legend representing the freedom of the American people from the English, and his name was adopted later by Jacob Barker, the grandfather of the late 19th century Philadelphia banker and Wyncote resident, Wharton Barker, as the name for his political clubhouse in New York City, Tammany Hall.

Many of the ancient Indian names survive today. Tinicum, originally "Blackbird Island" in the river near the airport, is used in several locations in the eastern part of the state, while Wissahickon ("catfish creek") describes a small river and its valley within the city of which, conversely, the Indians might still be proud. They might similarly recognize places along their Pennepack ("long still pond") creek. Manyunk ("place to assemble to drink," as in spirits) adjoins the expressway and still provides a location for that same social activity. Neshaminy and Nockomixon describe locations to the north and west.

Although the formal history of the area begins with Penn's grant in 1681, Europeans were evident in the area before then. English explorer, Henry Hudson, working for the Dutch East India Company, discovered the Delaware Bay in 1609 on his voyage to find a short trading route to Asia through the northern part of the continent. He did not spend much time in the Bay area – just enough to determine that.

Legacy Voices

Ken Benner
Hewett Road, Wyncote
Resident since 1971

In this oral history, excerpted below, Ken talks about finding Wyncote and his life-long interest in the Lenni Lenape Indians; collecting artifacts, and the history of the Indians.

TW: What brought you to Wyncote?

KB: My wife and I were looking for a place to buy a house. She worked downtown at Strawbridge and Clothier and I worked at the Upper Bucks Tech School. This place was just right, perfectly placed between the two, close to the train for her.

I was attracted to the house I guess because of the bird sanctuary out back. Coming from Quakertown which is very flat, I loved the hills. I loved the Victorian homes. It was a neat area and it didn't hurt that there was a tennis court up the street and I liked to play tennis. . . . I bought the house in 1971. . . . I have been very happy with Wyncote.

TW: How did you get interested in the history of the Lenni Lenape Indians?

KB: When I grew up in Trumbauersville, a lot of the locals told us that there were Indian villages many many years before, on the outskirts of Trumbauersville. When we had rainy weather and couldn't play baseball, we rode our bicycles out to one location, and we found arrowheads, and I got interested in the history of the Lenni Lenape Indians, and my collection grew and other people gave me their collections.

Recently I have been hunting in winter wheat fields, which have more narrow furrows than corn fields, but can still be productive.

We've got to keep in mind that the Indians have been here for 12 to 15 thousand years. We have been here for only three or four hundred. The evidence of their existence only remains in two ways: these artifacts that we find and the names that they left us.

I have no doubt that the Indians lived along the stream here as they did everywhere else. I am certain that things could be found around here. The problem is that nobody plows around here anymore.

TW: Judging from what you know, where would somebody who wanted to look find something along the Tookany Creek?

KB: Do you know where that Breyer estate was, there is high ground there, there are rock shelters there – Indians used to live in rock shelters. I would think that would be a good site. Going there after a storm . . . things could be found there. You have to look for shapes and colors. Arrowheads were made of flint or jasper, not common to this area. Jasper comes in yellow and red and brown and when it rains, dirt is washed off and they just stand out.

The full oral history can be found in the archives of the Old York Road Historical Society. http://OYRHS.org

his waterway pocked with shoals could not be a northwest passage. Hudson's report to his masters, while ignoring his detour from his northern route, extolled the apparent wealth of fur in the Delaware Valley region and later Dutch explorers exploited that resource by establishing trading posts and fur-trading networks with the Indians along the Delaware river basin. The various streams and creeks, starting with the Schuylkill river and Cobbs Creek, provided access to the interior for the traders and their Indian partners.

Tempted by the lack of Dutch investment in the new colonies of the Delaware, the Swedes ended the monopoly enjoyed by the Dutch in 1638 with the construction of Fort Christina near present-day Wilmington. Impressed by the supremacy of the Indians, they referred to the whole area of eastern Pennsylvania, southeastern New York, New Jersey and Delaware as "Lenapehocking" or "The Land of the Lenape." Schuyllkill ("noisy stream") is a remnant of the Dutch era and is used to name a county, river, and a noisy stream of highway through the city, (one suspects the Lenape would not be impressed!)

Finally, after Lord Baltimore concluded that his grant of Maryland included the lands occupied by the reticent Dutch, the British achieved control of the former Dutch areas with the Treaty of Westminster in 1674, setting the stage for the English settlement of the land to eventually be known as Wyncote.

Juliana's Cave
Juliana's cave can be seen along Chelten Hills Drive. According to local legend, it acquired the name from a member of Richard Wall's descendant family who, as a child, liked to escape the turmoil of a busy household and retreat to the cave to read. A remnant of the carriageway that John Wanamaker built to bring guests to his mansion from Church road along the scenic creek and past the cave can be seen as the horizontal line in the center of the photo. The last remaining lantern pylon can be seen in the foreground. The Breyer Estate townhouses now occupy the ground above.
Photo: Tom Wieckowski

Postscript

Juliana's cave has been known by that name in local lore for at least seventy years and most residents and local historians who can name the cave will mention the story of the young girl and her reading. Rev. S. F. Hotchkin, in his classic compendium of Old York Road sites, notes this landmark in 1892. He attributes the name to "Juliana Kirkbride, who was of a literary turn, and used to go there when she was living in Shoemakertown with the Shoemaker family" in the 1840s. (Hotchkin, 1892).

However, in 1941, resident Charles Sinkler, writing in his history of the Old York Road, takes the reader past the cave on his literary tour of the route. Sinkler writes: "there is still visible from the railroad St. Julian's cave, a favorite spot for swimming and picnicking." (Sinkler, 1941) Also, in a 1910 article in the *Public Spirit* (Hatboro) about John Wanamaker's improvements to his estate, the paper refers to the new road that "leads to Church road by way of Julian's cave along Tacony creek."

Interestingly, there is a Julian in history. St. Julian was a fourteenth century English mystic – and St. Julian was female. She was known as a hermit, once lived in a cave, and her writings are believed to be the first books written by a woman in the English Language. She is revered throughout England and Cheltenham in England has recognized St. Julian with a street, school, church, and a park.

How can this inconsistency in the local lore be reconciled? Perhaps myths change over time or multiple myths evolve lacking a solid factual base. Perhaps the British colonists endowed the cave with the lyrical reference to their hermit saint. Later generations, perhaps losing that original context, allowed the name to morph into a more familiar and secular form based on a more recognizable local figure. The answer remains elusive and wanting more data.

To add to the mystery of the name, the resident historian Horace Mather Lippincott tells the tale of Benjamin Lay, a member of the Quaker Meeting in Abington in the first half of the 18th century. According to Lippincott, Lay was an eccentric dwarf who was a vehement abolitionist and agitated widely against the institution of slavery in the colonies. The American Quaker poet, John Greenleaf Whittier, wrote about Lay in his introduction to a book on the problem of slavery. Whittier described Lay as "A figure only four and a half feet high, hunchbacked, with projecting chest, legs small and uneven, arms longer than his legs; a huge head, showing only beneath the enormous white hat, large, solemn eyes and a prominent nose." (Smellie, 1898) Like Julian, Lay also had hermit-like tendencies and lived in a cave on the property of Joseph Phipps from 1741 to his death in 1759. Phipps was one of the original land grantees in Abington Township (adjacent to Cheltenham) and his property lay across the township line from the property of Richard Wall, within walking distance to Juliana's cave.

As an example of Lay's antics, Whittier recounts the story of Lay's visit to one Quaker Meeting where leaders were gathered to confer about slavery:

In the midst of the solemn silence of the great assembly, the unwelcome figure of Benjamin Lay, wrapped in his long white overcoat, was seen passing up the aisle. Stopping midway, he exclaimed, "You slaveholders! Why don't you throw off your Quaker coats as I do mine, and show yourselves as you are?" Casting off as he spoke, his outer garment, he disclosed to the astonished assembly a military coat underneath and a sword dangling at his heels. Holding in one hand a large book, he drew his sword with the other. "In the sight of God," he cried, "you are as guilty as if you stabbed your slaves to the heart, as I do this book!" suiting the action to the word, and piercing a small bladder filled with the juice of poke-weed (*phytolacca decandra*), which he had concealed between the covers, and sprinkling as with fresh blood those who sat near him.

Lay was ultimately successful in his zeal as the Yearly Philadelphia Meeting of Friends adopted a resolution against the importation of slaves in 1758. Lay died one year later and is buried in the graveyard of the Abington Meeting, just a mile from the Olde Wyncote tract.

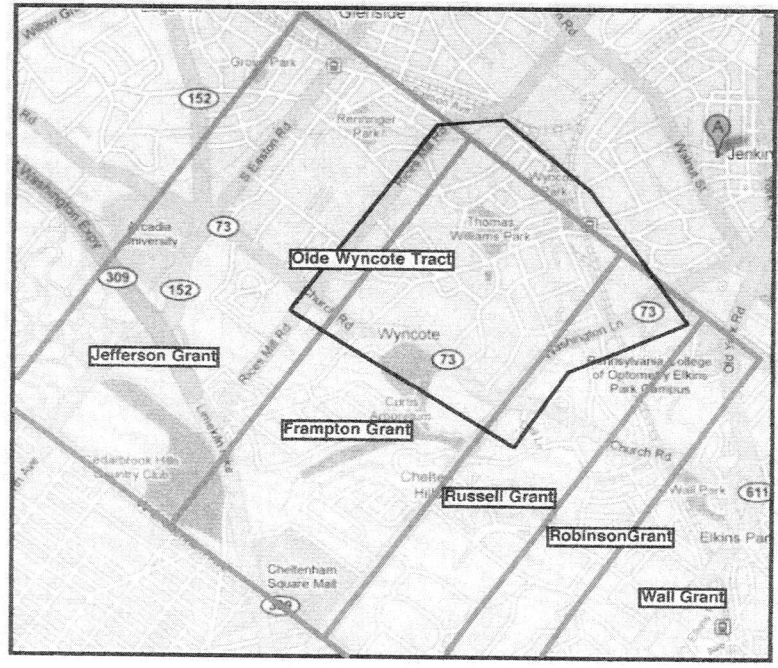

Penn's Colony - Grants by William Penn

The Cheltenham Penn grants in the area of the Olde Wyncote tract are superimposed upon a modern road map of the area. The only remnants of the original grant boundaries are Cheltenham Avenue (the city line), Township Line Road and Glenside Avenue (the Abington Township line), and most of Washington Lane. Note that the Paxson Avenue neighborhood (Beechwood Heights), shown here within the Olde Wyncote Tract, was originally on the Abington side of the township line, as was Knight's mill.

Chapter 2

PENN'S COLONY

Every countryman, even though he were the poorest peasant, had an orchard with apples, peaches, and such fruits. (Kalm, 1773)

If a new city should be associated with a particular man, the City of Philadelphia and the host province of Pennsylvania are immediately synonymous with the name of William Penn. While the founding of Cheltenham Township occurred concurrently with the founding of the city and the colony, the birth of the entity called Wyncote had to wait another two hundred years. However, the Quaker influence that Penn imported to his colony would influence both for many years in the future.

Born in London in 1644 to an Admiral in the Royal Navy, Penn left the state-approved Anglican religion to become a Quaker at the age of twenty-two. He traveled widely through Europe and Ireland, the latter the site of his father's estates, which he inherited. Although he lived well, Penn sought a way out of his financial debt, which, by 1680, had amounted to over a million dollars in today's value. His petition to King Charles II to repay a debt of eleven thousand pounds owed to his father from his activities during the Dutch war of 1665 resulted in an offer by the impecunious king of land in the new world. Although an outright payment would have resolved his financial problems quickly, Penn realized the potential of great financial rewards in creating a new colony. So, Penn's endeavors were first and foremost a business enterprise.

Penn's travels as well as his religious leanings led to distinct ideas of what an ideal city should look like, and when he received lands in the New World from King Charles II, Penn was eager to apply his developing religious and social ideas to the new colony. His efforts would be known as "The Holy Experiment." He himself bestowed the name of "Philadelphia" on the city, meaning the city of brotherly love. Among the ideals he reflected in his design were the pledge to treat the Indians fairly, the lack of ramparts to guard the city as other colonies required, and the desire to design a healthy "greene country town."

When his agents arrived in September, 1681, they set about selecting a site for the proposed city and found relatively high land on the west bank of the Delaware just above the Schuylkill river. They found about 2000 European settlers in the vicinity with less than 50 within the bounds of the city. By this time, the Indians were all but pushed back from the region but Penn still moved forward with his plan to "purchase" the land from them, leading to the famous if mythical meeting with Chief Tamanend at Shackamaxon.

Penn himself arrived in his new colony in August of 1682 aboard the ship *Welcome*. Penn's surveyor, Capt. Thomas Holme, laid out a city of precise grids from river to river, and divided the surrounding countryside in proportion to the investment each customer wished to make. His work is reflected in the iconic map of 1682 which identifies many of the original purchasers and is contained in the collection of the Historical Society of Pennsylvania.

Among Penn's most noteworthy attributes was his skill as a salesman. He had thrown himself into the work of promoting his new colony and, in 1681, published his pamphlet, *Some Account of the Province of Pennsylvania*. He depended on his Quaker confreres to distribute the pamphlet through England and Ireland, Scotland and Wales, and had it translated for distribution in Holland and Germany, thus assuring a diverse population by culture, but appealing to the Quaker principles of political liberty and freedom that he desired for his new province.

Penn's desirable sales price of two shillings per acre (about twelve cents) was far below the cost of land in England and Ireland, insuring him a ready market of buyers, but also inhibiting the profit he would make on his enterprise. (Penn would die penniless.) Anticipating a practice that today's professional marketers would call a "loss leader," Penn sought to insure sales of undesirable land in the wilderness by offering discounts on the more desirable city plots for large purchases on the outskirts, or directly requiring the outlying purchase in order to obtain choice city lots. This alluring bait proved to be very successful as groups of neighbors in Europe banded together to purchase large plots. Fifty shiploads of customers landed at Philadelphia in the first year of operation thus insuring the necessary critical mass for a successful venture.

Holme's map shows the parcels of such a group, at least two members of which were from Cheltenham, England, that purchased land in the northwest environs of the city. In fact, the Cheltenham "plantation" was part of Philadelphia County as Montgomery County was not created until 1784 when Cheltenham was split off as part of the new county. The fifteen purchasers of this block included William Frampton and John Russell who owned slices that were to contain the future village of Wyncote. Another innovation Penn allowed was to grant naming rights to group purchasers as well as the right to establish their own local government. Thus the Cheltenham group honored their plantation by choosing the name of "Cheltenham Township" for their new home. The relationship continues today as Cheltenham, in Gloucestershire, in south central England just northwest of London, is Cheltenham Township's sister city.

William Frampton had first settled in New York before purchasing his Cheltenham property. He may have been one of the forced investors in the outskirts as he opened a "brew and bake" house on the city waterfront and apparently never lived in Cheltenham. His plot forms the western half of the Wyncote tract.

Excerpts from

Some Account of the Province of Pennsylvania

Since (by the good providence of God) a country in America is fallen to my lot, I thought it not less my duty than my honest interest to give some public notice of it to the world, that those of our own, or other nations, that are inclined to transport themselves or families beyond the seas, may find another country added to their choice.

I shall take leave to say something of the benefit of plantations or colonies in general, to obviate a common objection.

Colonies, then, are the seeds of nations begun and nourished by the care of wise and populous Countries, as conceiving them best for the increase of human stock, and beneficial for commerce.

With justice, therefore, I deny the vulgar opinion against plantations, that they weaken England. They have manifestly enriched and so strengthened her, which I briefly evidence thus:

1st. Those that go into a foreign plantation, their industry there is worth more than if they stayed at home . . .

2dly. More being produced and imported than we can spend here, we export it to other countries in Europe which brings in money or growth of those countries . . .

3dly. Such as could not only not marry here, but hardly live and allow themselves clothes, do marry there, and bestow thrice more in all necessaries and conveniences for themselves, their wives, and children . . .

4thly. But let it be considered that the plantations employ many hundreds of shipping and many thousands of seamen, which must be in diverse respects an advantage to England, being an island . . .

> These persons that Providence seems to have most fitted for plantations are,
>
> 1st. Industrious husbandmen and day laborers . . .
> 2dly. Laborious handicrafts, especially carpenters, masons, smiths, . . .
> 3dly. A plantation seems a fit place for those ingenious spirits that being low in the world, are much clogged and oppressed about a livelihood.
> 4thly. A fourth sort of men to whom a plantation would be proper, takes in those that are younger brothers of small inheritances . . .
> Lastly, there are another sort of persons, not only fit for, but necessary in plantations, and that is, men of universal spirits .

John Russell's plot of 300 acres contains the eastern half of the Wyncote tract. Unlike Frampton, he moved to Cheltenham immediately and constructed a home just north of Cheltenham Avenue on what is now the Lynwood Gardens apartment complex. That home survived until 1949. His daughter's marriage to Joseph Mather in 1697, brought one of the most enduring names to Cheltenham and Wyncote and a grandson would eventually build the first home in the Wyncote tract.

Two other properties, while not a part of the Olde Wyncote tract, are of importance to the history of the village.

Mary Jefferson and her husband purchased three hundred acres immediately to the west of the Olde Wyncote tract. This plantation now constitutes the western part of modern Wyncote (to, roughly, Easton Road). Edward Jefferson apparently died on the voyage to the new land and Mary soon married Thomas Phillips, the owner of the next plantation to the northwest of hers. She also never lived in Cheltenham and, although she and Thomas were known to have lived at their city property, nothing further is known of their time in America.

Richard Wall Sr. and Jr. purchased slices of land in the Cheltenham plantation to the southeast of the Olde Wyncote tract. Wall built a house at today's intersection of Church Road and York Road immediately upon his arrival in 1682 and it became a center of development and the site of the first Quaker Meeting in the area. The house, greatly expanded through the years, still survives and serves as a Cheltenham Township museum.

It was at this time that the modest stream passing through the area achieved its distinctive name in Cheltenham. Although the stream was named "Tacony Creek" or "Frankford Creek" by the early settlers and by Holme on his map of the city, the settlers in Cheltenham enshrined what was probably a phonetic variation of the name into their usage. The early minutes of the Society of Friends indicates the desire of the Friends in the area of the "Tookany" in Cheltenham to establish a more convenient location. The result was that a "Meeting was settled near Cheltenham at the house of Richard Wall." (Quoted in Morgan, 1938) Morgan goes on to discuss the misspelling of his own ancestor's name and notes that such misspelling was common in an era when "education was scarce, handwriting was not too good, spelling inaccurate."

Penn himself would not stay long enough to see the beneficial results of his adventure first hand. He sailed back to England in 1684 and faced further problems with the finances of his colony. He eventually ended up with twice the debt that was owed his father and spent the bulk of his remaining years in debtor's prison.

In earliest colonial times, navigable waterways were virtually the only means of transportation of people and goods between settlements and outside of the population centers of the new colonies. The merchants of Philadelphia of the first half of the 18th century enjoyed a virtual monopoly in area trade as all waterways led to the city, which like all trading centers in the area, was on a waterway.

It is hard to imagine how Wall and Russell (and the other grantees) managed to find their inland property in the northwest environs of the city, let alone move there with their families. Movement through the unmarked backcountry in the early days of the colony was solely by means of walking the Indian trails with all belongings strapped to the back. In more heavily traveled portions of the trails, packhorses may have been used along wider portions of the well-used but rutted Indian paths. The route that Russell and Wall used was a well established "aboriginal trail," as the resident-historian Lippincott termed it, that stretched from the new city of Philadelphia, through Bucks county to today's New Hope, through New Jersey, to salt water at Elizabeth, New Jersey. The new plantations had to be self sufficient for lack of neighbors and long distances to the city center for the purchase of essential food and household goods. Even two hundred years later, Horace Mather Lippincott remembered the "blizzard of '88" (1888, that is) that kept his family indoors at his home at Washington Lane and Church Road for a week. He recalls that, "like every place in the country then, we were self-contained with horses, a cow, chickens, a root-cellar for potatoes, parsnips, turnips and beets, and a smoke house for dried beef and pork." (Lippincott, 1938).

The importance and accessibility of this trail is evident in the string of early settlements that fanned out from the city along it: Branchtown (Oak Lane), Shoemakertown (Elkins Park), Jenkin's Town (Jenkintown), Hill's Township (Abington), and Crooked Billet (Hatboro). As the population grew and the backcountry was developed, new means of transportation needed to be found. The construction of roads served this purpose. The initial sign of development in the area of the Wyncote tract was the construction of the road to New York.

Realizing the importance of roads to the development of the backcountry as well as for communication with other colonies such as New York to the north, the Provincial Council of the colony appointed a committee in 1686 to study the problem of roads and several were authorized north and south from the city as well as west to Lancaster. In 1711, the Council was petitioned by a group of landowners around Cheltenham to construct a road northwest out of the city and on to New York. The Council went on to specify a road from north to south that began "on the side of the River Delaware opposite John Reading's landing, . . . to Stephen Jenkins on the West side of his house, and from thence the most Direct & Convenient Course by the House of the late Richard Wall . . ." (quoted in Lippincott, 1943). The family of Stephen Jenkins gave its name to the town that eventually developed around his house and homestead and Wall's successors, the Shoemakers, gave their name to the village that surrounded their farm and mill. The surveyors appointed to the task of laying out the road apparently didn't see any better route for the road than the established and well-situated Indian trail and simply superimposed the route of the York Road directly on the path of the existing trail. Traversing open and mostly undeveloped land, one would expect this to be an easy solution, but politics intervened even then. Several land owners complained about infringements on the continuity of their various properties and the final route was stalled for almost a year. Members of the committee that authorized the road included Abington resident Isaac Knight (owner of a mill just northwest of the Wyncote tract later known as Rice's Mill), Toby Leech (an original Cheltenham purchaser to the north west of the Wyncote tract), Stephen Jenkins (of future Jenkintown), and George Shoemaker (heir to Richard Wall).

The course of the road was finalized on January 7, 1714 and thus the first official thoroughfare in Cheltenham Township was created. The building of the York Road was a considerable human accomplishment. Built through wilderness without benefit of dynamite or power machines, the road was only wide enough at first for an oxen team and wagon but it greatly improved access to the Olde Wyncote tract and its environs. The first wagons were used on the road in the 1740's followed by a stagecoach line in 1756. The coach ride took three days for the run from Philadelphia to New York at a cost of two pence per mile traveled.

In a similar nearby setting, Thomas Twining, the famous British tea magnate, described a stagecoach ride from Philadelphia to Baltimore during his visit of 1795. He noted immediately that the wagons were nothing like the luxurious coaches in use in Great Britain. He clearly was not impressed with this "rude conveyance."

The vehicle was a long car with four benches. A light roof was suspended from eight slender pillars. There was no place nor space for luggage, each person being expected to stow his things as he could under his seat or legs. There were no backs to the benches to support or relieve us during a rough and fatiguing journey over a newly and ill made road. (Twining, 1893)

The scale of the 18th century city and its environs were quite different from the present. Today's readers may experience a conceptual time-warp when confronted with a description such as Twining's continuing narrative:

At half-past ten the wagon started up High Street [now Market Street]. Upon leaving the city we entered immediately upon the country, the transition from streets to fields being abrupt, and not rendered gradual by detached houses and villas, as in the vicinity of London. The fields, however, had nothing pleasing about them, being crossed and separated by the numerous intersections of the intended streets, and surrounded by large rough-hewed rails, placed zigzag, instead of hedges. We soon reached the Schuylkyl.

The first road in the Wyncote tract itself was the Abington to Germantown Road, named for the access it provided to the Abington Meeting House from the Germantown Meeting House, which was administratively attached to the Abington Meeting. This road, later renamed Washington Lane to honor the general's Revolutionary War march to the Battle of Germantown, was constructed about 1715 along the boundary between the Mather and Frampton properties, although the path may have been in use shortly after the construction of the Meeting in 1702.

Off the northwest edge of the Wyncote tract, a road was constructed about 1715 as a result of an important discovery in neighboring Whitemarsh Township. In 1686, lime was discovered by an early settler, Thomas Fitzwater. Because of its value in the construction process, he erected a kiln to process the lime and a road was ordered to bring the lime to the Philadelphia market. The road is still known as Limekiln Pike today.

Next, Church Road, on the southern side of the Wyncote tract, was laid out in 1732 for the convenience of the minister of the Episcopal church who needed to move between Trinity Church at Oxford, north east of Wyncote, and St. Thomas Church at Whitemarsh, several miles west of Wyncote. Both churches were founded at the end of the 17th century and Ralph Morgan imagined the trials as "the good man conducted service at one end of the road on the Sabbath morning, and rode his horse through heat and dust or mud and cold the length of this highway to conduct a

service at the other end in the afternoon." (Morgan, 1938).
Bean identified the minister:

The Church road was so named from the fact of its being traveled
for a number of years by the late George Keith, then a celebrated
minister of the Society of Friends, who preached at Oxford and at
Whitemarsh. His oft-repeated journeys over this then crooked
path gave it the name of Church road, which it has since retained.
(Bean, 1884)

Keith, "the unhappy apostate," a friend of William Penn,
began his religious life as a Quaker but eventually rejected
that practice and associated himself with the Episcopal
Church as an itinerant minister.

In 1725, Isaac Knight, the owner of a large farm in
neighboring Abington Township, constructed a mill on the
northwestern edge of the Wyncote tract at what would
become Rices Mill Road and Glenside Avenue, although
Glenside Avenue was still more than a hundred years from
realization. The site of the mill was still part of Abington
Township at that time. This was the same Knight that served
on the jury authorizing the York Road. The mill stood in the
rolling countryside by the Tookany Creek with access from a
road leading north of the mill to the northern boundary of
Knight's property at Susquehanna Road. Access to the mill
on the Cheltenham side was created from Church Road in
1741 and the road simply was called Mill Road. After the
Revolution, the mill would belong to the Paxson family and
then to Daniel Rice, for whom the Cheltenham access road
was finally named.

Thus the boundaries of the Olde Wyncote tract were
framed within the first fifty years of occupancy in the area,
but, for the tract, time stood still as more roads would not
appear for more than a hundred years.

William Webster whose family owned large parcels along
the York Road strip in Jenkintown, purchased 200 acres of
property running along the west side of the Abington to
Germantown road in the Olde Wyncote tract in 1749 (for
600 British Pounds), from Thomas Carvel (or Carvell),
successor to the William Frampton grant. Carvel was a
church warden at Oxford Church, at the end of Church Road
no doubt became familiar with the area on his frequent and

Knight's mill about 1880
This picture was taken before the second level was added no later than 1897. By this time, it was owned by Daniel R. Rice who operated it as the Green Bank Flour Mill. The mill was of the internal wheel type, typical of the mid-Atlantic states, and probably used an "overshot vertical" water wheel which was fed by a mill race from further upstream. The mill race entered from the west, the other side of the building in this photo. The mill race became the road bed for Glenside Avenue between Easton Road and the mill. Today's Glenside Avenue is seen in the foreground. By the time of this photograph, the mill may have been converted to steam power as indicated by the smoke stack in the rear.
Photo: OYRHS

travels with Rev. Keith between the two churches at either end of the road. Webster established a farm on the fallow ground and probably built the first house in Wyncote. Webster's farmhouse, which later became the Heacock farmhouse, was built perhaps in mid-18th century, – some say at the time of or before the Revolution - on the hillside overlooking a small run to the Tacony Creek (now Heacock Lane) and facing the "Road from Abington to Germantown," as Washington Lane was still referred to at the time and in his deed as well. The best documentary evidence of the early date exists in Annie Heacock's memoir. She states: "The eastern half of the house in which I live stood during the Revolution." (Heacock, 1926) After Washington Lane was diverted, a driveway, the only access to the farm since Maple

Avenue, Heacock Lane and Glenside Avenue did not yet exist, ran from the farmhouse down into the trough of the small creek, and up the hill to intersect with Washington Lane opposite today's entrance to Serpentine Lane.

Another mill on the opposite side of Wyncote was established soon after Knight's. John Russell's plantation, the southeastern slice of the Wyncote tract, passed to his daughter Elizabeth and her husband Joseph Mather upon Russell's death in 1698. The Mathers lived in the Russell homestead on the Abington Road to Germantown (future Washington Lane) just north of today's Cheltenham Avenue along with their five children. Their son Richard inherited the property upon Joseph's death in 1724. Richard and his wife, Sarah, had three sons: Isaac, Bartholomew, and Benjamin. Benjamin continued to live in the family homestead but Isaac was given property at the north end of the plantation. He constructed his home and a grist mill along the Abington Road to Germantown in 1769. The home stood on the southeast side of Abington Road about halfway up the hill from the Tookany creek to present day Township Line Road. The mill was constructed about 50 yards north of Tookany creek, just a couple of hundred yards southeast of the Abington to Germantown Road. One visitor described the setting: "the click-clack of the mill could be heard from every hill. This one is at least a hundred years old and its approach along the water course leading up to it is most picturesque." (Chelten Hills, 1890) In order to power a water mill, water needed to drop at least a couple of feet in height to power the wheel that drove the grinding stone. Since there was no suitable natural drop in land along that part of Tookany creek, Mather purchased land about a quarter of a mile west, built a dam to raise the water level, and created a small lake. A raceway took the raised water on a course parallel to the creek to the mill. The mill served until about 1860 and later, John Wanamaker turned it into a powerhouse for his estate. The site today rests under a landfill for the south parking lot of the Wyncote House. Remnants of the mill survived until the construction of the new Washington Lane viaduct in 1958, and a section of the millrace survived a few more years until the Wyncote House parking lot was graded.

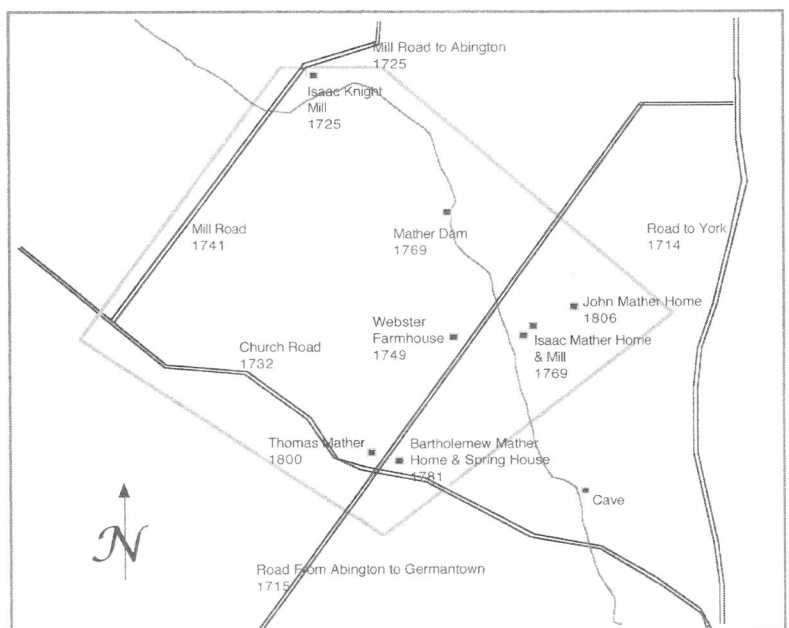

The Olde Wyncote Tract between Penn and 1800
In the hundred years since Penn's founding, the tract only gained three roads, two mills, and five homes. The first signs of industry appeared in the construction of two grist mills.

Isaac's brother Bartholomew, a wheelwright, inherited the central section of the Russell plantation. He had the distinction of holding the position of tax assessor in Cheltenham, the only public office in the township at the time and he constructed a residence at the northeast corner of Abington to Germantown Road and Church Road in 1781. This intersection saw the transit of numerous troops during the Revolutionary War and provided nourishment thanks to the spring at the site. The homestead stood deserted and vandalized for many years until demolished for an office building in 1980.

Mather Dam and Mill Pond about 1864
Nelson Collins, writing in 1954, noted that the pond silted up and for
"many years was a weed-grown meadow where Maryland Yellowthroats
and other swamp-loving birds nested." (Collins, 1954). The area in view is
now covered by the Jenkintown train station parking lot and Morgan
Park. The single track of the North Pennsylvania Rail Road is hiding in
the grass below the fence of the Kent estate.
Photo: Courtesy of the Old York Road Historical Society, Kent collection

The last homes of the colonial era were constructed just
after the end of the Revolutionary War. In 1800,
Bartholomew gave a piece of his land across Washington
Lane from his homestead to his son, Thomas Mather, who
constructed a home he called "Shadyside." The home
became the Hopkins Nursing Home and was demolished in
1976 for a modern expansion of the home. In 1806, Isaac
Mather built a house on part of his land just up the hill from
his own house abutting the line between Abington and
Cheltenham at the corner of today's Washington Lane and
Township Line Road, for his son, John. His son, Isaac P.
Mather, the "grand old man of Chelten Hills," obtained the
land – seventy acres of Isaac Mather's share of 100 original
acres - in 1853 at which time a "public Road" was opened
from the home along the township line to the York Road.

Isaac Mather lived there until his death at the age of one hundred and one in 1907. This home was demolished in 1962.

The allure of this countryside was captured by a British visitor to the area just before the Revolution. Riding out from the city through the northwest countryside with his host, he marveled at the beauty of the surroundings:

As we went on in the wood, we continually saw, at moderate distances, little fields which had been cleared of the wood. Each of these was a farm. These farms were commonly very pretty, and a walk of trees frequently led from them to the high-road. The houses were all built of the stone which is here commonly met with. Every countryman, even though he were the poorest peasant, had an orchard with apples, peaches, and such fruits. (Kalm, 1773)

Mather Mill, about 1893, from Washington Lane after Wanamaker converted it to a powerhouse.
Photo: Courtesy of the Old York Road Historical Society

Mather Mill about 1852
The mill was painted by American artist, Xanthus Smith, a resident of
Glenside. The view appears to be from the northwest judging from the
angle of the shadow of the tree and the position of the chimney. It shows
the original front of the building as indicated by the covered crane jutting
out from the roof. The crane was used to lift bags of grain to the top floor.
Photo: Courtesy of the Old York Road Historical Society

The Isaac Mather Homestead

The Isaac Mather home stood on the hillside above (north) of the mill. In this photograph taken near the end of the nineteenth century, additions erected by John or Rodman Wanamaker almost obscure the original stone structure. The chimney from the power plant in the old mill can be seen rising to the right. Washington Lane is to the left, although the building faced the original course of the "Road from Germantown to Abington" which was to the right. The site is now the Wyncote House apartment building. *Photo courtesy of the Old York Road Historical Society*

John Mather Residence
Isaac Mather built this home in 1806 for his son John just up the hill from his own home. Pictured here about the end of the 19th century, it became the home of John's son, Isaac P. Mather who lived here for more than a century. *Photo: Old York Road Historical Society*

Mather Residence 1962
The last vestige of the colonial era was left high and dry by the reconstruction of Washington Lane in 1958. It sat forlornly on a pedestal created when Washington Lane was widened and dropped by twelve feet. It was demolished to provide space for a swimming pool and a cabana at the new Wyncote House apartments.
Photo: Courtesy of the Old York Road Historical Society

The Bend in the Road

If you drive north on Washington Lane from the city, Cheltenham Avenue to Township Line Road to be exact, you might note that the road is straight as an arrow until you reach Maple Avenue, where the road bends to the right to go over the bridge spanning the creek and the railroad tracks. Yet we know that "the road from Abington to Germantown" was laid out in a straight line in 1715 along the boundary of John Russell's and William Frampton's original land grants. How did it get its curve?

The resident and historian Horace Mather Lippincott, in his 1910 history of the Mather family, confirms that the road was laid out in a straight line, but that "this turn was caused by Isaac Mather about 1800 so as to reach his mill which still stands at Chelten Hills Station." (Lippincott, 1910) The mill is gone but the curve is still there. The last vestige of the old route of Abington to Germantown Road is the boundary line of Joseph Heacock's purchase from Wm. C. Kent in 1857. The twenty-two acre property is almost a square except for a cut-out at the southeast corner that is marked as the property of Isaac Mather. This parcel is part of his original land grant that was east of the original road and colonial boundary. Heacock obtained this seven-acre wedge from Mather in 1859 to complete his twenty-nine acre farm. The property is also almost a triangle except for a small bump-out at the south tip of the parcel. This is the piece where the bend in Washington Lane began. In a deed dated April 5, 1787, Isaac Mather sold this strange little two acre triangle to William Webster, who already owned the farm to the northwest that eventually became the Heacock farm. This triangle represents the departure point of the new route of the road from the original route. The boundary going to the northwest from that point is the location of Heacock's future Maple Avenue.

This change explains several descriptions of troop movements during the Revolutionary War that indicate that the march up the road deposited troops in the center of Jenkintown rather than on its outskirts. An interesting exercise is to lay a ruler on the remaining original route and see that Washington Lane at one time went through the land about to the right of where the stucco twin houses at 108-110 Glenside Avenue stand today.

One wonders why Mather, wanting so badly to have immediate access to the Abington to Germantown Road, didn't just build his mill 567 feet to the west on the old route of the road?

This little land transfer also sheds light on another mystery.   Several earlier writers, including Lippincott, speculated that the Heacock farmhouse was not built by Joseph Heacock, but existed prior to his purchase in 1857, possibly even before the revolution.   No documentary evidence has come to light that establishes a date for the house, which, of course, is now gone thus barring any archeological research.   The location of the farmhouse relative to Washington Lane is problematic. If Heacock built it, why was it constructed so far (356.5 feet) from the nearest road, Washington Lane? Most farmhouses of that era were built directly on the road to provide easy access to the home and transportation. On the other hand, if Webster built it – in other words, if it were built before the 1787 land transfer, the analysis above indicates that the home was built right next to the old route of Washington Lane, a location that would have been expected.

One also can't help looking suspiciously at the location and size of the Mather-to-Webster bump-out. What was the reason for the dimensions and location of the odd parcel? Could it have been totally arbitrary?   The starting point makes sense, however. Note that it is on the line separating Isaac Mather's land from that of his brother Bartholemew. So if Isaac wanted to divert the road to his mill, that point of divergence is the first opportunity to do so on his own land. So then, what about the location of the eastern boundary of the bump-out? Note that the shift of route of the road would have left Webster's homestead landlocked, without access to the new Abington to Germantown Road. This would not be a tenable position for either Mather or Webster. Analysis of the 346.5 foot boundary indicates that it lies right next to the known 19th century driveway from the farmhouse to the new route of Washington Lane.

Thus it seems that the sale of the parcel to Webster, albeit reluctant (after all, Mather did not give up the adjoining seven-acre wedge for another seventy-two years), was a means of establishing Washington Lane frontage to Webster for his farmhouse. Therefore the farmhouse must have been there at least since 1787, and probably shortly after Webster purchased the property for his farm from Thomas Carvel in 1749.

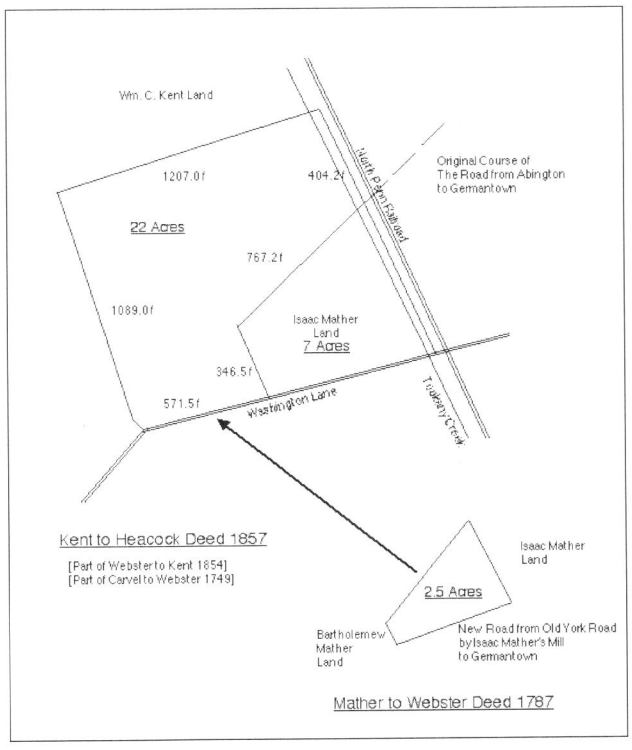

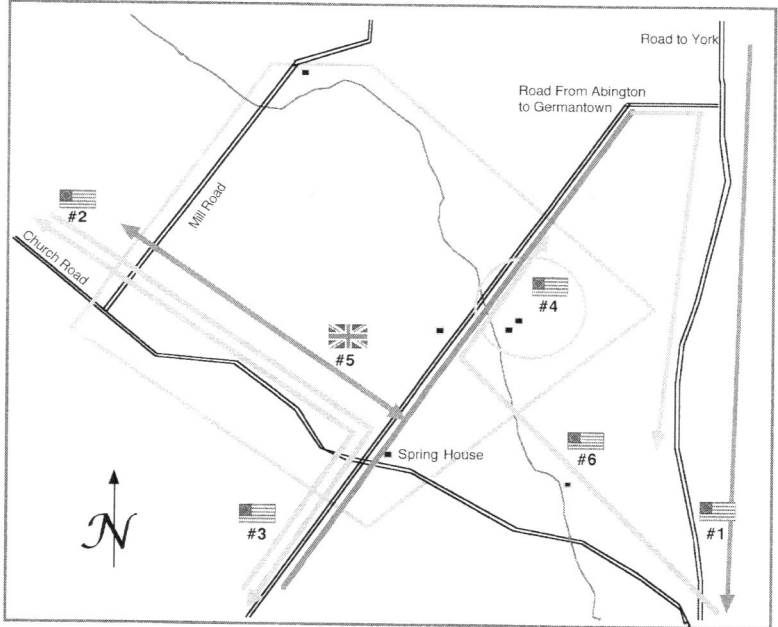

The War of Independence

The Olde Wyncote tract saw the movement of American and British troops through the area, including an encampment of American troops on Mather Hill after the Battle of Germantown.

Chapter 3

THE WAR OF INDEPENDENCE

Here was country hilly and wooded. McLane
swerved suddenly from the road,
bending low in his saddle as he galloped
across broken ground into the trees,
(Allan McLane, 1778)

The War of Independence was played out on two local stages. The more visible drama consisted of the activities of the troops on both sides as they maneuvered and met in battle. Although no important military conflicts occurred in the Olde Wyncote tract, it saw frequent troop movements due to its strategic location near key roads. Skirmishes occurred as close as Ogontz, Edge Hill, Germantown, and Crooked Billet (Hatboro). The other conflict was less apparent, but no less painful. It was the battle for loyalty among the population to either the new republic or the King of England. Both scenarios played out across the colonies and in the Olde Wyncote tract.

That glorious Wednesday, July 4, 1776, was the formal beginning of the struggle for independence, but a hostile environment had already existed for years in the colonies by that time. General Thomas Gage, the British North American commander-in-chief, supervised four regiments of British regulars from his headquarters in Boston. This force constituted about four thousand men. Another 4,500 troops arrived in June of 1775. The British presence would eventually reach 60,000. Also in that month, the Continental Congress created a regular army and appointed George Washington as commander-in-chief. General Washington rode out of Philadelphia on June 23, 1775, to proceed to Boston and begin the work of assembling the Continental army.

After Independence was declared the following summer, skirmishes in Massachusetts and New York erupted and the British, commanded by General William Howe, moved south to the capital city of the insurrection, Philadelphia. Conventional military thinking of the day stipulated that subduing the capital would cripple a rebellion. However, General Washington repelled the British advance, at least for the time being, with his surprise crossing of the Delaware on Christmas night in 1776 and the subsequent defeat of the British and the Hessian forces at the Battle of Trenton on December 26.

Afterwards, Washington settled the Continental army at Morristown, New Jersey for the winter while the British established an outpost at New Brunswick. Panic spread among the residents of the Philadelphia area as they learned of the large British force preparing for an advance on their city. A winter of reconstruction saw the Continental troops receive training, smallpox vaccinations, fresh recruits, and new supplies of muskets, powder, and clothing. But that winter, with its mild weather, would prove to be but a vague prelude of a more trying one to follow.

The army broke camp at six a.m. on July 31, 1777. Washington led his troops through Coryell's Ferry (New Hope) and down the York Road to Hartsville, just above Willow Grove, for an encampment. The next day, they continued through "Jenkin's Town" and Shoemakertown. (Movement #1 on the map) It must have been an awesome sight for the country folk of the Abington and Cheltenham area. It probably marked the first time that they saw the American army and, in an isolated farm area, such a mass of people. The size of the force was so large that when the troops marched into Philadelphia a month later, as John Adams wrote his wife, the troops took two hours to pass.

During the first week of August, the army camped at Carlton, the countryseat of wine merchant Henry Hill in lower Germantown near Wissahickon Avenue, as Washington waited for word of British movements to take the city. Although the mass of men was no doubt an impressive sight, their condition was not encouraging. In a review of the troops at Carlton on August 8th, the Marquis de Lafayette recorded his impressions:

About 11000 men, ill armed and still worse clothed, presented a strange spectacle to the eye. Their clothes were parti-coloured and many of them were almost naked; the best clad wore hunting shirts, large gray linen coats, which were much used in Carolina. . . . In spite of these disadvantages the soldiers were fine and officers zealous; virtue stood in place of science, and each day added to experience and discipline. (Eberlein, 1912)

Their "virtue" would be seriously tested in the coming battles.

When word arrived that indicated the British had given up the quest for Philadelphia, Washington moved the troops back to Hartsville a few days later in the sweltering late-summer heat and humidity to await further developments. (Perhaps the wine at Carlton posed too much of a temptation to bored troops.) Once again, they passed along the Old York Road. But that information was not correct: the British had not terminated their drive for the capital.

By August 23rd, Washington was informed that fifteen thousand British troops were being sent by ship from the north to sail up Chesapeake Bay and attack Philadelphia from the south. Washington once again moved his troops down the Old York Road and camped overnight at Stenton in Nicetown, the estate of the late James Logan. Logan had been Penn's secretary and chief justice of the provincial court. The army entered the city with a triumphal parade the next day (inspiring Adams' comment to his wife), and continued south to Brandywine for a confrontation with the British army on September 11. The battle did not go well for the Continental Army. Retreating towards Philadelphia, Washington sent word to Congress that the British were moving in from the upper Schuylkill region, and then took the army north to Pennypacker's Mills (above today's Skippack village, in Schwenksville). The alarm reached Congress at midnight on September 18, and all officials left the city "in the utmost consternation," according to a witness. (Gifford, 1976)

After a deadly skirmish in Paoli, the British army camped at Germantown and on the 26th of September, Lord Cornwallis, in splendid regalia, led three thousand troops into the city of Philadelphia. The American capital was occupied. A British line protected the city on a line just below Germantown from the Schuylkill River to the Old York Road below the Chelten Hills.

Washington immediately planned a counterattack with his force of eleven thousand. He divided his army into four columns and set them off at seven o'clock in the evening on October 3rd. On the western-most route, General John Armstrong descended along the Ridge Road to the mouth of the Wissahickon and was to attack the Hessians stationed there to protect the main force at Germantown. In the center, General John Sullivan, who had been a delegate to the first Continental Congress from New Hampshire, took a column to march down the Skippack Road to the Germantown Road and attack Germantown head on. General Washington accompanied this contingent. Also part of this force was a young cavalryman who was universally described as the most dashing figure of the war, Allan McLane. Captain McLane, scouting ahead of the main marching body, was the first to engage the enemy at Mt. Airy just as day broke.

General Nathanael Greene led the largest contingent down Skippack Pike and Church Road, and over the Abington Road to Germantown. (Movement #2 on the map.) Colonel William Smallwood, marching with the Greene column, continued down Church Road to the Old York Road, turning west at Branchtown, (Oak Lane today) to outflank the British. This contingent consisted of militia from New Jersey and Maryland.

On October 4th, a confusing battle ensued in Germantown complete with fog and mistaken identities that resulted in a British victory. The result after a day of vicious warfare was disastrous for the new Continental Army. Despite the nominal loss, it is a marvel to think of four groups of rookie soldiers, moving without any communication along four separate routes, marching sixteen miles on foot, moving overnight, and expecting to be in their position at the same hour for a four a.m. attack. No wonder that, despite the loss, they were encouraged to fight on.

After the battle, Washington withdrew along the Abington Road to Church Road and thence up Skippack Pike, (Movement #3 on the map.) stopping at the spring for refreshment. Lippincott notes the treasure of the new republic's leadership that trudged through the Olde Wyncote tract on that discouraging day: besides Washington, were Colonel Alexander Hamilton, first secretary of the treasury; Lt. James Monroe, a future president; and Lt. John Marshall, chief justice of the Supreme Court after the war. (Lippincott, 1938) The haggard elements of the Continental Army made their way to encampments in Pawling's Mill, Kulpsville, and Methacton, before settling at Whitemarsh for an encampment on November 2. Meanwhile the British settled in at Philadelphia and Germantown. Washington's army formed a defensive line that extended from Militia Hill on the west of the Bethlehem Road to Camp Hill on the east. Between that line and the British Germantown defense line was a no-man's land, including the Chelten Hills where patrols skirmished for the next several months while seeking supplies and attempting to stop each other from that task.

Despite the fringe location, Washington established an outpost in the Chelten Hills to guard his left flank. (Movement #4 on the map.) An encampment of about a month populated the hills above Tacony Creek on Mather property. One historian described the scene:

"Mather's Place was half arable ground and half dense woods. Chestnuts and oaks vied proudly with each other aspiring to the skies; and from their gnarled roots miniature rivers bubbled forth and ran riotously down the hillsides into the bosom of Tacony Creek. Further up, upon the banks of this quiet stream, the flower and pride of the Continental Army eked out a miserable existence during that wretched winter of 1777-78. The rolling plateau lying between the York Road and the old road to Germantown formed an admirable lookout for the Continental outposts, and many a signal passed from there to the headquarters at Fort Washington. " (Cushing, 1893)

A memorial in the form of a granite slab was placed sometime after the war on top of a grave of an unknown soldier who died either from hardship or during a skirmish with the British. It was mentioned in the Cushing history of the Wanamaker estate and rested at the corner of Township Line Road and Old York Road for many years until the widening of Township Line Road in 1958. The memorial is remembered by long-time residents of the area, but its disposition after the road project is unknown and, regrettably, it is considered lost.

On December 5th, General Howe ordered a British excursion to test the Continental defenses. The peripatetic Captain Allan McLane discovered the British forces at Chestnut Hill and reported their progress to Washington. According to Major Leopold Baurmeister, a commander of the Hessian mercenary troops, Howe's force turned off Germantown Road "to the left on Abington Road and reached Jenkintown, two and a half miles to the left of the enemy's camp, at daybreak." (Baurmeister, 1957)

Baurmeister itemized the British contingent assigned to this mission:

- The British light infantry and grenadiers
- The Hessian grenadiers
- The 4th English Brigade
- Two light 12-pounders and two howitzers
- The Brigade of English Guards and the 1st brigade
- The 7th and 26th regiments
- Two light 12 pounders
- The Hessian Leib Regiment
- One officer and twenty horse of the 17th regiment of Dragoons
- The 3rd English Brigade
- The entire Hessian Jaeger Corps
- The Queen's Rangers

What a formidable sight these troops must have presented to the patriots and residents along the line of march on the narrow and rural Abington Road.

Patriots found along the way were driven back to Edge Hill in a series of skirmishes on December 6th and 7th. Edge Hill formed a ridge to the north of the Abington Road overlooking the path of the British march. (Movement #5 on the map.) It extended from Conshohocken on the west to Roslyn on the east. The American position was so well effected on the ridge that the patriots were able to repel several attempts to assault them along the Edge Hill line. In one skirmish in the center of the line above Edge Hill Village, Colonel Joseph Reed and General John Cadwalader were cut off from their troops and fell from their horses. A Hessian contingent led by British General Grey was prepared to attack the Americans with bayonets when a cavalry unit under Capt. Allan McLane rode in to rescue them.

Baurmeister again reported the action at Edge Hill to his superiors:

I went in front of the English grenadiers and found the rebels entrenched as follows: Before and behind their strongest abatis [rows of bent and twisted tree limbs with sharpen points aimed at the enemy], which went up the slope of the hill, they had dug trenches with embrasures every two to three hundred paces. There were no batteries behind the abatis, but on the entire flank I counted nine uncovered pieces, all of which were manned by French officers and soldiers. They were all determined to wait for whatever might come, but at the same time there was much excitement among them. I do not know even yet why their artillery remained silent. They could not only hear us approach through the woods, where the leaves rustled, but their advanced posts and our skirmishes exchanged many a shot.

Baurmeister then concluded that the rebels had gained a "very disadvantageous position from which to attack them," and withdrew. In all, each side suffered about 40 casualties in the two days of skirmishes.

On December 8th, General Sullivan and his troops arrived to assist the Edge Hill troops and, finding the British gone, rested themselves in one of the inns that stood at the intersection of Edge Hill road and Limekiln Pike. Upon their retreat back to Philadelphia along the Old York Road, the British were brutal to the citizens of the area. Lippincott mentions the loss at the Shoemaker homestead of all horses, grain, and cattle.

Seeking more distance between his troops and the British, but ordered by Congress to protect the residents of the countryside as well as block British access to the temporary capital at York, on December 11th, Washington ordered the army to move to Valley Forge for the beginning of a long and disastrous winter encampment that has inspired our history and culture for more than two hundred years. Washington rejected more remote posts in Bethlehem and Lancaster in order to be close enough to spy on the British and provide security for the citizens of the intervening countryside. Over the winter, scouts patrolled the areas northwest of the city. William Hutchinson, a member of the militia from Chester County and only 20 years of age, described his experience.

In the month of February, 1778, I again entered the service as a volunteer in a company commanded by Capt. John Taylor . . . and rendezvoused at Doylestown for the equipment of the men. . . . From thence we were ordered to a place called the Crooked Billet, now known as Hatborough, and from thence to and through the various towns and places in Philadelphia, Montgomery, and Bucks counties, constantly performing the same kind of service . . . for the purpose of preventing the enemy from foraging in that district of the county and also of preventing the disaffected of the vicinity from having any intercourse with the enemy. (Dann, 1980)

One patrol in particular, typical of this period of the conflict, was led by Capt. Allan McLane. His biographer described McLane as "a handsome man of medium height, lithe, agile, intense." (Cook, 1959) Allan McLane was a native of Philadelphia, "born on the 8th of August 1746 on Walnut Street in a house built out of the populous woods near the Schulkill in 1740." (McLane, 1779) McLane served unscathed through to the end of the war and became the port collector for the City of Wilmington until his death in 1829, living to the "patriarchal" age of eighty-three.

Another biographer observed that McLane was "known to everybody as the constant hero of enterprise and daring. Having been personally acquainted with him in his elder days, I had gathered many facts of his exploits. It was the pleasure of himself and his men to make it a matter of frolic and fun to attack or alarm the enemy, wherever and as often as they could." (Watson, 1857)

On June 8, 1778, McLane set out on a patrol from Frankford to Shoemakerstown when he was ambushed by a squad of British Dragoons. Attempting to escape, McLane rode across the countryside past Shoemaker's Mill and through the woods reaching a country lane, and, "being familiar with the country, he feared to turn to the left as that course led to the city, and he might be intercepted by another ambuscade. Turning, therefore, to the right, his frightened horse carried him swiftly beyond the reach of those who fired upon him." (Bean, 1884) McLane continued down a hill on the road and "stepped out of a small brook, which crossed the road" when McLane saw dragoons approaching from the opposite direction. Cook describes the resulting action in words evidently taken almost directly from McLane's journal, which he himself wrote in the third person.

Quietly, offering no resistance, McLane sat his horse, obviously waiting for the inevitable, his unused sword dangling against his hip. Sure that now, at last, he was ready to surrender, the British troopers galloped up on either side. The one on the left let his sword slip back into the sword strap. The one on the right followed suit, and as he came abreast of McLane, he reached out with his sword hand and grasped the Captain's right shoulder. Then, at the last possible second, McLane acted. He whipped out one of the pistols concealed under his coat and fired its ball directly into the chest of the dragoon on his left. Whirling in his saddle, he used his free hand to grasp the sword of the dragoon on his right, and while this startled trooper struggled to grip the handle and wrench the blade clear, McLane rose in his stirrups and put the whole weight of this body behind two savage blows, crushing the skull of the dragoon with the lock and barrel of his discharged pistol, wielded like a club. . . . In the struggle with the second dragoon, a deep gash had been inflicted on his hand by the sword he had grasped, and McLane began to feel faint from loss of blood. Near him was a millpond, and, McLane, dropping in exhaustion from his horse, tottered to this and immersed himself in the cold water. (Cook, 1957)

    McLane's description suggests that the action took place at the crossing of Tacony Creek at Abington Road in the location of Mather's Mill. (Movement #6 on the map.)

    The McLane episode in Chelten Hills was apparently well known enough to inspire literary and artistic recognition. Charles Willson Peale, the famous and prolific colonial artist, celebrated the incident in a significant oil painting that hung in the Peale museum in Independence Hall for the first half of the 19th century.

The episode was also recognized by Philadelphian, Silas Weir Mitchell, in his 19th century book *Hugh Wynne, Free Quaker*. That book chronicles the Revolutionary War adventures of the fictional Hugh Wynne, grandson of Dr. Thomas Wynne, one of William Penn's advisors and personal physician. Wynne receives a commission as an officer in the Pennsylvania militia at the beginning of the war and is placed under the command of Captain Allan McLane. In the version of the Chelten Hills incident offered by Mitchell, Wynne, of course, was the victim and he was ambushed by the British in an even more gory confrontation than McLane himself recounted.

The Battle of Crooked Billet also brought British troops through the area. Twenty-three year old John Lacey had just been appointed Brigadier General and commander of the Pennsylvania militia in January when he was ordered to the northwest to interrupt the flow of goods to the British. Camping in the village of Crooked Billet, now Hatboro, Lacey spent the month of April, 1778, attempting to rebuild his force of civilian soldiers. General Howe attempted to destroy this operation by sending a force of British rangers and Hessians up the Old York Road under the command of Major John Graves Simcoe. He confronted a sleeping and unprepared Lacey in Crooked Billet on the night of April 30, and, on May 1, a vicious skirmish ensued which left a wasteland of carnage and atrocities across the small village. At the end, the British and their mercenaries withdrew back to Philadelphia along the Old York Road.

The War of Independence quit the Philadelphia theater with the withdrawal of the British from the City of Philadelphia to New York in June of 1778. Washington followed by breaking camp at Valley Forge and moving his army, rejuvenated after a spring of training, on to the next phase of the war in Monmouth, New Jersey.

The second stage upon which the war played out came into focus after the military operations were removed from the area. It was the battle for the allegiance of the people and, no longer hampered by military dangers, the citizenry took their retribution against those who ended up on the wrong side. The American Revolution forced ordinary people to choose between two difficult positions: support of one meant the treasonous rejection of the other. In the

Philadelphia area, the Quakers were a major presence, and their beliefs prohibited them from taking sides. Thus, their loyalty was questioned by both elements in the war. The Knights and the Mathers were particularly imperiled both by the fact that they were Quakers and by their ownership of mills that were a mainstay of food production in the Chelten Hills area.

In Abington, the three sons of Isaac Knight, Isaac, Jr., Joshua, and John had all preferred the British side in the war. Heirs to the large land holdings of their father which included most famously the mill at today's Glenside Avenue and Rice's Mill Road, their properties covered the area known as Baederwood all the way to the corner of Edge Hill Road and York Road in Abington. They were accused of treason for aiding the British and on May 8, 1778, their names were listed on the first proclamation of "attainder" issued by the administration of the Commonwealth of Pennsylvania. The eventual result of long legal proceedings was the confiscation of most of their land. As a result, their name, unlike the Mathers, disappeared from the succeeding history of the area.

In Cheltenham, some of the Mathers also found themselves in trouble for participating in the war effort. Bartholomew and his son, Thomas, were castigated by the Abington Meeting for aiding Washington's troops. Bartholomew had provided wagons for transporting food and material to the continental army and Thomas had provided his services as a driver to deliver the goods to the troops camped at Valley Forge. Lippincott tells a family story about Thomas' narrow escape from the British by hiding in a barrel.

As the war moved on to other areas of the country, the area of the Olde Wyncote Tract once again became a quiet agrarian outpost far from the action and far from the growing City of Philadelphia.

~~~~~~~~~~~~~~~~~~~~~~~~

Charles Willson Peale was one of the foremost – and prolific – Colonial American painters. He moved to Philadelphia at the beginning of the Revolution where he met and painted most of the important figures involved in the American conflict. He knew Col. McLane and they became strong enough friends that McLane acceded to Peale's request to testify during the divorce trial of Peale's son, Franklin, in 1820. At the trial, Franklin's wife, Eliza, was found to be mad (possibly due to her Quaker zeal in promoting the abolitionist position) and the marriage was annulled. Peale, in writing to his son Rembrandt in 1819 to inform him of his new painting of McLane, called McLane "the greatest partisan we had during the American Revolution." (Sellers, 1952) Peale's painting, executed in 1811, was entitled "A Recontre Between Col. Allan McLane and Two British Horsemen," and was hung in Peale's Museum, which occupied the upper floor of Independence Hall for a period at the beginning of the 19th century. The painting allegedly memorialized McLane's close call in Chelten Hills sometime after the battle of Germantown and has been described as a "large" painting. It was listed in the acquisitions catalog for the museum in 1818. A copy of the painting was made and presented to Col. McLane.

Peale was credited with over a thousand paintings. His profligacy was not entirely without support. Charles' younger brother, James, who was a somewhat less accomplished and successful artist than Charles, came to work for Charles as his assistant in 1769 until he received a commission to serve in the Revolutionary militia in 1776. James served with Col. William Smallwood and was a member of the contingent that marched through Jenkintown and down Abington Road during the Battle of Germantown. After the war, James returned to Philadelphia to again work for his brother. Among James' duties was to do detail work on Charles' paintings and make copies of his works. James apparently was asked by Charles to begin work on the "Recontre" painting.

Lippincott refers to seeing a painting of the incident in his brief account of the McLane incident in his history of Chelten Hills, indicating some level of post-19th century awareness of this work. Unfortunately, the "Recontre" painting was not listed in the sale catalog when the museum was disbanded in 1854. Sellers, who completed an inventory of Peale's subjects, lists the whereabouts of the painting in 1952 as "Unlocated."

It is not known what the relationship of James' "Encounter" painting is to the "Recontre" painting. Given James' duties as a copyist, it is entirely possible that this is a duplicate of Charles' work or at least another version. The title of the painting has undergone change through the years and an original title of the painting has been identified: "Revolutionary Subject." (Edson, 2001)

"Encounter Between Capt. Allan McLane and a British Dragoon" by James Peale. Circa 1819.
Courtesy of the United States National Archives. 111-SC-91311

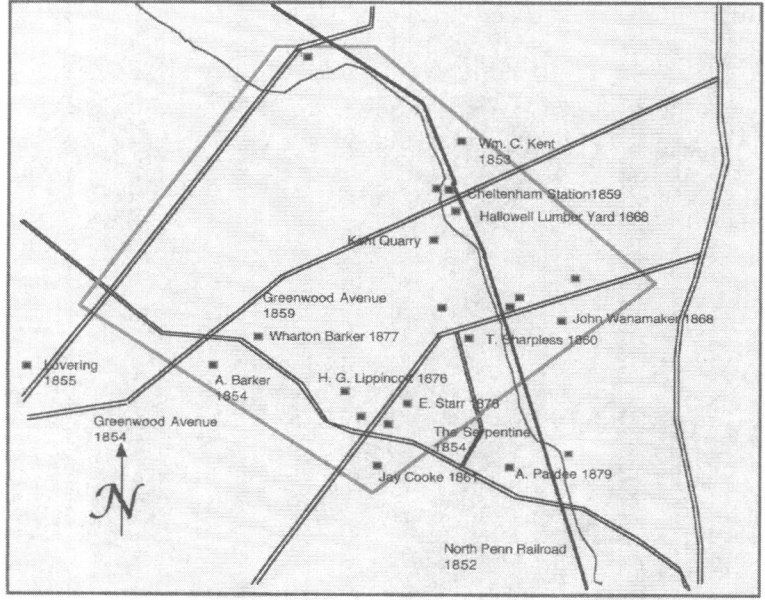

Development During the Gilded Age

The period between 1852 and 1876 saw the development of the railroad and the first of two important crossroads that would form the framework of the new village. Estates of important Philadelphia businessmen began to populate the tract around the Washington Lane and Church road corridors.

Chapter 4

THE GILDED AGE

*Here one may live in real country, yet share few
of the disadvantages usually attending
country life. Here, girls, you can pick berries
and gather wild flowers, and all of you, young
and old, feel generally free and independent.*
(Hale, 1859)

In the Olde Wyncote tract in 1852, life had continued largely unchanged for one hundred and sixty eight years from the granting of the first deeds by William Penn. Interrupted only by the turmoil of the War of Revolution, the verdant countryside supported several generations of farmers and a few millers in relatively comfortable circumstances. Professor Charles Trego of the University of Pennsylvania described the successful agrarian nature of the area:

Montgomery is in a high state of cultivation, and its agricultural productions are numerous and important. Most kinds of grain cultivated in the state are grown here, and hay, potatoes, butter, fruit and other articles for the Philadelphia market are produced in abundance. The products of the dairy alone are estimated to amount to $402,681 annually. Lime, limestone, and marble also constitute a considerable item in the wealth of this county, producing an annual income of more than $250,000. (Trego, 1843)

Even after a century and a half, the Olde Wyncote tract could not yet be called a "community": the population was still too scarce in the tract and the few Quaker farmers found their social sustenance in the broader assembly of congregants at the Abington Friends meetinghouse in nearby Jenkintown. Land had passed from generation to generation within the family, sometimes dividing to accommodate children – as in the multiplication of "Mather" names resident in the tract, or through marriage – as in the introduction of the Lippincott name into formerly Mather territory. But, although not apparent to them, the time and manner of doing things of the legacy Quaker farmer was about over. By the end of the century, significant changes would ensue and life in the tract would undergo a complete facelift. Three factors fomented this transition: the construction of the railroad, the commercialization of land development, and, a little later, the post Civil War expansion of the economy.

1852: The Railroad

The grand changes that were forthcoming were, in 1852, just brewing in the still distant social and geographical reaches of the Philadelphia business world. In that year, a group of industrious business activists received authorization from the state legislature to form a new railroad. Perhaps in no other aspect of late nineteenth century life had the benefits of the industrial revolution been so manifest as the railroad frenzy that gripped the nation and would continue to build steam throughout the period. In 1830, the first rails in the United States totaled only twenty-three miles. By 1850, nine thousand miles covered the country. In another twenty years, after the Civil War, the growth in railroading and the country produced a total of fifty-three thousand miles. Every investor with money to spare hurried to find a railroad to harbor his investment. On April 8, 1852, an Act of Legislature granted life to the Philadelphia, Easton, and Water Gap Railroad. The name bore testimony to the business war that pitted Philadelphia industrialists and merchants against those of neighboring

New York. It was not the commuter railroad we know today, as the founders were more concerned about moving freight and goods to the city. Passengers were almost an afterthought as long as the coal got to the city. An announcement of a public meeting in the city called citizens to a "Philadelphia Mass Meeting" with the cry "Philadelphians, Hark!" and continued with the harangue:

The Forks of the Delaware echo to the whistle of the locomotive that is come to bear away to a neighbour city in a neighbour state the trade and treasure of the Keystone valleys. THIS CAN BE PREVENTED BY A DIRECT RAILROAD TO THE LEHIGH VALLEY. Therefore, arouse, for where the interests of all are at stake, it is the duty of all to ACT. (Hare, 1940)

By the following year, the railroad had changed its name to a "shorter and more appropriate name" (in the words of the board of directors), North Pennsylvania Rail Road, and authorized the survey of a route that would connect existing downtown railways near the docks with New York bound lines leading from Easton. The president amplified the goal to the board:

It is proposed to bring back to Philadelphia the trade of the Lehigh, which has been diverted to New York by means of better facilities than we, unfortunately, possess at this time, and which would be constructed by those directly interested in that trade who transacted their business in the northern part of the city, or those who owned real estate to be benefited from the location of the road. (North Pennsylvania, 1854)

The annual report of the chief engineer, submitted on April 30, 1853, recommended a route that traced in part through the region of the Olde Wyncote tract:

. . . the best line that could be obtained was that which left the Wissahickon by the valley of Sandy Run, crossing the Bethlehem turnpike near Hirsh's tavern, thirteen and a half miles from Philadelphia by the turnpike, passing through Edge Hill by a deep cut at the village of Edgehillville, descending the Tacony to the vicinity of Shoemakertown, where the Old York Turnpike Road is crossed. (Miller, 1854)

As with the Indians and the Dutch, the creek that had already cut a level course through the countryside, would be the preferred route through the area.

In one report, Chief Engineer Edward Miller noted his policy of establishing stations along the way:

In regard to way stations on the route of the road, I have already advised that they should be numerous, and not of an expensive character. Private enterprise in a district so populous and wealthy as that traversed by your road, will soon alter greatly the relative importance of different points; and I have no doubt that the first division from Philadelphia to Plymouth Road will develop an amount of trade and travel that will astonish the most sanguine, under a liberal and judicious management. Until this development takes place, it is impossible to determine the extent of the accommodations which will ultimately be required at particular stations, and temporary buildings will generally best meet the exigencies of the case. (Miller, 1854)

Miller's list of stations included a modest wood station at Washington Lane, the Chelten Hills station, but there was no accommodation of Jenkintown in his plan, let alone the future Wyncote. The next station outbound beyond Chelten Hills was Tacony, located at the mill road. That station shortly proved inconvenient and was moved to the Germantown Willow Grove Plank Road (today's Easton Road), named Abington, and later renamed Glenside.

Construction of the line began in 1854 and apparently proceeded at a rapid pace. By that year, $1,538,600 had been raised for construction of the line and a final cost was estimated at $2,980,000 for the entire length of the line to Bethlehem. These costs did not include land acquisition, a topic that was not addressed by the board until 1856. By New Year's Day of 1855, the right-of-way had been graded from the city terminus to Plymouth Road in Gwynedd and construction commenced on laying down a single track from the city to the end. In a piece of either good planning or rampant optimism, construction from the very beginning included provisions along the right-of-way and bridges for a second track. Locomotives had been purchased from the Baldwin Company in Philadelphia by the end of 1854 along with passenger cars from Kimball and Gorton of Philadelphia. (Fires were an everyday event in mid-century urban life and Kimball and Gorton met its own demise after

Chelten Hills in 1859
This illustration of an agrarian Chelten Hills area was published in a 1859 guide book to the North Pennsylvania Railroad. The train can be seen chugging through the Tookany Creek valley. The view arguably could be either from the south or the north: other illustrations in the book appear to be historically accurate, lending authenticity to this view of Chelten Hills.
Courtesy of the Hagley Museum and Library

a disastrous fire in 1862.) By opening day, Baldwin Locomotive Company had delivered a new steam engine, the "Cohocksink" and her sisters, the "Aramingo" and the "Shackamaxon" would be delivered later in 1855 and early 1856 respectively. It was customary in railroading to give locomotives names and the NPRR locomotives did not get numbers until the Reading Railroad took over in 1879. Each locomotive, the most modern model of the day, weighed 49,000 pounds, had 54-inch drive wheels, pressure cylinders 12.5 inches in diameter and a six-wheeled tender with a water tank for 1,000 gallons.

It is no small cause of wonderment by today's expectations of legalities, regulatory gridlock, and NIMBYism how a railroad formed, funded, surveyed a route, obtained the land of right-of-way, laid level the route, blasted through solid rock cuts, obtained rolling stock including three complicated locomotives, laid nineteen miles of rail – all within a period of three years. One railroad

The Original Route of the NPRR
The nineteen mile route began near the Philadelphia docks to facilitate the line's original purpose of transporting goods from upstate regions to the city for distribution.
Courtesy of the Old York Road Historical Society from Hare, 1940

Chelten Hills Station, 1924
The view looks toward the Jenkintown Station. Washington Lane is the horizontal line in the middle of the photo.
Photo: Courtesy of the Hagley Museum and Library

historian explained that "black powder, as the chief explosive, and the pick, hand shove, dump wagon, and wheelbarrow were still ranking contractors' equipment in railroad construction." (Hare, 1944) But Baldwin itself, the largest manufacturing operation in the world at the time, produced the locomotives for the railroad on a sixty-day production schedule. Compared to the excruciating wait for today's SEPTA rail car replacements, the whole enterprise seems an accomplishment nothing short of miraculous.

One element that contributed to this alacrity lay in the problem of land acquisition that was so conveniently deferred by the board during their first meetings. The 1853 charter and, by reference, the 1849 Pennsylvania law regulating railroads allowed the company almost total authority to go where they wanted and assume any land for their road. Section 10 of the law specified:

That the President and Directors of such Company shall have the power and authority by themselves, their engineers, supervisors, agents, artisans, and workmen to survey, ascertain, locate, fix, mark, and determine such route for a Railroad as they may deem expedient, not however passing through any burying-ground or place of public worship. (An Act Regulating Railroad Companies, 1849)

Only the dead or the praying could escape the voracious appetite of the railroaders and of course, with such prerogatives, the company could move quickly. In the case of the Olde Wyncote tract, the railroad did not get around to settling with William C. Kent and Edward M. Davis, two owners represented in the tract, until July of 1857, almost three years after the route was settled and two years after the trains started running through their land.

The first ride from downtown Philadelphia to Gwynedd on the North Pennsylvania line occurred on Monday, July 2, 1855. Pulled by the new "Cohocksink" steam locomotive that was delivered in May, a train-full of dignitaries boarded at the "new and very commodious station" at Front and Willow streets (near the docks and today's Waterfront Square Condo complex). The event was recorded by the *Philadelphia Inquirer* and indicated the excitement that accompanied the affair.

Yesterday was celebrated by an important and auspicious event, which may be termed the harbinger of an increased traffic for Philadelphia, through a new and highly interesting region of Pennsylvania. We refer to the opening of the First Division of the Northern Pennsylvania Railroad to Gwynedd, a distance of about nineteen miles. A Committee of the City Councils, representatives of the press, and many prominent citizens were invited on the occasion, and the party assembled must have been nearly one hundred in number. . . . We were whirled along with great speed over an exceedingly beautiful country, in which highly cultivated farms and fields were agreeable [*sic*] alternated with majestic and park-like groves, hill and dale, and watered with sparkling brooks and streams. (*Philadelphia Inquirer*, July 3, 1855)

The "Cohocksink," successful on this celebrated day, would survive until its dismantling in 1878 due to old age, but her sisters would soon be destroyed in a conflagration of their own making within a year in a tragic head-on collision at nearby Fort Washington.

The railroad grew quickly. The Board of Directors boasted of the health of their enterprise in their 1858 annual report:

The equipment is now equal to a business of about $400,000 per annum and consists of sixteen locomotives, fourteen first class passenger cars, four baggage cars, twenty-four lime cars, four eight-wheel dump cars, and fifty-four wheel dump cars. (North Pennsylvania, 1870)

Designed to bring coal and other goods to Philadelphia, the railroad would soon find other uses more profitable. By 1861, revenues from the transportation of passengers, milk, and pig iron would supersede coal. The annual report for 1861 lists milk shipments at 11,664 gallons and 7,688 gallons respectively for the Abington and Old York Road stations, out of a total of more than a million and a half transported.

One mellow sightseer summed up his experience on the new railroad in 1859:

If you have been on it before, you do not need to be told of its careful and obliging conductors, the smoothness of its track, the elegance and comfort of its cars, and the beautiful and interesting scenery through which it passes. (Hale, 1859)

At the advent of the railroad, two land transfers in particular marked the transition between the old and the new in the Olde Wyncote tract: the purchases of the Kent estate and the Heacock farm. The Kent purchase was the prototype of the new style of land use in the tract and the surrounding region. It represented the first time that a wealthy Philadelphia businessman purchased a large amount of property solely for its recreational value – for the pleasure of the surroundings and as a summer retreat - rather than for its farming value. It was a bellwether of the wave of wealthy industrialists to follow. Conversely, the purchase of farmland by Joseph Heacock was the last major purchase of farmland for farming purposes to occur in the tract. It singularly marked the end of an era.

1853: William C. Kent

William C. Kent was a founder and partner of the Philadelphia dry goods wholesaler, James, Kent, and Santee & Company, which had its offices at 237-41 North Third Street. An article in the *New York Times* of 1890 referred to Kent's firm as "the greatest wholesale dry goods house in Philadelphia." The firm became deeply involved in the burgeoning cotton industry in the United States and is credited with dabbling in the earliest forms of a cotton futures market. Indicative of the abolitionist fervor that percolated in mid-century Quaker Philadelphia, the firm found itself on a "black list" of merchants who were deemed "enemies to the institutions of the South." (*New York Times, 1860*) It is not known what specific activities earned the company this opprobrium, although the anti-slavery beliefs of the owners would have been enough, but it is a telling commentary on the tenor of the times that a vaunted northern newspaper would print such a libel.

Kent was also a director of the North East Pennsylvania Railroad (not to be confused with the previously mentioned North Pennsylvania Railroad) that was chartered in 1870 to construct a line from Abington Station to New Hope. The line began operations in 1874. It is the branch that crosses today's Mt. Carmel Avenue on the way to Willow Grove and Hatboro. Kent purchased almost two hundred acres of woods and fields in Jenkintown in 1853 and the Chelten Hills on March 31, 1854, at the cost of $20,710 and ten cents. His Cheltenham purchase consisted of one hundred and three acres and extended from the township line at the southern limit of Jenkintown to today's Maple Avenue on the south, and all the way over to Washington Lane on the east. In other words, at one time he owned most of what today we know as Olde Wyncote. The previous landholder was Benjamin Webster, grandson of William Webster who worked a farm on the site. Kent built a summer retreat, *Beechwood,* a blocky federal-style mansion on the

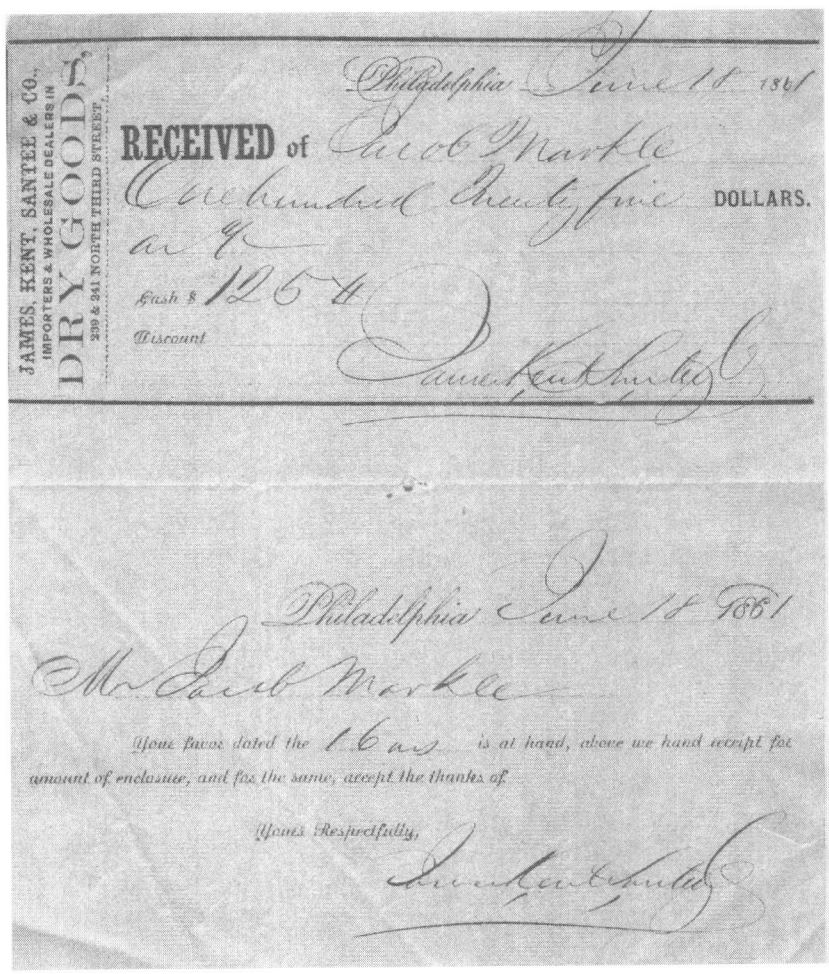

James, Kent, Santee & Company Receipt
Dated June 18, 1861, the document portrays the formality of business at the time of the civil war.
From the collection of the author

Jenkintown hillside with a wide porch facing the south that must have provided a most relaxing and favorable view of the woods. (One sign of the transition in land use was the proclivity hereinafter for labeling the new estates with lyrical Anglo names.) A long lawn descended the hillside from the porch to the rustic old Mather millpond below and cooling woods were the site of family picnics along the creek in this peaceful glen. One visitor to the area, historian William J. Buck, on a hike through the sylvan setting from Glenside to Shoemakertown, remarked:

This desire [to explore the area] arose from trips I had made at various times on the railroad, while proceeding to and from the city. I had thus observed, while journeying along here a section of country of remarkable beauty and romantic wildness. It is one of the loveliest places imaginable, surrounded by hills and precipices which are covered by woods and bushes, and no signs of residences or cultivation in sight. (Buck, 1857)

In the City, Kent became involved in the controversy over the construction of the new City Hall. Besides the corruption and indecision that attended the plans to build in Center Square, the plan to consume all four blocks of the public park with one large building, called the "Intersection" plan, dogged the project for years. It triumphed over a plan to surround the intersection with several smaller buildings. In 1872, Kent joined a protest committee and signed a public petition protesting the plan along with other luminaries from Cheltenham including Jay Cooke, and Edward Townsend. Kent withdrew from his firm in 1873 at which time the firm changed its name to "James Santee & Company." It survived a takeover but was liquidated in 1883. The firm was stressed by the Civil War which disrupted is business in southern cotton as well as a devastating fire, in February 1866, that destroyed its premises on Third Street, as well as the rest of the block. The final blow to Kent may have been his investment in Jay Cooke's Northern Pacific Railroad venture which collapsed, also in 1873, causing a nationwide financial panic. But Kent still owned property, and a lot of it, in what would become a "hot" market.

Kent's intentions in moving to the Olde Wyncote tract may have been aesthetic or recreational, but his subsequent actions indicate a more pragmatic element. As a shrewd man of business, he certainly must have known of the impending railroad when he purchased his land, although there was no evident construction yet underway. He was not involved in the forming of the railroad company either as a charter member or a director, but his two partners, John O. James and Charles Santee were both charter signatories and founding directors of the North Pennsylvania Rail Road. Whatever reticence he experienced in 1853 disappeared by 1856 as Kent participated in the first mortgage of the railroad, a million dollar venture, by investing $90,000 privately in the mortgage securities. This was the second highest investment amount of all investors in that offering. He no doubt figured, as did engineer Miller, on the development and prosperity that would attend to its construction.

Following his first sale to Joseph Heacock after just three years of ownership, Kent made sixty-four individual sales of parcels of his property over a twenty-four year period. The sales ranged from the Heacock sale in 1857 to a homesite for Horace G. Lippincott in 1876 with his final sale in the summer of 1881. After his death that year, the executors of his estate made the final disposal of his holdings with an additional fifteen property sales over an eight-year period. These included a large tract in "Beechwood Heights" to the developer Willis P. Hazard in June of 1885 and the disposal of the last parcel to Thomas Nicholson in 1889. Ironically, Nicholson's purchase on July 20, 1889, was for an extension to his coal yard at the train station to serve the booming population of the village. The transition from farmland to suburb was symbolically complete. Although the grand estate was gone, three more generations of the Kent family, spanning 123 years, lived at various places in Wyncote, enjoying the benefits of the fine suburban village that the vast estate had spawned.

Beechwood
William C. Kent's estate is pictured about 1865. The porch looks over the
Tookany Creek Valley into the woods beyond.

1854: Edward M. Davis

This period also represented a new way of selling land. The
traditional mode that endured in the tract for so long - and
in society in general - was the transfer of discrete parcels
from individual to individual. In the case of this farming
area, that meant from farmer to farmer. But Kent's disposal
methods foretold a new way of doing business. That method
was formalized by Edward M. Davis with the incorporation
of the Chelten Hills Land Development Company in 1854.
Unlike Kent who sold his land to suit the interests of
individual buyers on demand, Davis filed a complete plot
plan with Norristown, the county seat, indicating the
subdivision of the properties he obtained.

A Picnic Along the Creek
A summer picnic along the Tookany Creek at the bottom of Kent's hill, about 1864, just below the Mather dam. A nascent Greenwood Avenue crosses the creek on a simple wooden bridge in the background. The flow of the creek seems low, but that would be caused by the millrace for the Mather mill flowing from the dam which diverted about half of the flow of the creek. The millrace is just out of the picture to the left.
Courtesy of the OYRHS, Kent Collection.

Edward M. Davis, from Philadelphia, was a descendent of a Revolutionary War officer who was an aide to General Washington. He was a faithful Quaker and ardent abolitionist who made (and lost) several fortunes as a man of many business interests. In 1848, he became a business partner of Morris Longstreth Hallowell, who would become part of the family when his son, Richard Price Hallowell, married Davis' daughter Maria in 1859. As a partner in a large wholesale dry goods business that dealt in southern cotton, he found his business suffering as a result of his involvement with abolitionism, and switched to imported silk and wool as a main line of business. An article in a Philadelphia newspaper of September 1879 summarized the difficulty in pursuing both business and his moral crusade.

As early as 1834, he attached himself to the American Anti-Slavery Society and remained an enthusiastic member until he witnessed the triumph over the evil which it opposed. Often his goods lay untouched on the shelves until sold at auction, because his customers feared to offend Southern sentiment by dealing with an Abolitionist. [*sic*] No consideration deflected him from his determination to release the slave. (Chorley, 1973)

In 1850, Davis purchased "Oak Farm" just across the northwest city line and moved his sister, her husband, their children and his mother-in-law, to share a farmhouse, renamed "Roadside." Davis' mother-in-law was Lucretia Mott who also was deeply involved in the abolition movement and turned the farm into an important stop on the underground railway. One can only imagine the excitement, if not tension, in the household as Lucretia Mott and her associates pursued their clandestine activities. His granddaughter described their home in more pacific terms:

The house at Roadside was a sunny old place, surrounded at first by cherry and apple and pear trees; afterwards by maple and oak. The windows commanded pleasant, though limited views of the adjacent country, and looked up and down the much-traveled Old York Road, formerly the highway for stage-coaches between Philadelphia and New York. (Hallowell, 1884)

Davis also purchased farmland extending south to the city line from the homestead and planned a community there that would feature integrated living, a radical concept in the pre-war era, and enabled perhaps only by the vibrant abolitionist atmosphere of the Philadelphia region. The success of today's LaMott community testifies to the value of his vision. Over the next couple of years, he assembled another large tract in Chelten Hills from the Mathers and others and planned over one hundred lots to be marketed to wealthy businessmen of Philadelphia. Despite his business setbacks, by 1854, he was a director of the Pennsylvania Railroad, the president of Barclay Coal Company, a partner of Morris Longstreth Hallowell - the father of his daughter's future husband - and prime partner in the new land venture, buying up large parcels of outlying land from farmers and selling individual building lots. He was very successful in the

Davis and the Anti-Slavery Committee
Edward M. Davis is pictured second from the left in the top row along
with other members of the committee. Lucretia Mott is at the bottom
right with her husband James.
Courtesy of the Friends Historical Library, Swarthmore College

area northwest of the city in his Oak Lane development and
moved further out, betting that the railroad would bring new
opportunities for development to the countryside just
outside of the city limits in Cheltenham Township. Unable to
observe the war from the sidelines, he joined the staff of
General John Fremont and served as a quartermaster. For
his militarism in defiance of Quaker passivism, he was
expelled from the Quaker community. After the Civil War,
he would continue his activism by supporting the woman's
suffrage movement.

Piecemeal development continued in the Chelten Hills
area of the Olde Wyncote tract for several years after the
construction of the railroad and the marketing by Davis. Not
surprisingly, a nascent village sprung up around the station
at Chelten Hills, spurred by what was still the only major
road near the station in the tract, Washington's route from

Germantown to Abington. Davis' activities impacted land values in the tract. In 1855, his mother-in-law, while writing to a friend with advice on where to settle, noted that cheaper country living could be found anywhere except "near Chelton [sic] Hills where Ed. Davis & Co. have raised the price of land &c. so much," that another location being considered in West Chester might be better. (Mott, 1855) Fortunately for Davis, his mother-in-law's negativism apparently did not retard land sales, but she had a point. When Abraham Barker purchased his estate in 1854 from Owen Cadwalader, he paid the princely sum of $14, 800, or about $300 per acre. Cadwalader had purchased the property in 1847 at about $100 per acre.

1854: Barclay Lippincott

Lippincott moved to the Olde Wyncote tract just a month before Abraham Barker. He was the first Lippincott to move here. Barclay was a partner with Edward T. Taylor in a clothing store on the southwest corner of Market and Fourth Streets in Philadelphia, Lippincott, Taylor & Company. Merchant John Wanamaker had started in the dry goods business as a clerk at Lippincott's store in 1851 at a salary of $2.50 per week before moving on to Oak Hall, another clothing store closer to Center Square. Lippincott sold his property to Abraham Barker six years later and moved back to the city. By 1877 when Lippincott sold the rest of his property to Wharton Barker, Lippincott was conducting business as an auctioneer in the city.

1854: Abraham Barker

Barker had established the firm of Barker Brothers Bank with his brother Sigourney in 1842 after being emancipated at the age of eighteen by his father, a businessman in New Orleans. Louisiana law required such freedom for a minor before allowing him to engage in business. The youngster must have been very industrious: in the four years that he worked before leaving for Philadelphia, Barker had accumulated a stake of fifty thousand dollars. He was just 21 years of age when he moved; his brother was three years younger. Barker also married in the year 1842, and married well. Sarah Wharton was a descendant of a Philadelphia mayor and sister of Joseph Wharton, a successful industrialist and co-founder of Bethlehem Steel who later found the Wharton School of Business at the University of Pennsylvania. Barker was admitted to a seat on the Philadelphia Stock Exchange in 1845. Among his accomplishments on the Exchange, he was credited with improving operations through the publication of printed lists of transactions for each day and the establishment of a financial clearinghouse. The Barker Bank was the American agent for Barings Bank of London, one of the most prominent banks in what was then the banking capital of the world.

He was apparently successful enough to purchase his first property in the Olde Wyncote tract in 1854. Although he did not purchase from Edward M. Davis, he was probably influenced to invest by him, as a fellow Quaker and having worked with him among the active abolitionist community in Philadelphia. The 1860 census shows Barker to be comfortably established as a resident of Cheltenham Township along with his wife Sarah, sons Wharton and Sigourney, daughters Deborah and Elizabeth, as well as five servants. Barker likely named his estate *Lyndon* to honor his ancestral home of the same name in Rutland, England.

In 1863, Barker co-founded the prestigious Union League of Philadelphia whose purpose was to support President Lincoln in the War between the States. His activities extended to a committee that established the first training camp for Negro soldiers at Camp William Penn. The committee turned to Jay Cooke, a fellow founding member of the Union League, for land for the camp and it was established in 1863 at Cooke's new estate at the southeast corner of Washington Lane and Church Road.

Barker's property consisted of two lots totaling fifty acres on the corner of Church Road and a new road not yet named leading from Church Road to the Limekiln Pike (today's southern Greenwood Avenue). The lot closest to the corner, previously owned and farmed by Owen Cadwalader, already contained a "mansion." Barker added on to his estate with purchases of properties to the east and north in 1858 and

1860. The 1860 purchase was property on the northeast side
of Church Road, across from his home, that was owned by
Barclay Lippincott. Barker was apparently more than a
country gentleman as he actively farmed the land during the
years he lived there.

Barker would lose his estate in 1890 after his bankruptcy
due to an international banking crisis and panic. He died
after falling from a streetcar while visiting New York City on
April 8, 1906, at the age of 85 years.

1855: Joseph S. Lovering

You could say that Joseph S. Lovering was a sweet guy,
but then you too would be chided for being corny: Lovering
was one of Philadelphia's leading sugar magnates. He is
perhaps the most obscure of the luminaries that lived in the
Olde Wyncote tract in the Gilded age: not even a road is
named after him. Joseph S. Lovering was born in
Wilmington, Delaware, in 1800 and embarked on a career as
a grocer at 2nd and Pine Streets. In 1836, he purchased the
1792 Sugar Factory on Church Street and embarked on a
career that led to international renown. Through a series of
later mergers and acquisitions, the company ended up as
Jack Frost Sugar. Taking on the skills of a chemical
engineer, he developed a secret steam process for refining
sugar that did not involve the need for animal blood. Other
refiners were desperate to learn his secret:

For the purpose of deceiving and misleading them in their
attempts, he had a room in his refinery fitted up with a great
number of pipes and valves, also intricate looking machinery, into
which at certain times, he would go and turn valves and
manipulate levers, simply as a blind, the whole arrangement being
a mere fake, that had nothing to do with the real process of
refining. (Schenick, 1990)

By 1845, Lovering was listed as one of Philadelphia's
twenty-five millionaires. He was described as "dignified and
imposing, with a white beard that extended past his
collarbone." He spoke French and insisted on carrying on
his firm's correspondence in that language. Lovering's older

daughter, Mary, married Charles Wharton in 1849 and Lovering's younger daughter, Anna, married Charles' younger brother, Joseph Wharton in 1854, thus solidly connecting the Lovering family to the famous and wealthy Whartons. Joseph and his wife Ann Corbit purchased a country estate in the Olde Wyncote tract from Charles William Wharton in 1857. Named *Endsmeet*, the estate was a working farm and contained one hundred and ten acres and a farmhouse at the southern part of the tract just off the Road to Paxson's Mill. Greenwood Avenue would be laid out along part of the southeastern border of the estate. It is not clear how much the Loverings used the farm as they inherited a substantial property, *Oak Hill*, located near the Logan section of the city. The farm would stay in the family for many more years as it would become the country home of their granddaughter, author Anna Wharton Morris. Joseph S. Lovering died in Philadelphia on May 14, 1881

1857: Joseph Heacock

At the eastern end of the Olde Wyncote tract, Joseph Heacock purchased his farm. Heacock was born in Rockhill Township, Bucks County, in 1800, but had moved to Jenkintown in 1822 and worked as a blacksmith on the Old York Road strip below Greenwood Avenue. He had accumulated some land in Abington below his shop before turning to farming. In 1824, he married Esther Hallowell of the Abington Hallowell family. He first purchased twenty-two acres from William C. Kent in April 1857, Kent's first sale. The land included part of the Benjamin Webster farm and homestead. He then obtained an additional seven acres from Isaac Mather (the grandson) next to the southwest corner of his property (around the Heacock Lane and Glenside Avenue intersection) in April of 1859. This made a square that included today's Maple Avenue on the south to the railroad tracks on the north and Webster Avenue on the west to Washington Lane on the east. Heacock's farm was successful for many years and he accumulated a notable dairy herd that grazed on the land south of today's Maple Avenue and in the field along the Tookany Creek across from the Mather mill.

Heacock Farmhouse
This photograph taken in the late 1890's shows the addition on the left
that was added when the home became the Heacock boarding school.
Photo: Courtesy of Nancy Wood, Wyncote

1859: Jenkintown Station and Greenwood Avenue

If North Penn Railroad Chief Engineer Miller was
penurious in passing the Jenkintown area without a station,
he was also prescient about growth. By July of 1859, the
railroad had received a petition from residents and
merchants of the Jenkintown area for a station closer to that
community. The historian, William Buck, apparently knew
of this road and station initiative at the time of his 1857 hike
through the area. Speaking of the isolated Chelten Hills
station at Washington Lane, he noted:

It is intended, I believe, by next spring, to move this station about
a half a mile further up where a new turnpike is now making from
the railroad to the village of Jenkintown, which will be about three
quarters of a mile in length. This road promises to be a great
improvement to that neighborhood, and will have a summer road
on each side of the stone track, be well graded and about fifty feet
in width. (Buck, 1857)

This indeed was a first class undertaking by Jenkintown interests as evidenced by the stone surface in the middle of the road and its generous width. Standard road width at that time was just thirty feet. As a turnpike, it was a private development that indicates there were definitive business interests at work, even before the formal request was made to the railroad, to connect the business center of town with a future station. No doubt enterprising interests in the Jenkintown community saw other development opportunities in the area of the prospective station. The road was extended southward to Church Road in 1859 and connected with an existing new road from Church Road to the Limekiln Pike. It was named Greenwood Avenue in 1860, possibly to honor a resident of the area. If so, that would make Greenwood Avenue the first road in Wyncote named for a resident.

The North Penn responded to the Jenkintown plea by constructing a station at the "new road" in late 1859. Testing the waters of development as predicted by engineer Miller, the company designated the station for "accommodation" trains only. In other words, it was a local flag stop. (Today, the Jenkintown station is the busiest in the SEPTA system outside of center city.) The company included a wood shack and a wood platform at the station on the Jenkintown side of what was still a one-track railroad line. The western side of the station was bounded by the marshy remains of the Mather millpond and the Tookany Creek. Originally named "Cheltenham," by 1862 growing use of the stop prompted a name-change to "Jenkintown," again as a result of a petition from area residents. Within a few years, the success of the railroad led to the installation of a second track as far as Abington, which was completed on June 1, 1869. Development pressures also prompted the railroad, needing to insure access on both sides of the now double-track line, to construct a new wooden station building at Jenkintown. A more fitting stone edifice was constructed in 1872, and in 1932, the renowned architect, Horace Trumbauer, constructed a grand new station fitting of the growing suburb.

In 1879, Edward C. Knight, president of the Bound Brook Railroad that was connected with the NPRR at Jenkintown, recommended to the NPRR and the Reading that the three companies would enjoy a considerable efficiency of scale if they unified. (The NPRR had already taken over the operation of the NEPRR in the previous year.) This was accomplished on May 14 of that year when the Reading Railroad leased the two railroads for a period of 990 years. Reading president Franklin B. Gowen, pondering what technological advances would happen in the ensuing years, drolly but correctly predicted that none of the three railroads would survive that long. The NPRR survived another hundred years after the takeover, although its only function was distributing rental payments to shareholders, thus guaranteeing a job for life to the NPRR president, secretary and treasurer. All other employees of the NPRR were dismissed upon the merger. It was ultimately a bad deal for the hardy little railroad. The larger Reading, under Gowen's questionable management skills, went bankrupt in just a year and a chastised Gowen eventually resigned and shot himself.

1860: Townsend Sharpless

Townsend Sharpless, born in Philadelphia in 1793, was an early resident of the developing tract. Like Kent, Sharpless was a partner in a major dry goods business located at 32 South Second Street Philadelphia, just a block from W. C. Kent's establishment. The firm was founded as the Townsend Sharpless Company in 1815 and, by the time his son, Charles, purchased his country home, Sharpless Brothers (the succeeding company after founder Townsend Sharpless' death in 1835) was the oldest firm of its kind in the United States. Sharpless was described as a man "of ample means" as a result of his business activities and was able to retire early to pursue his social activities. As a devout Quaker, Sharpless was involved in several major social movements of the day as an ardent abolitionist and a prominent member of the Philadelphia Prison Society. The Prison Society was instrumental in establishing a new kind of prison, the Eastern Penitentiary on the fringe of the city in Fairmount in 1829. Sharpless is credited with introducing the concept of "commuted sentences" for good behavior into the judicial system.

Townsend's first wife, Mary B. Jones, died at the age of forty-one in 1856. In 1859, at the age of sixty-six years, he was enticed by his sister to visit Virginia and meet her friend, Elizabeth, "the sweet Quakeress of the Valley," who had the most "lovely character" of any woman. He discovered shared interests with the woman and married Elizabeth McAllister Jolliffe of Alexandria Virginia. Elizabeth was thirteen years younger than Townsend. After a year-long honeymoon in Europe, Townsend purchased a lot from Edward M. Davis and built a summer home. It was located in the Chelten Hills side of the Olde Wyncote tract along the Road from Abington to Germantown, just opposite the entrance to the Heacock farm. Davis had just opened "The Serpentine" – today's Serpentine Lane – to gain access to interior lots that he laid out. Sharpless may have been introduced to the area though his association with Kent as well as by the efforts of fellow Quaker activist Davis. Sharpless purchased two more lots from Davis in 1862 and 1863 to extend his property along the creek to the Church

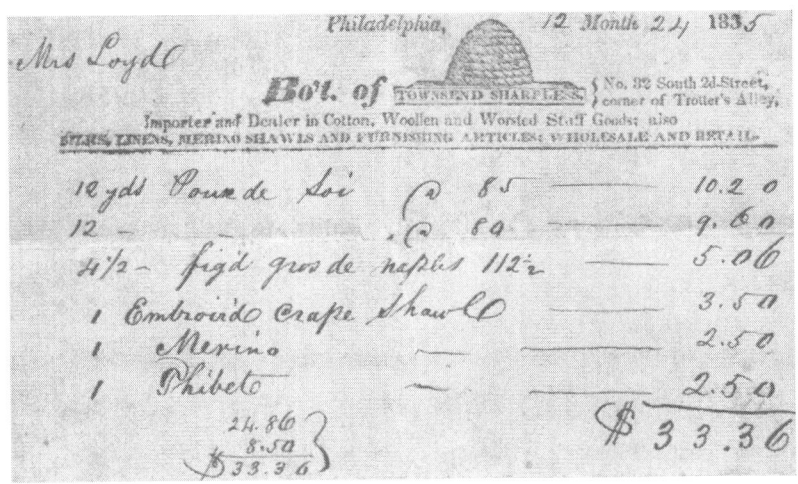

Townsend Sharpless Receipt, 1835
An early invoice for fine cloth from the Townsend Sharpless company,
Courtesy of the Villanova University Library

road. Unfortunately, Sharpless died in 1863, soon after moving into the new home and purchasing the new lot. Elizabeth, by all accounts very much a gracious southern lady, lived there until her death in 1883.

1861: Jay Cooke and the Civil War

At the far southern reach of the Olde Wyncote tract, financier Jay Cooke – "the financier of the Civil War" - assembled a large estate by purchasing several properties from Edward M. Davis and Thomas Mellor from 1861 through 1865. Cooke initially occupied a small farmhouse on the property near the southeast corner of Washington Lane and Church Road when he was in attendance at his farm, awaiting the construction of his grand mansion, *Ogontz,* on a hillside further south on Washington Lane. Although the Civil War had little direct effect on the tract, Cooke's activities were an important component of the war effort. On May 22, 1863, the War Department established the Bureau of Colored Troops. As the war continued, Cooke was approached by Abraham Barker representing his committee for the establishment of a union army training ground for Negro soldiers. Cooke responded by volunteering his property for the camp. However, officers soon determined that the rolling hillside of the property between Church Road and Rock Creek, a tributary of the Tookany Creek, was not appropriate for the military uses intended at the camp, so a sympathetic Edward M. Davis was recruited to the effort. Davis leased some of his land that was intended for his integrated community, located about a quarter of a mile south of the original site on flat farmland near the northern city line of Philadelphia. Camp William Penn was established during the summer of 1863 in Lucretia Mott's backyard. Recruits were brought to the camp by means of the North Pennsylvania Railroad through its Chelten Hills station. Over 11,000 troops were trained there, acquitting themselves well in most major battles of the war.

1865: Charles L. Sharpless

Charles, born in 1821 in Philadelphia, was the son of Townsend and joined him in the business in 1835. Upon Townsend's death in 1863, Charles became the sole proprietor of the firm. In 1870, he admitted his two sons, Charles W. and Henry W. into partnership of the dry goods business, operating as Sharpless and Sons until 1885, when the sons assumed control of the company as Sharpless Brothers. Charles oversaw extensive improvements to his business including the installation of steam heat and an electric power plant to light the premises. The "immense" size of the firm is indicated by its six hundred and fifty employees, not including overseas buyers and agents. Twenty delivery wagons plied the streets. A directory of the day indicates the scope and prosperity of the operation: "The firm's commercial relations are widespread, its facilities unsurpassed, its connections the best possible, while its wise management has ever been noteworthy." (Pennsylvania Historical Review, 1886) He also found time in 1865 to serve as a director of a new Philadelphia bank, the National Bank of the Republic, also at 8th and Chestnut Streets.

Charles purchased most of the Sharpless property from Townsend's widow in 1865, except the house and grounds in which Elizabeth resided. He constructed a new residence, *The Oaks,* on the eastern part of the property near Church Road and, despite his apparently vigorous endeavors to expand the company, also established a model dairy farm in the Olde Wyncote tract that became nationally known. Charles visited the island of Jersey in 1865 to personally select the Jersey cows that would be the hallmark of his farm. His herd eventually included twenty Alderneys as well, and one Jersey, "Dutchess," had the distinction of being the most expensive cow of that type yet purchased in the United States.

One visitor described the business as "carried on with the neatness, the order, the elegance of a first-class commercial house, the *ne plus ultra* of cleanliness and taste in the dairy business." (Commissioner of Agriculture, 1868) His property was further described in that report as "so disposed around the hill on which he has built that all the fields are under his eye as he stands on the slope south of his house." The milk house, with a floor six feet beneath the outside surface of the ground, was flooded with spring water to chill the milk and maintained a constant temperature of fifty-two degrees, varying little "whether people outside wear overcoats or are dropping down with the sunstroke." His livestock interests extended to fine horses, a "fine selection of brood mares and four stallions – two, Post's Hambletonian and Cheltenham, by Hambletonian, and one, Magnolia, by American Star." (Report of Transactions, 1871) His main interest was in breeding efficient road-horses as his Quaker education "inclines him away from everything like racing, " said the report.

Sharpless also possibly holds the distinction of being the first resident of the Olde Wyncote tract to appear on the docket of the Supreme Court of the United States. In 1881, he and his firm were sued by Schreiber & Sons, a publisher, who claimed copyright infringement. Unknown to Sharpless, a subcontractor producing a line of clothing had used an image of a baby elephant as part of the label. The image was copyrighted by Schreibner and, upon discovering its use, the company sued for damages in district court. When the complaint was dismissed, the publisher appealed to the Supreme Court on a technicality involving the other partners' level of liability. The suit was dismissed in an opinion delivered by Chief Justice Morrison Remick Waite in 1884.

By 1870, the various Sharplesses owned most of the triangular parcel of land bounded by Washington Lane, Church Road, and the railroad tracks and four generations of Sharplesses lived there. Charles died in his home on July 1, 1882, at the early age of sixty-two after a two-year battle with kidney disease. At the time of his death, the company was conducting over five million dollars of business per year. Sharpless Brothers lost all of their inventory in a disastrous fire that consumed the 800 block of Chestnut Street on December 11, 1897, which led to the company's demise later that year, ending an eighty-two year run of business.

1867: Hallowell Lumber Yard

The initial commercial development of the Wyncote tract
was the establishment of a lumberyard at the new
Jenkintown station by William Hallowell in 1867. Of course,
the land was purchased from Kent. Hallowell was part of an
extensive family in Abington, Cheltenham, and Moreland
that had deep roots in the area. Isaac Mather was married to

The Sharpless Buttery

If one wishes to see the grazing and dairy business
carried on with the neatness, the order, the elegance of a
first-class commercial house, the *ne plus ultra* of
cleanliness and taste in the dairy business, he should visit
Mr. Sharpless's farm. He has 160 acres so disposed
around the hill on which he has built that all the fields
are under his eye as he stands on the slope south of his
house. The farm buildings are in a valley at the rear of
the house, protected from the winter winds and easily
reached from all parts of the farm. He keeps from 20 to
25 Alderneys, and has what we saw at ery few other
places, a milking house – a large and airy structure, with
hard clay floor well rammed, and stanchions with the
name of each animal tastefully printed and nailed over
the place where she regularly stands. The house is kept as
clean as a dining room. The cows remain there only
during milking time, when a little green corn or other
food is thrown in the mangers, so a cheerful entry and
quiet standing are insured. Close by stands his milk-
house, the walls about 10 feet high, 6 feet being beneath
the surface.

In fact, we may as well here disclose the grand
secret of the Philadelphia butter. From the time the milk
leaves the cow till the butter graces the table, milk,
cream, and butter are near the temperature of 60
degrees. In churning, 62 degrees is found the best figure
for the mercury, the cream is kept as cold as possible.

The skimming is done with a concave tin scoop, perforated with a great number of small holes. This separates the cream from the milk more perfectly than any other instrument or process. Milk is allowed to stand 36 hours before skimming; the depth of the milk in the pans is generally two and a half inches; the same with the cool water on the outside of the pans. These people use the barrel churn driven by horse-power.

Even in the heat of July, and through these dog-days, many of them churn but once a week, and never more than twice. Cream is a great absorbent, and no ill odor of any sort should be allowed in a milk house. If a gentleman happens to be smoking he throws away his cigar when he enters that cool and hallowed retreat, as though the dairymaid were the lady of the manor.

How do these farmers get such a price for their butter? First, they always make a first-class article. . . . Second, they bring in their butter in a showy and attractive condition. . . . A Large tin vessel, designed expressly for the business, has chambers at each end into which ice is put. Thin wooden shelves about three inches apart rest on little projections from the sides. A layer of balls is placed on the bottom and covered with its shelf, but not so as to touch or mar the handsome print of a sheaf of golden grain, which stands out on the top of each ball; on this shelf another layer of prints, and so on till the vessel is full, then containing 40 or 50 pound prints. The tin with ice in each end, is then set into a wooden tub which has been cooled with ice or spring water. Over this is drawn a cover of padded carpeting, with oil-cloth on top. Thus hot air and dust are wholly excluded, and the butter rides to the city and opens in the market-house in as fine condition as when packed in the spring-house. In just this way, with this degree of care and skill, is the best Philadelphia butter made, marked, and marketed.

Report of the Commissioner of Agriculture, 1868

a Hallowell and the family was represented in other families that would move to the village in the next twenty years. Lewis Dannenhower and Thomas Nicholson of Abington, utilizing the necessary and easy access to the rail line, purchased the Hallowell yard and opened for business as Nicholson Coal and Lumber in 1874 just on the other side of Greenwood Avenue from the station.

1868: John Wanamaker

John Wanamaker, born in 1838, would achieve notoriety as the inventor of the "department store" opening his first store, Oak Hall, at Sixth and Market Streets on April 8th, 1861 less than a week before the first shots of the Civil War. On that day, the men and boys' clothing store sold $24.67 worth of clothes. His "Grand Depot" at thirteenth and Market Streets opened in 1869 and revolutionized shopping. Among his retail innovations were sales, refunds for returned merchandise, specified pricing for all items, and the departmentalization of goods. He provided free medical care to employees and pension plans before they became standard practice in business. He was a marketing genius who raised the practice to the level of a science, while famously noting "Half the money I spend on advertising is wasted: trouble is, I don't know which half."

He was successful enough not only to expand his store but also to enable him to purchase property for a summer home and retreat in the country. Wanamaker was just thirty years old when he became a Chelten Hills land owner, purchasing his first parcel of land along York Road in 1868 from Augustus Trego, the son of the Penn professor. The land consisted of three properties with a total of thirty acres and was located close to today's intersection of Meetinghouse Road and Old York Road. Wanamaker used an old farm house on the property for his summer home.

Additional purchases in 1880 and 1883 from Isaac Mather and Edward M. Davis would bring his estate to one hundred and three acres. The Olde Wyncote tract Mather property, on the Township Line Road between York Road and Washington Lane, would be the site of his grand mansion, *Lindenhurst*, which he built over three years and occupied in the summer of 1882. Wanamaker engaged the prolific American architect, Edward A. Sargent, for the design task. Built in the Queen Anne style with snow-cone roofs and angular parapets and dormers, the building rose from stone quarried on the property. Complementing the mansion were a barn, stables, greenhouses, a two-story dollhouse for the children, natatorium with a bowling alley, and a herd of cattle consisting of full-blooded Alderneys, Jerseys, and Ayrshires, "with pedigrees as long as their tails." Wanamaker particularly enjoyed the serenity and beauty of the area, making it a perfect escape from the busy world of Philadelphia business. Wanamaker was in the habit of taking an early morning walk "among the flowers and trees and birds" when he was in residence at the estate, claiming that it made "the day easier when he carries some of the morning freshness into his office." *Lindenhurst* was floridly described by an admiring late nineteenth century historian:

The natural beauty of the land made artificial embellishment in some cases unnecessary; but Mr. Wanamaker spared no activity or thought to make the place as beautiful as possible. Nature was improved upon here, or left in its primeval grandeur there; in one place a too precipitous hillock was leveled or a deep ravine filled up. The touch of art brought forth from the arid ground wide sheets of water and crystal fountains. The monarchs of the forest were spared whenever possible. The natural vigor of the broad lawns was intersected by innumerable shady footpaths, until the place became a veritable park of parks. (Cushing, 1893)

Wanamaker not only enjoyed the fine work of nature in his gardens, but also was an avid art collector. Cushing went on to describe the interior of the house:

Handsome oil paintings adorn the walls; but one that is prized above all the others is that of the elder daughter, painted in 1888, by the celebrated Brozik in Paris. Adjoining this apartment is the dining room, furnished throughout in dark, warm colors. The immense old-fashioned sideboard groans under its load of plate, while in another corner the most valuable of the familial china, principally fine old Louis Phillip, may be seen through the glass doors of walnut cabinets. The room is lighted from the west by a single window of stained glass representing Millet's famous painting "The Angelus." Over the broad doorway leading to the breakfast room are several specimens of art in stained glass depicting biblical scenes, each complete in detail and of great richness of coloring. The walls are entirely surrounded by large open cupboards containing many thousand pieces of Dresden and Limoges dinner ware.

Cushing later described his library:

There is one masterpiece in particular which catches the eye as soon as the visitor enters the room. It depicts a young girl, in whose face rests an expression soft and intellectual, seated gracefully in an easy chair, in a setting of palms and flowering plants. It is a portrait of the younger daughter, and in the corner appears the signature of the artist and the date: "M. de Munkascsy, 1889." The room is filled with articles of virtu [*sic*], many of fabulous worth, no doubt.

Wanamaker was an admirer of Munkacsy who painted a celebrated biblical trilogy from 1882 to 1896 consisting of "Christ Before Pilate," "Golgotha," and "Ecce Homo." Wanamaker purchased them all for an untold small fortune, ranging from $100,000 to 175,000 for each, and displayed them in the library of his country estate.

The great businessman by all accounts was very generous with his exquisite country domain. He frequently brought the Sunday School class he taught to the estate for picnics, and *Lindenhurst* was the site of the one of the first Abington Hospital June Fete Fairs, a June tradition that continues today at the June Fete Farm in Huntingdon Valley. Wanamaker was a Republican activist and was the main fund raiser for the 1888 presidential campaign of Benjamin Harrison. Harrison rewarded Wanamaker with the post of Postmaster General, a position that he occupied from 1889 to 1893. Many innovations flowed from his tenure including the initiation of "country free delivery," which would benefit the new village of Wyncote, and parcel post delivery. Critics of course noted that this subsidized service would greatly favor the owner of the largest department store in the country. On February 8, 1907, tragedy struck *Lindenhurst* when a fire broke out in the early morning hours. The mansion was a total loss. Wanamaker himself put the loss at a conservative $1,500,000 although he stated "It is almost impossible to place a valuation on the property

In the News

Wanamaker Mansion

It is supposed Mr. Wanamaker's new house will cost about $50,000.
Public Spirit April 3, 1880

What promises to be, when completed, as pretty and as stately a mansion as can be found in this section of the State is now receiving the finishing touches at Chelten Hills, on the line of the North Pennsylvania Railroad, for Mr. John Wanamaker. The building is located on a rising slope, which commands an elegant view for many miles. The domes and turrets are of Jenkintown stone. The well-executed wood-work and the beautiful array of stained and plate glass quite bewilder the visitor who is unprepared to see such magnificence.
Public Spirit August 15, 1882

On Tuesday one of the plumbers employed by Mr. Wanamaker, was a passenger on an early morning train on the North Penn. Railroad. At Chelten Hills the train did not stop and he threw off a heavy piece of lead, which was to be used by some workmen at that place. He did not notice the watchman at the crossing, and the piece of lead struck him. He was knocked down and his shoulder and leg broken. Persons who witnessed the occurrence say it was purely accidental.
Public Spirit September 15, 1882

The damage sustained by John Wanamaker of Philadelphia, by the burning of his barn, near Jenkintown, this county, a few nights ago, and which was insured in the Montgomery County Mutual Fire and Storm Insurance Company, and the Union Mutual Fire and Storm Insurance Company of Montgomery County, was adjusted on Wednesday by M. McGlathery and Charles Hurst, the respective Secretaries of the two Companies. The amount awarded was $3,377.05. Both these companies are first-class, and the prompt settlement of this claim speaks volumes in their favor.
Public Spirit, December 30, 1882

John Wanamaker is fixing up the old mill at Chelten Hills and putting in a new water wheel to force water to his residence.
Public Spirit April 28, 1883

Mr. John Wanamaker has started to build a wall around a portion of the handsome property. He has torn down the old mansion, and it makes a decided improvement to his beautiful domain.
Public Spirit April 4, 1885

Mr. John Wanamaker has put up a high fence through a portion of his woods thereby forming a park for his poultry.
Public Spirit April 25, 1885

John Wanamaker has sixty acres in his country property at Jenkintown, and it is all in lawn and wood. He bought Samuel Felty's place to get some farm land.
Public Spirit May 23, 1885

Lindenhurst
John Wanamaker's first mansion on the Isaac Mather property.
Photo: Courtesy of the Old York Road Historical Society

destroyed, including as it did priceless books, statuary, and paintings which can never be replaced." Remarkably, two of the paintings by Munkacsy, *Pilate* and *Golgotha*, were saved by neighbors – including young Ezra Pound, future poet - who streamed to the site and labored through the night to remove treasures before the advancing flames. The two Munkacsy masterpieces were stored with other belongings in the stable before being sent out for restoration and for years afterward, they were exhibited in Wanamaker's downtown store during the Easter season. It was a good thing they were moved: a month later, another fire consumed the stable destroying the balance of Wanamaker's possessions.

John Wanamaker's son, Rodman, took charge of building a new mansion for his parents. Even more luxurious than the original, it contained 300 rooms and was built in the French chateau style. Mary Wanamaker died at Atlantic City in August of 1920 at the age of eighty-one and her funeral was conducted at *Lindenhurst*. Her obituary in *The New York Times* noted that "she lived a retired life, caring little for the social activities of the world. . . . Her interests were centered on her home and her family." In early December, 1922, Wanamaker caught a cold on a trip to his New York store and was confined to bed for several weeks at *Lindenhurst*. He died after being moved to his downtown home on December 12, 1922, at the age of eighty-four, leaving an estate valued at one hundred million dollars. The vacant and financially unviable mansion was demolished in 1944.

1870: Kent Quarry

Kent's quarry is located on the southwest side of today's Glenside Avenue just east of Greenwood Avenue. This quarry may have provided the stone for the Kent mansion and is now occupied by a residential street, Cliff Terrace. The quarry expanded further up the hill to the southeast in the '70s, the size indicating a much more extensive business in stone as the cut is quite substantial. That part of the quarry is now occupied by the Lincoln Investment building. Kent rented this parcel to O'Neill and Son who developed a large business producing building stone. Felix O'Neill of Jenkintown was a prominent plasterer, stone mason, and builder, responsible for many of the era's stone bridges in Jenkintown and vicinity.

Several earlier authors have indicated that the larger quarry was the source of foundation stone for the construction of City Hall. Most recently, the issue was resurrected in 1959 when the railroad siding leading into the quarry was uncovered as part of the construction of the new post office on the other side of Glenside Avenue. However, the records of the Commission on Public Buildings – the Philadelphia agency responsible for building the new City Hall in the last quarter of the 19th century - include a list of six bidders for the stone contract in 1871, but none are the O'Neill or Kent quarry. The winning bid later that year was to the Conshohocken Stone Company, although a relative of William Hallowell, the neighboring lumberyard proprietor, Charles H. Hallowell, was awarded one of the contracts for 500,000 bricks. The size of the quarry indicates that a substantial project or projects in the city were supported by the operation. If it was not City Hall, then the actual use of the stone has yet to be discovered.

The quarry reached the limits of its development in 1886. Residential construction was impinging on the once-remote operation, but the big problem was that the operators had excavated to the limits of their property lines. The *Public Spirit* noted on July 10, 1886, that neither Joseph Heacock nor Henry Lippincott, who owned the adjoining properties, were pleased with this operation as they felt it depreciated their own land. They were also unwilling to sell to the Kent estate to increase the size of the quarry. The newspaper noted sardonically that O'Neill could drill downward, but "there is danger that one of their heavy blades will kill a chinaman or two and they are so tenderhearted that they would not do that."

Besides the economic implications of closing an operation that employed sixty men, the paper rued the day when the station will be "without the occasional fun of dodging rocks and the music of bombardment." In April of the next year, one particularly big blast showered rock on the Harper Restaurant on the other side of the tracks. The newspaper noted that one patron who was in the act of eating was so startled that he nearly dropped his glass of water. He thought that "the dom prabitionists was blowin' up the house," a reference to the activities of Jenkintown's temperance society and the fact that Harper's restaurant had problems with the law regarding the service of liquor. In a following article on April 30 of that year, the paper noted another large blast and commented that after an explosion, "people in the neighborhood are accustomed to look above them to see if any rocks are falling in dangerous proximity." Definitely not a prime neighbor in a growing community!

1875: Joseph Heacock, Jr.

Joseph Heacock, Jr., assisted his father on the old Webster farm while attending the Abington Friends School and after graduation. Falling into debt as a young man, he left the farm at the age of twenty-six to work for hire in upstate New York. He briefly kept a diary recording his adventure and recalled the day that he left home:

I walked to the York Road Station so as to go in the 6:15 through train. Arriving in Philadelphia, I went at once to the conductor of the through freight and asked him to take me up the road as far as Bethlehem. He spoke very kindly to me and told me that he would gladly help me on my way. Left Phil.a. at 10 o'clock. (Heacock, 1871)

When he got to New York, he noted the spectacle of the steam engines, a memory that will resonate with residents of Glenside Avenue up to 1950 as they tried to keep fresh-washed clothes clean:

I thought that I had seen pretty black smoke made by the engines on the North Penn Railroad. But all that I had seen was as nothing as what the engines on the Northern Central made.

His mother, Esther, died in 1874 while he was away from home. Upon satisfying his debts, and perhaps allaying some personal concerns, he returned to the homestead in 1875 and rented his father's farm. In 1876, he married Elizabeth Walker of Valley Forge. Proving to be quickly successful, he purchased the assets of his father's farm in 1876 as Joseph Sr. faced infirmity at the age of seventy-six. The total cost of outfitting such a farm in those days was $583.25 - which included the cows. Joseph, Jr. continued the work of the farm and began raising a large family on the old homestead. The senior Joseph Heacock died in 1883 on his farm. Joseph and Elizabeth bore their first four children in the farmhouse, although their firstborn, Fannie, and fourth, Mary, both died in infancy.

1876: The Lippincotts - Joshua W., Henry H., Horace G.

In the Centennial year, several more members of the extensive Lippincott family moved to the Olde Wyncote tract, confirming the trend of making Wyncote a "family affair." Contrary to local belief, these Lippincott's were not directly related to the famous Philadelphia publishing company of the same last name, founded by Joshua Ballinger Lippincott. They may have been somewhat distantly related as they were born in the various areas of

Heacock Bill of Sale
Joseph Heacock turned over the farm to his son in 1876, although he
maintained ownership of the property until his death. Note that Mr.
Heacock did not give up his buffalo robe.
Courtesy of the Friends Historical Library, Swarthmore College

central New Jersey, but there doesn't appear to be any
immediate connection.

Joshua W. Lippincott was born in Cinnaminson, New
Jersey, in 1840 and attended Haverford College, class of
1860. He was president of Lippincott and Parry, a wholesale

dealer in woolen goods and other cloth, founded by his uncle, Joshua Lippincott, in 1828. In 1863, after the death of Joshua (the senior) and the retirement of co-founder Samuel Parry, the firm changed its name to Lippincott & Johnson with the admission of two new partners, and conducted business at 1021 Walnut Street in the city. Also in that year, Joshua married Mary Elizabeth Parry, Samuel and Martha's daughter. (Coincidentally, Mary Elizabeth's paternal grandmother was a Lippincott.) Unfortunately, Mary died in 1866, age twenty-seven, shortly after their marriage and Joshua then married Eliza Greenough in 1869. He was a member of the board of the North Penn Railroad which may have introduced him to the area. Joshua purchased land from Mary Sharpless in the Olde Wyncote tract in 1874 and constructed a new home on Washington Lane in 1877. The company prospered but was crippled by an extensive fire at their new location at 629 Market St. on November 9, 1891. Although suffering $300,000 worth of damage, the firm recovered and conducted business for many more years. His son by Eliza, Horace G. Lippincott, also lived in Wyncote and assumed the business of the firm upon Joshua's death in 1896 at his home. This Horace G. is variously referred to as "Jr." or "2nd" as he was named for his older cousin, Horace G. Lippincott, son of George and Mary. Horace (2nd) resided at *Squirrel Corner,* the renamed former homestead of Thomas Mather.

Henry Heulings Lippincott was born in Westfield, New Jersey, in June of 1832. He entered the mercantile business, operating as a wholesale grocer on Delaware Avenue just north of Market Street. In 1861, he incorporated as H.H. Lippincott & Trotter with his younger brother George and William Trotter. In 1858, he married Priscilla Parry in Philadelphia, daughter of the founding partner in his brother, Joshua's, firm of Lippincott and Parry. They had three children, including Mary W., who never married and became a significant presence in the burgeoning community of Wyncote. In September of 1876, Henry purchased property from Mary Sharpless and Joshua Lippincott for his country home. Four more purchases through 1888 extended his property in a wide swath from Greenwood Avenue, across Washington Lane, and curving down to the railroad tracks. He died at his home in Wyncote on August 25, 1893.

The first Horace G. Lippincott was born in 1844 in Philadelphia to George Lippincott and Mary Greenough. Mary was the sister of Eliza who had married Joshua in this intricately intertwined family. Horace was an 1862 graduate of Haverford where he was a member of several organizations including the Dorian Cricket Club, playing the position of "long-leg" and on which he distinguished himself by earning the team's batting honors. Soon after graduating, he was a co-founder of the Haverford College Alumni Association. He married Caroline Rowland of Philadelphia in 1873 and had six children. In 1876 he purchased a parcel of land from William C. Kent and a larger piece from old-time resident Isaac Shoemaker across the South-central part of the Olde Wyncote tract and built a country estate named *Stonehouse*. He was a member of the Union League and shared an interest common to so many area Quakers, prison reform, as a long-time supporter of the Prison Society.

1877: Wharton Barker

Wharton Barker may be one of the most active and successful Philadelphians of the era about whom practically nothing was written or is now remembered. He was born in Philadelphia in 1846 to Abraham Barker and Sarah Wharton Barker, successors to distinguished Quaker families that included a former mayor of the city. He has not the honor of a biography recording his life and deeds and the Web site "Political Graveyard" sullenly notes that even his burial place is "unknown" following his death in 1921, also in Philadelphia. (He is buried at Laurel Hill.) Upon graduation from Penn in 1866, he immediately joined the Barker Brothers firm. Donehoo's history of the state notes that Wharton "almost immediately manifested those qualities of the sanely progressive banker, which won for his house and for himself a wide and valued acquaintance in financial and political centers of Europe, so that the house of Barker realized handsomely from foreign contracts." (Donehoo, 1926) These contacts led to a commission as the American representative for the Russian government in procuring warships from the Cramp shipyard (C.D. Cramp was a later Wyncote neighbor) in Philadelphia as well as a commission from the government of China to assist in the planning of a telephone system, railroads, and banks. One can imagine the force of his personality as well as credibility as these were two of the most unapproachable nations of that era. In 1870, Abraham and Wharton Barker along with Joseph Wharton (Wharton Barker's uncle and mentor) moved the Wharton Railroad Switch Company from Philadelphia to Jenkintown. The company provided many of the railroad switches for the rapidly developing railroad systems of the day, many of which were financed by the Barker bank.

Barker satisfied his interest in economics and world affairs by founding several publications, most of a political nature and including the influential newspaper, *The American*. His interests turned political and as a political amateur and private citizen, he masterfully engineered the upset nomination of James A. Garfield in the 1880 National Republican Convention in Chicago. Later, Barker was the candidate for president of the United States for the Populist party in the election of 1900. His candidacy was based on his interest in "bimetallism" as the basis for currency management among other issues. The local newspapers of the day are replete with detailed debates between Barker and Edward M. Davis on the proper monetary policy of the United States.

Through all of his political and business activities, Barker accumulated an influential set of political friends. Major policy issues that occupied him included sugar tariffs, trade with Canada, and bimetallism and monetary policy. He was considered a national expert in all three areas. Business relationships with Russia, China, and Brazil, kept his name current in the State Department. His chief political crony and frequent correspondent was Senator John Mitchell. Barker was stayed close to both Benjamin Harrison and James Garfield and Congressman William Darrah Kelley of Philadelphia was constantly in touch with Barker involving political matters of interest and patronage.

Barker married Margaret Corlies Baker in 1867 and presumably lived with his parents at *Lyndon* for the first years of his marriage. By 1877, he purchased a large parcel of land on the northwest side of Greenwood Avenue to the Mill road, and stretching from Church Road on the Southwest to today's Maple Avenue. The lot consisted of seventy-seven

acres and a residence in the area of today's Barker Road. By
1881, he invested in an additional nineteen acres on the
northwest side of the mill road bounded on the southwest by
Church Road and on the Northwest by today's Royal
Avenue. However, by 1876, Abraham had constructed a new
home for Wharton across Church Road on the second
property he purchased from Barclay Lippincott. This was his
home for ten years. Shortly after moving in, about 1878,
Wharton laid out a road to connect the back entrance of his
estate on Greenwood Avenue with the mill road. Perhaps by
popular usage, the road became known as "Wyncote Lane"
by the end of the eighties. Wharton, interested in enhancing
the natural beauty of his holdings, lined the road with trees
and into the new century, the road was renamed Deaver
Road to honor a later resident. Wharton moved to a new
home constructed on the 1881 Church Road property that
became his last home in Wyncote. That site later became the
estate of George Horace Lorimer, *Belgraeme*.

1877: J. Wesley Pullman

Pullman was a hard working mining engineer and iron
manufacturer who did not fit the mold of a Gilded Age
tycoon. His modest home in Wyncote, unremarkable except
for its situation on a country hilltop, indicates he was there
to enjoy the sylvan setting, although he, too, provided a
name for his estate; *Dogwood*. Just four days after
purchasing his first parcel in the Olde Wyncote Tract,
Wharton Barker split off a five-acre parcel for Pullman.
Pullman and Joseph Wharton were colleagues through the
iron ore business and were involved in the Hibernia mines of
Northern New Jersey, which Wharton finally purchased in
1904 through his acquisition of the New Jersey Iron Mining
Company. Given the short turn-around, perhaps the
transaction was a favor to a family-friend as Barker would
not dispose of any other parts of his property until his
bankruptcy almost twenty years later. Pullman may have
been attracted to the area due to his marriage in 1873 to
Julia Kent, a relative of William C. Kent and their new home
adjoined Kent's holdings in the new village.

Wharton Barker Circa 1866
Taken about the time Wharton graduated from college and joined his father's banking firm. The pose suggests a serious man with great aspirations.

Photo: Courtesy of Rodman Barker, Council, Idaho.

The driveway to his home would become North Bent Road in the twentieth century and he became a permanent resident after his retirement in 1907. The Pullmans traveled extensively through Europe, the Pacific Coast, Mexico, and Puerto Rico.

1878: Edward Starr

Edward Starr was born in Philadelphia in 1844 and followed his father into the finance industry. As a star cricket player at Haverford College, Starr acted as umpire in the first intercollegiate sports contest in any sport in the United States. It was a cricket match against the University of Pennsylvania played at the Haverford cricket field, actually a meadow in front of one of the academic buildings. Starr's counterpart from Penn was Beauveau Borie, a future resident of Cheltenham and Jenkintown. The Haverford team felt under-talented due to the loss by graduation of one of the best cricket players of the era, Horace G. Lippincott. As any American who has tried to understand this indecipherable sport will appreciate, the contest, despite starting in mid-morning, was declared over as darkness fell after only the first innings (note, a singular term) was complete. The competitive unit, "innings," became singular in form by dropping the "s" only after the sport was morphed by American culture into the new sport of baseball. The modest (for cricket) score after the first innings was 89 to 87 in favor of the home team. The victorious Haverford players hosted the visitors at dinner at a nearby restaurant thus missing evening Bible services on campus and incurring the wrath of their vigilant president. The historian Horace Mather Lippincott said that cricket particularly appealed to the "Quaker habits of Philadelphians." He explained that the sport is planned for the participant rather than the spectator and "the length of time taken to finish a game is founded upon the idea that it is pleasant to prolong an intermingling with one's friends." (Lippincott, 1917)

Starr, a broker and member of the Philadelphia Stock Exchange for thirty years, was the founder of Starr & Company, with offices at 4th and Chestnut Streets in Philadelphia. In 1866, he married Townsend Sharpless' daughter, Mary Williams Sharpless, in a grand wedding ceremony at the Sharpless estate on Washington Lane. He died at his Chelten Hills home, *The Orchard,* in 1914 at the age of seventy.

1879: Ario Pardee, Jr.

General Pardee, born in 1839, inherited the coal empire and assorted companies of his father in upstate Pennsylvania, the A. Pardee & Co. of Hazelton. The company conducted business with the Whartons and the senior Pardee was a founder of the Reading railroad. Pardee took over management of the companies immediately after his graduation from Rensselaer Polytechnic Institute in 1858. Joining the 28th Pennsylvania Infantry in 1861, Pardee served in the Civil War and distinguished himself at the battle of Gettysburg where the field that saw his most important engagement is named after him. His father had financed the creation and outfitting of the entire brigade with which he served. He also served during the Atlanta campaign and, for his service, he received a battlefield promotion to the rank of Brevet Brigadier General. Having contracted dysentery during the war, his health was impaired and he moved to Philadelphia in 1875 in order to be closer to medical care and manage his company's operations in that city. He received a directorship of the North Pennsylvania Rail Road and in 1879 purchased a twenty-five acre estate in the Olde Wyncote tract from Richard J. Dobbins, who had obtained it two years before from Charles L. Sharpless. Pardee died at his home on March 16, 1901.

General Ario Pardee, Jr.
The General and his wife on their front porch about 1900.
Courtesy of Pardee Resources Company, Philadelphia

The Gilded Age, a term invented by Mark Twain in his book by the same name, afforded some very successful and very wealthy businessmen the opportunity to escape the city at will and establish alternate lives for themselves and their families in a verdant country setting. It also provided an opportunity for them to increase the wealth by speculating in land that would soon see spectacular development and growth in the flush post-Civil War and post-Reconstruction era. The Age manifested itself early in Philadelphia, with the Olde Wyncote tract serving as a precursor to the even more extravagant homes that would be built elsewhere by the likes of Flagler, Carnegie, Frick, Vanderbilt, Morgan. At the height of the Gilded Age nationally, Wyncote would be surpassed locally by the sumptuous estates of the Main Line being marketed by the Pennsylvania Railroad in Philadelphia's western suburbs. But the Gilded Age itself would soon be transformed into a new life for the Olde Wyncote tract. That new form would include opportunities "for the rest of us," as the old computer commercial stated, and an integral community in every sense where once only farms and magnificent private estates stood. If the physical trappings of wealth represented by the estates could not survive the development pressures of the approaching twentieth century, the attractions of a naturally beautiful setting and the pursuit of a good quality of life would survive in the institutions and social structures of the new community. It just needed a few more years of development – and an official name.

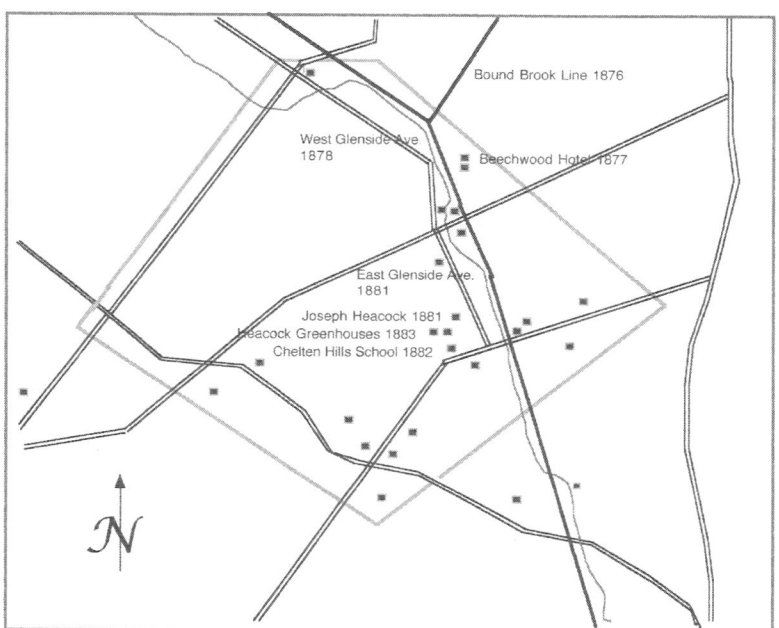

Gestation - A Decade of Slow Growth
The ten years between 1876 and 1887 saw the completion of the crossroads, Greenwood Avenue and Glenside Avenue, which would become the new center of the village.

Chapter 5

GESTATION

*His guests [arrived] through a neighborhood which is that of
a highly improved and picturesque landscape of hill and dale and
wooded heights, crowned with magnificent country seats.*
(Public Spirit, *June 16, 1877*)

Philadelphia of 1876, "the First City," was the center of the celebration of the birthday of our nation. The Centennial Exhibition of that year marked a hundred years of survival and achievement and an astonishing ten million people would visit the glittering buildings and grounds of the grand fair. The Pennsylvania, the Baltimore & Ohio, The North Penn and the Reading railroads would channel many of those visitors from far-away places to the West Philadelphia grounds of the giant party. With the Civil War behind the country, new prosperity favored the city and its people. The population of the city during the Centennial was about 725,000 and in just twenty-five years more, that number would rise to 1.3 million. Affluence and convenient railroads would push increasing numbers of Philadelphians out to the new suburbs that began to flourish near rail lines.

But more than just celebrating the nation's survival, the Centennial pointed the way to a new age of growth and prosperity powered by the great technical inventions of the day that would be demonstrated at the affair. From the large to the small, these inventions promised new conveniences and comforts. The hallmark of the exhibition, the immense Corliss steam engine, promised unlimited power to various industries and would increase their productivity many times. That power would even reach the small mills that lined the Tookany Creek. It would soon be tapped to drive whirring electric dynamos to dispel the nighttime gloom of streets, businesses and homes. Professor Bell's talking device would facilitate not only business but also the social and cultural life of the community. These innovations would find their way to the Olde Wyncote tract over the next twenty-five years and lead to the emergence of a modern community. Residents of the Olde Wyncote tract would play a role in the conduct of the venture. Area residents - William C. Kent, along with his former partners John O. James and Charles Santee, and John Wanamaker - were involved in the planning of the exhibition along with Abraham Barker who served on the finance committee. Wharton Barker obtained a role as the banker for the Russian delegation, a position that would lead to further relations with that nation and formal recognition from Czar Alexander II. In the ensuing years, the flow of Gilded Age wealth would diminish in the Olde Wyncote tract, but a larger, better equipped, and more complete community of more modest means would evolve and flourish in its place.

1876: Bound Brook Line

While the Vanderbilts, Kents, Barkers, Cookes, and Drexels of the world seemingly captured the market for railroad building, an unknown entrepreneur, Henry Martyn Hamilton of Montclair, New Jersey, thought he had a way of elbowing in on the action. Capitalizing on widespread sentiment opposed to the monopolistic tendencies of the B & O railroad in the Washington to New York market, Hamilton thought he had a solution: create a railroad that would thread a back-country route through Easton, Reading, and Lancaster. Work on a new railroad called "The National Railway" began in 1867. Hamilton proceeded by cobbling together small railroads through New Jersey and Pennsylvania. The effort degenerated into interminable

NEW YORK AND PHILADELPHIA NEW LINE.
BOUND BROOK ROUTE.
Depots, Foot of Clarkson Street and foot of Liberty Street.

TRAINS FROM NEW YORK, BOUND BROOK, AND TRENTON
To PHILADELPHIA.
OCTOBER 9th, 1876.

☞ Trains are run on New York time between New York and Bound Brook, and Philadelphia time between Bound Brook and Philadelphia.

Distance from New York	STATIONS.	128 Yardley Accom.	184 Trenton and Centennial	102 Philad'a Express.	104 Philad'a Express.	106 Philad'a Fast Line.	110 Eastern Express.	130 Philad'a Bund Brook Local	114 Evening Fast Line.	132 Trenton & Bnd Brook Local	118 Evening Express.	SUNDAY TRAINS.	
	Leave.	a. m.	a. m.	a. m.	a. m.	a. m.	p. m.	p. m.	p. m.	p. m.	p. m	a. m.	p.m.
	New } Clarks'n St			6.35	7.35	9 05					6 20		
	York } Liberty St.	5.40	6.45	7.45	9.15	1.30		5 00			6.30		
1.0	Jersey City	5.50	6 56	7 53	9.25	1 41		5.11			6.41		
12.5	Elizabeth	6.17	7 17	8.17	9 47	2 02		5.34			7.05		
15 1	Roselle	6.23	7 23										
17.2	Cranford	6.28	7.26										
19.5	Westfield	6 33	7 30										
21.7	Fanwood	6.35	7 34										
24.1	Plainfield	6 44	7 39	8.34		2.19				7.22			
26.9	Dunellen	6 50	7 44										
31.2	Bound Brook	6.57	7.50	8.40	10.10	2.25	2 30	5.55	5.56	7.30			
33.4	Weston	7.02	7.58				2.45		6 03				
37.1	Hamilton	7.06	8.02				2 52		6 07				
41.3	Vanskta	7.12					3.02		6 18				
42.7	Harlingen	7.15					3 07		6.24				
45.1	Skillman	7.19	8.15				3.15		6.31	7.55			
47.0	Stoutsburg	7.23					3.21		6.37				
48.6	Hopewell	7.27	8 21		10.35	2 56	3.27	6.27	6.42	8.02			
53.3	Pennington	7.32	8 32		10.45		3.42	6.55	6.52	8.12			
57.4	Ewing	7.43					3.52		7 00				
58.3	Trenton Junction	7.45	8 43	9.20	10.52	3.12	4 00	6.42	7 03	8 20			
	TRENTON.. } Arr.	8.05	8 55	9 35	11 05	3 30	4.30	7 00	7.15	8.35			
	Lve.	7.35	8.15	9.25	10.20	3.00	3.45	6 30		8.05			
59.8	Yardley	6 55	7.55	8.50	9.25		3.18	4.15	6.48		8.28	7.00	7.00
62.9	Palmer	7.02						4.23				7.05	7.07
64.7	Woodburne	7.07						4.30				7.13	7.13
67.3	Langhorne.	7.13		9.03			3.30	4 40			8.42	7.20	7.20
69.4	Janney	7 18						4 46				7 25	7.25
71.3	Trevose	7.23						4.52				7.30	7.31
73.0	Somerton	7.28	8.15	9.14				4.55	7.13		8 53	7.35	7.35
76.7	Bethayres.	7.36		9.21				5.07	7.20		9.00	7.44	7.43
78.3	Beneret	7.41						5.17				7.48	7.48
79.2	Noble	7.43						5 15				7.50	7.50
80.3	Jenkintown June.	7.50	8.27	f 9.30	f 9.58	f 11.27	f 3.53	5.25	f 7.28		f 9.00	7.55	7.55
	Green Lane.												
88.4	Berks St. Depot..	8.25	8.40	9.50	10.15	11.45	4 10	5.50	7.45		9.25	8.15	8.25
	Centennial Depot.		8 55	10 05	10 26	11 50	4 23						
	Arrive.	a. m.	a. m.	a m	a. m.	a. m.	p. m.	p. m.	p. m.	p. m.	p. m.	a. m.	p. m.

No through trains are run on Sunday. Passengers for Elizabeth and Plainfield will not be taken on westward trains. No. 102 will stop on signal at stations marked § for passengers west of Bound Brook only. Trains marked "f" at Jenkintown Junction stop to let off passengers for Main Line North Pennsylvania Railroad. All trains stop at Green Lane to leave passengers for Germantown. Pullman Cars on Nos. 104 and 106 for Centennial Grounds.

TICKET OFFICES:
FOOT OF LIBERTY ST.   FOOT OF CLARKSON ST., NORTH RIVER,
       529 BROADWAY.   N. W. CORNER SPRING ST.,
              AND AT THE PRINCIPAL HOTELS.

Schedule to New York

Residents of Jenkintown and the Olde Wyncote tract could go directly to New York in just two and a half hours. Notice the warning about the time difference between New York and Philadelphia. In 1876, the country still depended on solar time for calculating local time; that is, noon was determined in your town by when the sun was directly overhead. As fast train travel became more common in the late 19th century, this led to inconvenient discrepancies in train schedules. In this case, noon in New York was five minutes before noon in Philadelphia. The railroads first solved this problem by establishing their running time based on solar time in the town of their headquarters. But this became problematic when a route was served by two or more railroads, such as this trip to New York. This method created additional headaches in places where several railroads funneled into the same terminus. The Pittsburgh station for example, maintained six different clocks. The problem was resolved in 1883 by the nation's railroads which devised a system of standard time zones.

squabbles between competing railroads and the forces of the major railroads that stalled development at every step. Investors were timid due to the volatility of the structure and the scandals involved. In 1874, the North Penn Railroad, running through the Olde Wyncote tract for almost twenty years, took over the operation of the National Railway a spur line from Jenkintown to Yardley, the Delaware River Branch, which would connect with lines coming from Bound Brook, in central New Jersey. In 1875, acquisition of land took away additional property at the base of William C. Kent's hill for the line that headed north. The line opened in May of 1876, just in time to facilitate travel to the Centennial Exhibition in Philadelphia that guaranteed the success of the railroad venture, and that of the exhibition as well.

1877: Glenside Avenue West

A new road "on the township line between Abington and Cheltenham" was opened in 1877. It extended from Rice's mill to Greenwood Avenue and the Jenkintown station. Public interest in a shorter route between the two stations probably inspired the road, saving a long trip by way of the Church road. In addition, the mail for Abington was carted from the mail depot at Jenkintown station to the Abington station for distribution to that community several times a day, so postal authorities also had motive for instituting a shorter route. The road would serve another important purpose in the early days of the community as a dump sprang up at the top of the Glenside Avenue hill, just off to the northeast side of the road overlooking the old Mather millpond.

1877: The Beechwood Hotel

The first wave of the public in large numbers to discover the beauty of the Olde Wyncote tract was composed of vacationers from the city seeking recreation and restoration in the country. In 1870, William C. Kent, perhaps facing the infirmities of advanced age and having retired, sold

In the News

The Joys of Riding the Rails

The artists who have employed their elegant leisure in portraying in pencil, the mysterious workings of their degraded minds upon the walls [of the station house] and who have in consequence rendered it impossible for a pure minded man or woman, except they be stone blind, from sheltering themselves from the rain or wind in these buildings, ought to be kicked with stout cow-hide boots all the way from Hartsville to Abington station for the dirty work they have done. The whipping-post and cat-tails would suit their case.
Public Spirit, February 17, 1877

It is unpleasant to be constantly reminding others of their duty, but when the necessities of the case demand it, we think it time to speak out. There is a cesspool behind the Jenkintown railway station that emits so unpleasant an odor that it is with difficulty passengers sit in either waiting room any length of time with any degree of comfort. Can't the railroad officials remedy this. Surely they are not aware of it, else it would have received their attention.
Public Spirit, July 19, 1884

A well has been dug behind the Jenkintown Station by the railroad company to supply its patrons with good water. A spring was struck at twelve feet.
Public Spirit, September 27, 1884

Beechwood to George F. Lee and moved to a smaller house just east of *Beechwood* on the property he had purchased from Joseph Heacock in 1853. Lee, described as a "Gentleman of the City of Philadelphia" according to the deed, owned the mansion for only two years.

In 1872, Lee sold the property to Richard J. Dobbins, an aggressive land speculator who already owned several parcels in the Old York Road area. He also "owned" the Old York Road as a director of the company that owned and managed the Cheltenham Turnpike Company, as the road was known along its Cheltenham stretch. Dobbins was a Philadelphia contractor who had constructed Memorial Hall, and other buildings, for the Centennial Celebration in West Philadelphia. His local holdings included a farm near Willow Grove and his palatial estate along the Eastern portion of Old York Road near the Stetson and Mott properties, and, later, the estate of Charles L. Sharpless that he subdivided in 1880. He is credited with bestowing the name of "Ashbourne" on the area of his estate, after a similar named area in England that he favored. As a director of the North Pennsylvania Rail Road, Dobbins intended to capitalize on the growing popularity of the area and the trend of developing resort properties near the new country train stations of the railroads. He was not new to the hotel business as operator of the Congress Hall hotel in Cape May and having just sold a resort hotel in Long Branch, New Jersey, as well. He would conclude his interests in the Congress Hall after it suffered a devastating fire in the following year. He opened Kent's former estate in 1877 as "Beechwood House" under the management of one Mr. Boothby. (In one of the never-ending coincidences sparked by Wyncote's Anglo heritage, there is a Beechwood House in Scotland that was the home of one Lord Boothby.)

On the day of the grand opening, June 14, Dobbins met 400 guests, some of whom arrived by special train from the city, to a "picturesque landscape of hill and dale and wooded heights, crowned with magnificent country seats," according to a newspaper report of the day. The mansion was augmented over the previous years by an addition of 135 by 44 feet in order to accommodate a total of one hundred and fifty overnight guests. A band "discoursed sweetest melody on the noble piazza" as croquet parties in "light summer costumes dotted the lawn close cropped as velvet." After a sumptuous dinner, the men partied downstairs in the billiard room "and iced champagne was as plentiful for the gentlemen as claret punch was abundant in the upper room for the ladies." (Beechwood House, 1877) Guests included neighbors such as Joseph Bosler, Edward M. Davis, and Abraham and Wharton Barker, as well as Philadelphia dignitaries such as future Attorney-General Wayne McVeigh; the mayor of Philadelphia, Daniel Fox; F. A. Comly, president of the N.P.R.R. and Senator John H. Mitchell. Each gentleman was accompanied by "his Lady," of course.

The Hotel prospered for seventeen years amid the steady growth of the area. By 1884, the local newspaper would say of the hotel:

Among the many beautiful summer resorts within a radius of 10 miles from the City of Brotherly Love, we know of no one more tastefully beautiful and more beautifully situated; certainly we can say there is no place more healthfully located than the "Hotel Beechwood," situate on the hill top opposite Jenkintown Station." (*Public Spirit*, 5/31/1884)

The Beechwood Hotel, as it came to be known, thrived under the ownership of Dobbins and became a regional center of entertainment that included "hops," concerts, equestrian competition, as well as plain old relaxation in the country. In 1884, Dobbins constructed another building on the northwest side of *Beechwood* that increased the occupancy to three hundred guests. For many visitors, it would be a chance to experience the new world of suburban living and many returned to purchase the first houses of the new community.

1881: Glenside Avenue East and Joseph Heacock's Home

It may have been inevitable that once a road connected the Abington and Jenkintown train stations, residents would start thinking about a similar road connecting Jenkintown station with the Chelten Hills stop. In 1877, a jury of local residents was appointed to examine the prospect for such a

road that would eliminate an otherwise two-mile route by
way of Church Road to travel from one station to another.
Joseph Hunter, the ubiquitous surveyor and magistrate of
Jenkintown, performed the survey of the short route.
Nonetheless, it took four years to bring the road to fruition.
The first part of the road was probably an easy decision as it
followed the cart-way from Greenwood Avenue that accessed
the quarry at the top of the hill. From there, the road
followed the Heacock pasture and pond to intersect with and
end at Washington Lane. The first house on Glenside
Avenue was built that year by Joseph Heacock, Jr. No doubt
feeling crowded in the old homestead at the top of the hill
which he shared with his elderly father and his father's five
unmarried sisters, he built a hulking gray mansion,
Netherhouse, overlooking a peach orchard, new road, and
the pond, for his wife and two children. Two more children
would be born in the new home. The mansion would pass to
Joseph's older son James upon his death and last until the
property was further subdivided in 1962.

An unfortunate and sensational event occurred in front
of Joseph's house on August 1, 1886, "while residents were
"peacefully slumbering on Sunday morning all unconscious
that a murder most foul had been committed the night
previous." While a boarder at Heacock's house had reported
hearing a commotion in the direction of the Chelten Hills
Station, early the next morning, track workers found the
body of a man floating in Heacock's pond. A folded coat left
by the train track led observers at first to believe the death
was a suicide. But the victim bore the signs of being beaten
to death, according to an inquest by Squire Joseph Hunter.
His pockets contained several objects: a pocket book, $2.64
in money, a piece of a Ridgeway park programme, a Chinese
Laundry ticket, and a piece of bloody string. No retail
consumer card or driver's license to aid in the investigation
in 1886! Armed only with the victim's description –
"strongly built, apparently about fifty years old, about 165
pounds, thin moustache" - and the fact that a piece of coal
was found imbedded in his skull - Squire Hunter and
Constable Bates identified the place of death as the
Nicholson coal yard and the man as Jacob Hoffman.
Hoffman was known as "Dutch Jake" of West Philadelphia

Netherhouse
The home of Joseph Heacock, Jr., constructed on Glenside Avenue in 1881. Children from the Heacock School are sitting on the porch.
Photo: Courtesy of Nancy Wood, Wyncote

Chelten Hills School
Viewed in 1896, the school accommodated children from the neighborhood as well as from other countries who boarded at the Heacock farmhouse. About fifty five children and teachers are pictured in this view.
Photo: Courtesy of the Old York Road Historical Society

In the News

On Monday, the Hatboro train knocked a cow higher than she could jump off the track at John Larzelere's place.
Public Spirit, October 24, 1874

The boarders at the Beechwood postponed their fireworks until Tuesday, on account of Monday's rain. There were several very fine set pieces, a number of bombs each containing 150 colored balls, a fountain consisting of four dozen Roman candles fired at once, which filled the air for several minutes with innumerable balls of fire.
Public Spirit, July 10, 1880

Does your heart ever seem to stop and you feel a death-like sensation, do you have sharp pains in region of your heart – you have Heart Disease. Try Dr. Graves' Heart Regulator. $1 per bottle.
Public Spirit, December 15, 1883

Bad temper often proceeds from the painful disorders to which women are subject. In female complaints, Dr. Robt. Pierce's "Favorite Prescription" is a certain cure. By all druggists.
Public Spirit, December 22, 1883

A. J. Rice, miller of this place, while cleaning part of his machinery had his hand caught in the shaft, losing thereby one finger at the first joint and one at the second. On his right hand he is still quite weak after having been administered ether to perform the operation of sewing the mangled parts together.
Public Spirit, December 22, 1883

who was working in Doylestown and had been seen at a bar in Jenkintown on Saturday before his death. Philadelphia newspapers lauded the investigatory skills of Hunter and Bates – "Justice Hunter, who has charge of the Hoffman case, is a quiet, bright young man." But, despite the posting of a reward by residents led by H. H. Lippincott, no murderer was identified. The investigation was finally dropped, noted the *Public Spirit,* "because there are no funds available with which to carry it on."

Joseph Heacock himself had a close brush with death in 1893. As he was driving his carriage to Jenkintown and approaching the Chelten Hills railroad crossing, his horse was frightened by an oncoming train and swerved onto the track. He jumped clear but the flagman stationed at the crossing attempted to rescue the horse. In the process, the flagman was swiped by the passing train and lost his arm.

1882: The Chelten Hills School

The growing population of the region created a demand for schooling. Responding to this need, Joseph Heacock's sister, Annie, teamed up with the younger Joseph's new wife, Elizabeth Walker, to begin a school. Given the rural and isolated setting, it would be easy to think that such a school would be a one-room, one-teacher outpost for farmers of the region. But just the opposite was the case.

The preponderance of affluent residents in the Olde Wyncote tract helped fuel the demand and shape the expected experience. The impetus for a local school came principally from the Lippincotts - Horace, Henry, and Joshua - and Edward Starr, who lived adjacent to each other along Washington Lane across from the Heacock farm, and had young children. As well-to-do, well-educated, and influential residents, the quality of their children's education was a serious concern and they would not be inclined to accept anything less than a vibrant educational experience. Annie, and Elizabeth possessed the experience and skills that would be equal to their patrons' expectations. In 1882, the two ladies established the Chelten Hills School in the old homestead on the top of the hill.

Their credentials for conducting such a venture were impeccable. Annie attended the Philadelphia Normal School (the prestigious forerunner to the Philadelphia High School for Girls). In the days before the trains came, she commuted by stagecoach every day for four years from the stop at the Cottman Hotel (Old York Road and West Avenue) in central Jenkintown to Center City. After graduating in 1857, she was a teacher in the Philadelphia Public Schools until 1863, when she accepted an invitation to go South during the war. As an ardent Quaker abolitionist, she was drawn to the opportunity to teach at a school for "colored" people who were devastated by the war. Her sister Gayner joined her on Port Royal Island, South Carolina, where they remained for six years. Upon her return, Annie accepted a position at the Friends Central School. In 1869, she became acquainted with the suffrage movement and was elected the secretary of the Pennsylvania Suffrage Society. (Edward M. Davis was a vice-president.) She was a participant in the first women's suffrage parade in Philadelphia. She maintained her interest in the movement throughout her life and her brother, as a state senator, proposed the first suffrage bill for Pennsylvania early in the 20th century.

When they opened their school in 1882, Elizabeth had resigned her position at Friends Central School in Philadelphia to become a farmer's wife in Chelten Hills. They were joined by another sister, Eliza, who had been teaching at the "Coloured Orphan's Home" in Washington, D.C. For their classroom, they occupied part of Elizabeth and Joseph's new house on Glenside Avenue, where a large room was equipped with many windows to accommodate pedagogical activities. (There is no record of what Joseph thought about this arrangement, having just escaped a cramped household of women at the old homestead.) The boarding students were housed at the farmhouse under the care of Gayner while Annie served as the principal. Despite their affluent patronage, the Quaker teachers established a select school with an egalitarian twist as they also accepted other residents of the neighborhood who were of a more working-class background. A teaching staff would be assembled of such quality that several of them eventually showed up in "Who's Who of America":

- Nannie Adaire: 1227 W. Lehigh Av., Philadelphia, Pa. Educator; b. Philadelphia, Pa.; grad. Girls' High School, 1900; Bryn Mawr Coll., A.B., '04; A.M., '06. Teacher of English and history in the Chelten Hills School, Wyncote, Pa., 1905-06; principal of Medford (N.J.) High School, 1906-07; teacher of English in Norristown (Pa.) High School since 1907.

- Margarethe Urdahl Anderson: Charleston, Ill. Educator: ed. Univ. of Wis., B.L. '96: Univ. of Berlin, 1898-999; Univ. of Heidelberg and Univ. of Christiana, '99; Fellow in Teutonic philology, 1900-02; special fellow,, 1902-03, Bryn Mawr College; Ph.D. '04; m. 1906, Lewis Albert Anderson. Teacher of German and Latin, Chelten Hills School, Wyncote, Pa., 1903-04; teacher of German and history, Eastern, Ill., State Normal School, Charleston, Ill.

Other teachers included Dr. John W. Ridpath, pharmacist and civic activist of Jenkintown who taught Science and several graduates also appeared in Who's Who.

Elizabeth and Joseph's daughter, Priscilla, later recalled the environment of the school from which she graduated:

During the eighties, Glenside Avenue was lighted by kerosene lamps wherever property owners cared to stand the expense and trouble. Cows grazed in our meadow by the railroad where a good-sized pond was dammed to supply ice for the two homes. From it also good spring water was pumped to the old Heacock homestead to a tank in the attic that stored the drinking and bathing water for the boarding school. In those days, Wyncote possessed but one store, a corner grocery, and post office. Greenwood Avenue, skirted by open fields, led to Jenkintown village as did Washington Lane. (Heacock, 1942)

By 1892, the success of their school left their quarters in the house very cramped: they were holding classes in the stairwell and the dining room according to Annie's memoir. They purchased land from Joseph along the new Mather Avenue, just across from the farmhouse and erected a school complete with a meeting room large enough to accommodate the entire student body. The capacity of the room allowed it to serve as community meeting place for

Recess, Circa 1888
In this precious photograph, a group of older children from the Chelten
Hills School pose during an excursion to play tennis in the Heacock
pasture. The charm of seeing the children is matched by the rustic view of
the Heacock farm in the last days before suburban development began.
Glenside Avenue runs across the top left corner of the view and
Netherhouse is just beyond view to the upper left. Farmland extends up
the hill in the background at the upper left where houses will soon sprout
on the new Webster Avenue. At the upper right, Heacock's ice pond
shimmers on a fine June day. Horace Mather Lippincott, in his memoir of
the school, recalls the day when he fell into the pond on such an outing.
Mary Elizabeth Hallock, pianist, is fourth from the left and Virginia
Lippincott, daughter of H. G. Lippincott, is the last on the right. She
married Admiral Hilary P. Jones, USN, hero of the Spanish American war
and commander of the U.S. fleet. The ground was built up to street level
in the 1940s as the township used the property as a fill for autumn leaves.
The site today is a township park, courtesy of Elizabeth Heacock's
donation of the land.
Photo: Courtesy of the Old York Road Historical Society

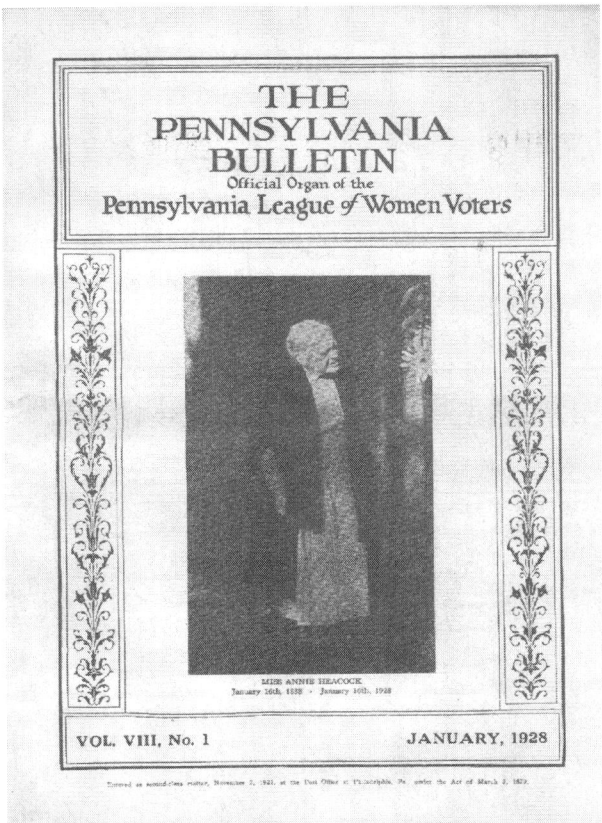

THE
PENNSYLVANIA
BULLETIN
Official Organ of the
Pennsylvania League of Women Voters

MISS ANNIE HEACOCK
January 16th, 1838 · January 16th, 1928

VOL. VIII, No. 1   JANUARY, 1928

Annie Heacock
Upon her death in 1928, Annie Heacock was lauded by the Pennsylvania
League of Women Voters in their *Bulletin*. Her ardent support of abolition
was followed by her work on behalf of women's rights. The article noted
that her "interest and sympathy were keen in all the worthwhile affairs of
the day."
Photo: Courtesy of the Friends Historical Library, Swarthmore College

In The News

The Harper Restaurant

[This neighborhood institution was in a small wood-frame building at the southeastern corner of the railroad and Greenwood Avenue. Its site today is under the embankment leading up to the railroad bridge.]

Thieves broke into the restaurant of Mrs. Harper at the station on Wednesday night. They cut a piece of glass out of the window, pushed the catch aside and entered. They stole all her best cigars, and regaled themselves on her pies. The loss was about $50.
Public Spirit, December 30, 1882

Mrs. Harper, who keeps the restaurant at Jenkintown station, has been proceeded against for selling liquor on Sunday. The Grand jury has found a true bill and it went before court on Friday. The complaint was made by two German hired men at the instance of Hastings and other prohibitionists of the town.
Public Spirit, June 6, 1885

Mrs. Harper was acquitted of the charge made against her. She had to pay the costs. The evidence was not worthy of credence. Last Sunday night, she shut up and neither gave nor sold. In this she was wise.
Public Spirit, June 13, 1885

Jenkintown boasts of a very knowing goat, who lives at the restaurant at the station. He wanders about on the tracks in the most nonchalant manner, and up to date has succeeded in dodging both the fast express and the slow freight, but he does it in such a way that spectators have great expectations of seeing him ground into P&R sausage.
Public Spirit, May 21, 1887

civic groups, lectures, and recitals. The school catalogue for the academic year 1899 specified tuition of $120 per annum and room and board fees of $250 per annum, which included "washing of a dozen pieces per week. White skirts, shirtwaists, dresses, extra." An ambitious curriculum was outlined which included physical exercise, Latin, Arithmetic, Science, piano, daily group vocal activities, and other courses "to keep pace with the many improvements that are constantly made." A class trip to Washington, D.C. resulted in a meeting and a handshake with President Grover Cleveland.

The rise of public education and the improvement of educational facilities at other schools led to a steady decline in students in the twentieth century. In 1898, Elizabeth retired and the school finally closed in 1912. After her retirement, she served as an accountant for the Joseph Heacock Company until she was forced, against her will, at the age of eighty-eight to see an oculist to get glasses. She persuaded him to put plain lenses in the spectacles insisting there was nothing wrong with her eyes. The final words of her memoir were: "Eighty-eight is a good old age. I have had my share of blessings, and it is quite time to see what the future life may be." Annie Heacock died on January 16, 1928, in the old farmhouse where she had lived since 1857.

1882: Rodman Wanamaker

John Wanamaker added to the size of his estate with the purchase of the Henry Lippincott property on the northeast side of the railroad tracks at Washington Lane. This property included the old Mather homestead and the mill. In so doing, he obtained valuable water rights that would be useful in the management of his property. In the following year, Wanamaker installed a water pump in the old mill to supply water from the Tookany to his mansion, the Mather homestead, and his farm operation.

The mansion would be turned over (at a price of $20,000) to his younger son, Lewis Rodman for a residence after his graduation from Princeton and marriage to Fernanda de Henry in 1886. The sale did not include the mill. Rodman named the estate *Millrose* and made substantial improvements to the old house and grounds. The affable and dapper Rodman was an avid and internationally known sportsman. He sponsored record-breaking aviation projects, such as a transatlantic crossing of his airship *America*, and aircraft speed contests. In 1908, he founded the now-famous Millrose games in track and field at Madison Square Garden in New York and, in 1916, he founded the world's first professional association for golfers, the PGA. He funded the first PGA championship tournament that was held later that year. In 1888, he was assigned the task of managing Wanamaker's Paris operations where he greatly expanded the store's business in fine arts and antiques and, consequently, was credited with fueling the American preoccupation with French goods. Rodman assumed control of the company after his father's death in 1922.

An article in the *New York Daily Tribune* of April 26, 1903, announced the issuance of a life insurance policy in the amount of $1,000,000 to Rodman Wanamaker. The policy was called the largest of its kind to date and named Wanamaker "one of the most heavily insured persons in the world," except for King Edward VII. The Prudential Life Insurance Company of America featured the policy in its advertising indicating "Mr. Wanamaker's Selection of the Prudential is a Striking Demonstration of – The High Esteem in which This Company is held by Farsighted Business Men." (Mitchell, 1903) The extravagant use of capital letters no doubt was intended by clever publicists of the day to reinforce the significance of the event. He died in 1928 at his seashore home in Atlantic City of kidney disease that left him increasingly disabled over his last several years (thus ensuring a large profit from insurance despite the hefty $30,000 per annum premium on his Prudential policy). *Millrose,* though exquisitely and completely furnished and fully staffed, was sporadically used as the globe-trotting Rodman owned townhouses on Spruce Street in Philadelphia and on Washington Square in New York.

John Wanamaker later purchased another home just on the other side of the railroad tracks in the new Heacock development for his daughter Mary and her husband Barclay Warburton. Warburton was the publisher of a Philadelphia newspaper, *The Daily Evening Telegraph*, and the treasurer of one of the early automobile manufacturing concerns in the country, the Searchmont Automobile Company, based in Philadelphia. Part of his notoriety was achieved when Warburton championed and publicized the development of a system of public baths, The Public Baths Association of Philadelphia, in a city where most houses of working class neighborhoods still did not have running water and bathing facilities. The bath facilities were intended to "afford to the poor the facilities for bathing and the promotion of health and cleanliness." The Association lasted until after the second World War. The charitable organization was announced at a dinner sponsored by John Wanamaker and received his support as well. Among other important accomplishments of the Warburtons, Mary Warburton is credited by entertainer George Jessel for being at the right place at the right time, a bar in Palm Beach, Florida, in 1927, as the bartender was inventing a new drink with tomato juice. The barman at the Paddy LaMaze asked her to taste it and bestowed the name "Bloody Mary" on the drink to honor her contribution. The Warburtons built a large home in Jenkintown and suffered a fate similar to her father's, a fire that severely damaged their home in 1912, just five years after her father's catastrophe. Like her father, she lost a significant art collection.

Mary served on numerous charitable boards, usually in the company of Mrs. E.T. Stotesbury, her former Jenkintown neighbor. During the World War, Mary served on the Emergency Aid of Pennsylvania Committee that raised over two million dollars for the relief of victims of the war. Mary became involved in Republican politics and served on the Commission on Constitutional Amendment and Revision for the State of Pennsylvania in 1920 and served as the assistant chairman of the Pennsylvania delegation of the Republican National Committee in 1921. In that capacity, she had the honor of being the first woman to preside at a meeting of that group. The Warburtons purchased property in Palm Beach, Florida, where they built a winter home. Barclay served as mayor before his death and Mary served on the planning committee that submitted a comprehensive development plan for the new town in 1929.

Thomas B. Wanamaker was the financial and operations officer of his father's store and was the publisher of a

Philadelphia newspaper, *The North American*. John also purchased a home in the Heacock tract to house his son and daughter-in-law. Thomas eventually moved out of his Wyncote home to a more upscale estate in nearby Meadowbrook where he, too, suffered a complete loss of home and possessions in a disastrous fire in 1901. Thomas, who had assumed major responsibilities for the new emporium at Thirteenth and Market upon his graduation from Princeton, nonetheless had a distant relationship with his father. He was known as a no-nonsense businessman who had little of the warmth of his father or his gregarious younger brother. His liberal policies expressed in *The North American* irritated his father as well as his policy of publishing a Sunday edition that offended his father's religious beliefs. John went as far as purchasing space on the front page of the newspaper to deliver a lecture on the sanctity of the Sunday observance. Enduring serious health problems, he found it necessary to write a letter to his father in 1906 telling him of his intentions to resign and relinquish all business interests. An extended business trip to Egypt after his retirement resulted in a worsening of his illness and he died in a Paris hotel on March 2, 1908, at the age of forty-seven. He left two young sons and a will that would later be vigorously contested by his re-married wife.

1883: Joseph Heacock and Company

Following the senior Joseph's death in 1883, the farm passed entirely to his two sons, Joseph, Jr., and Edward, who continued truck farming on the family farm. Joseph Heacock, Jr., was active in politics, a rare Democrat in this heavily Republican neighborhood. Nonetheless he was so well respected that he was elected to serve as Montgomery County auditor and in the Pennsylvania Senate. At about this time, Joseph Heacock, Jr., built his first greenhouse to satisfy his nascent interest in indoor flowers and plants. The glass house was the largest of its kind, attracting envious florists from a wide area, and it was the first greenhouse to be heated by steam. The hobby took off and by the time subdivision of the farm began in 1888, Heacock had a substantial investment and infrastructure in greenhouses, and a national reputation as well. Over two acres of the farm was covered in greenhouses that ran in ranks along Maple Avenue. The location was perfect for the use as Maple Avenue rises to the North at that location, enabling each greenhouse to sit slightly above its predecessor, bathed in unhindered sunlight. He specialized in roses, carnations, and palms. By the turn of the century, Joseph had incorporated his florist business and rose production had moved to a new facility in Roelofs, Bucks County, leaving the Wyncote facility to specialize in palms and orchids.

Heacock suffered a tragic family catastrophe in 1907 when his youngest child, Edward, was drowned in a freak accident while exploring mountainous territory in British Columbia. Edward Rockhill Heacock was born in *Netherhouse* on August 10, 1885 and graduated from the Chelten Hills School in 1901. At Chelten Hills, he was known for his love and knowledge of biology and, in particular, his ability to name all of the spring flowers that could be found in the fields around school and the Chelten Hills railroad station. He was an accomplished pianist and loved opera. His best friend, Hensel Eckman, described him:

He cared little about "dress" and so called "society." He had thick, bushy red hair of a golden hue which he did not bother brushing many times a day, rather scorning the habits of the rest of us who were continually plastering down our locks as many times a day as we could get to a mirror, going to the other extreme. (Eckman, 1964)

Ironically, Eckman went on to describe Heacock as an excellent swimmer and recounted the times that the two of them went swimming in Wanamaker's natatorium.

Ned could swim fairly well. We used to open a window of Mr. Wanamaker's swimming-pool building across the way, a low vine-covered building of native mica-and-garnet-bearing rock, and spend the afternoon swimming in the inviting but little used pool. Either our trespassing was never discovered or else Mr. Wanamaker in his kindly manner decided "to forget it."

Heacock Greenhouses, circa 1890
This view looks toward the Northeast from the Southwest corner of
today's Maple Avenue and Heacock Lane intersection. Maple Avenue
climbs the hill to the left of the greenhouses and a nascent Heacock Lane
is visible to the right of the horse and wagon going to the right. The
greenhouses were an impressive operation. The houses contained 80,000
feet of glass, one house contained only orchids and another had over
75,000 palms.   His steam plant boasted a boiler capacity of 220
horsepower that typically consumed 1,200 tons of coal in the winter. The
steam plant is the white building on the right seen with its smoke stack.
Residents of the 1960's development of homes along Maple and
Stonehouse Lane still report digging through buried beds of glass shards
when gardening.
Photo: Courtesy of Nancy Wood, Wyncote

Advertisement for Heacock Company
Times Chronicle, 1908

Joseph Heacock, about 1910
Courtesy of the Friends Historical Library of Swarthmore College

As a student of Biology at Penn, Edward excelled in his studies, winning the 1904 J. S. Harrison prize in Biology and a prestigious faculty award. He began participating in field trips with faculty to the still-uncharted Canadian Northwest in his junior year and thus was experienced in wilderness exploration. He signed off a letter to Eckman as he was leaving his base camp by commenting that he was "stepping off into the unknown." Upon receiving word of his son's disappearance, Joseph left Wyncote for the Canadian Rockies and hired a guide to continue the search for his son. No trace of his son was ever found.

Joseph died at the age of 72 in 1918 after a being hospitalized for minor surgery. His wife, Elizabeth, survived him and continued to live in the home until 1924 when she moved into the old homestead. Their son, James, took possession of *Netherhouse* after her move and raised his family there.

An Ill-Fated Summer
Excerpts from Herbert Ives
The Alumni Register
The University of Pennsylvania
August 1908

One of the least explored parts of British Columbia lies north of the Canadian Railroad in the Selkirk Mountains. The traveler who goes by train, after passing through the Rockies by way of Banff and Field, crosses the Columbia River twice; first near Beavermouth, where it flows north, later at Revelsticke, where it flows south.
. . .

It was to explore this virgin territory that two parties set out in the summer of 1907. Had accident and death not prevented we should have followed this plan: Merkel Jacobs, '05, and Edward Heacock, '06, who had already spent two summers in the Northwest, were to attempt the crossing of the mountains from the east. They counted on starting from Beavermouth by canoe, early in June, before the melting of the snow made navigation too difficult, going down the Columbia, and placing caches of supplies up Gold River, which runs into the Columbia from the heart of unknown country.
. . .

The summer as it worked out was very different for some of us. Jacobs and Heacock, much hindered by the exceptionally late snows, succeeded after heroic exertion in placing two caches on Gold River. . . . I had been away from the Emerald Lake camp for a three-day "hike" in the Yoho Valley. On returning I found everything upset, and Heacock was there. He had arrived the day we left, bringing word that Jacobs had broken his leg. A huge rock had turned over on him; they had pried it off with their guns to find the leg broken above the knee. Heacock had dragged Jacobs to shelter, set his leg, cooked food and left to come to us for help.

Heacock had hiked four days to reach camp. Ives set out the next morning with another colleague on a mission to rescue Jacobs by a route that took them up the Beaver Canyon to a ridge west of the Columbia River.]

That climb was the worst experience Stiles and I had ever had. We left Beavermouth at five in the morning each carrying a fifty-pound pack, not counting the weight of guns and other equipment. Now the climb we had ahead was one which a man unencumbered would have found sufficiently difficult; for men new to packs, as we were, with our feet sore and blistered, it was a long ordeal of agony. We first walked in the boiling sun for three miles along the railroad in Beaver Canyon until it crossed the Beaver River by bridge to the north side. Here we started to ascend the mountain that rose almost straight up for three thousand feet. . . . Often we made our way over loose earth only by clutching at trees and bushes, and again the undergrowth of willows and alders was so dense we could scarce force our way at all. The sun beat relentlessly upon us. Swarms of mosquitoes bit our arms and faces, and even through our thickest clothes. Our thirst became intense, but there was no water.

. . .

All about us were snow-covered mountains as far as the eye could see. Frequently our way lay over snowfields where were tracks of bear and caribou, then again over huge rock slides of shifting, teetering boulders, difficult and dangerous from the chance of a misstep starting an avalanche. We were not properly equipped for walking in the snow, and with our heavy packs would sometimes sink in to our waists and have to be dug out.

. . .

Our camp arrangements were all with the one view of taking care of Jacobs. The relief party had found him in some scrub just above our "island" whither Heacock had dragged him. They had carried him here and laid him in an improvised rock bed between two trees. Over his head was slung the small silk tent with which he and Heacock had traveled. This was far too small to cover him, and in the rain and at night we drew the tent together and covered his exposed legs with rubber blankets. Day had bandaged him to a long board so that he could not bend his body and had hung a stone on a rope over a log at the foot of the "bed" for a stretching weight. All summer long Jacobs lay on this rock while we tightened the bandages, fed and tended him. A less troublesome invalid I am sure never lived.

. . .

Tuesday, July 24th, Heacock and Bob Jacobs departed northward for Gold River to find the canoe and secure a cache on the north shore. I, as the least expert canoeist, staid [*sic*] in camp. We expected them to return in about three days. Late in the afternoon of the third day Bob returned alone, empty-handed, to tell us of a disaster worse than the first. In crossing the river, now swollen with melted snow, their canoe had been overturned. They clung to it until it began to sink, then Bob had struggled ashore. Heacock disappeared around a bend.

Courtesy of the American Alpine Club, Golden, CO

Edward Heacock, 1906
Graduation portrait from the University of Pennsylvania
Photo: Courtesy of the University of Pennsylvania, Gatter Research Collection on Ezra Pound, Rare Book & Manuscript Library

Legacy Voices

Nancy Wood
Heacock Lane, Wyncote
Resident Since 1921

TW: When did you find Wyncote?
NW: I was born on Mather Avenue, at 120, two houses up. After we were married, we lived on Webster Avenue, 118 Webster, for thirty-some years before moving here for another forty years.

TW: I guess you remember when Heacock Lane ended at Maple Avenue.
NW: Yes I do. It ended at the Haydock house. It was very woodsy up there. We always used to find the Beaver girls sneaking up there and smoking. The big hill in the cow pasture was great for sledding.

TW: You knew the Heacocks of course?
NW: I remember the walk that went down the hill from the farmhouse to Jim's house [on Glenside Avenue]. When they cut the farmhouse in half, it sickened me. People can't image all the greenhouses that were up there. A number of us put our hands through the glass but they never said anything.

TW: Who was Priscilla?
NW: Esther's sister. Priscilla was the artist. Priscilla was very laid back: lovely lady, used to ride her bike around. Esther hated cats. She liked the birds, so she used to trap cats that came around. You would hear a gun going off and you knew she shot another squirrel for eating her bird seed.

TW: Anything else you remember in particular?
NW: I remember the blacksmith shop. Across from the investment company. It was next door to the old building that looks like a gas station next to the post office. The blacksmith was Chris. There was Pat who lived up the stairs. My friend and I would climb the steps to see him. He had a coal stove and was always cooking bread and apples and raisins. He was pleased to give us some. We used to stop at the ice factory at the top of the hill and they used to give us chips of ice as a treat.

TW: What did you do for fun when you were small?

NW: We used to go over to Wanamaker's for fun. I went through the big house. Before they tore it down. It was a beautiful house. The wood in the library and all the bathrooms with gold fixtures and marble sinks. There was an elevator to the servants' quarters on the third floor. My brother was always getting us in there. There was a doll house. You could walk through it and everything was in miniature. There was a pool house with a dance floor above it. There was a spring house further down the creek. We imagined the parties they must have had: swimming and then dancing afterwards. There was a barn over further. You know the [Abington Hospital] June Fete was held there for years. Where the sunken gardens were. We came up the back way and my Aunt didn't want us to get in without paying. We spent a lot of time playing in the pond.

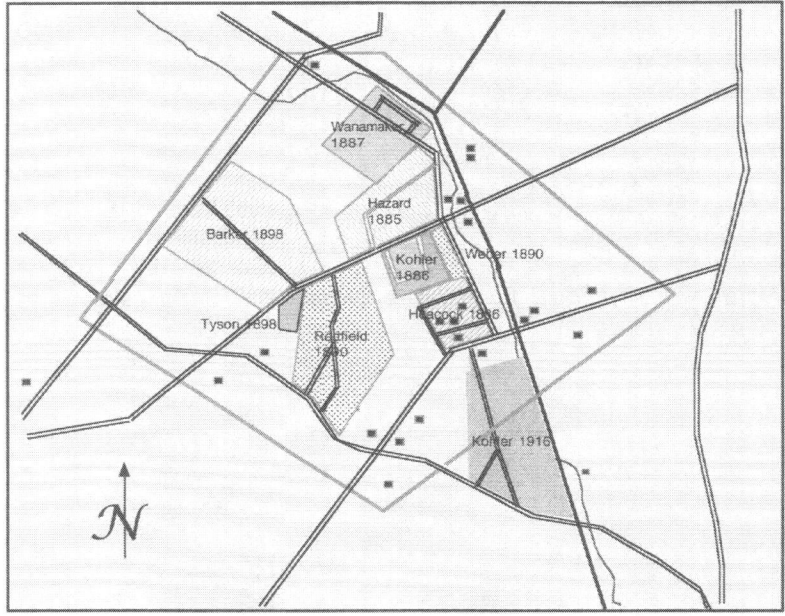

Major 19th Century Developers

Seven entrepreneurs in the late 1890's developed most of historic Wyncote in just 15 years. They added new residential roads to gain access to the building lots in their holdings.

Chapter 6

THE DEVELOPERS

---

*Beechwood Heights will soon be covered with fine
country seats. The eighth house is now underway.
The Queen Anne style of architecture seems
to prevail, though there are others.*
(Public Spirit, *August 14, 1886*)

In the short fifteen-year period between 1885 and 1900,
the frenzy initiated by the first land purchase for popular
development would result in the creation of most of the
roads and homes that define Wyncote today. It was the
prelude to developing a true community with all of the
amenities and services that a community required. Just
seven developments accounted for most of the homes that
would be built in the new village.

1885: Willis P. Hazard

Things changed forever in the Olde Wyncote tract on
May 27, 1885. On that Wednesday, the executors of the Kent
estate sold a nineteen-acre parcel of land to investor Willis
P. Hazard of Chester County. Loosely called the Kent tract or
Beechwood Heights, the land was on a wooded hillside
across the Tookany Creek and Mather millpond from the old
Beechwood estate. Hazard quickly put in a road, later to be

named Woodland Road, across the top of the hill and subdivided the property into fifty-seven parcels.

Hazard does not seem a likely candidate for this groundbreaking role. In an age full of entrepreneurs and multi-tasking dilettantes, Hazard was a prime example of a polymath. Though having family roots in Philadelphia, Willis was born in 1825 in Huntsville, Alabama, and moved back to Philadelphia at a young age. He was the grandson of Ebenezer Hazard, confidant to General Washington and first postmaster-general of the United States. In 1904, all of Ebenezer's papers that Willis had faithfully preserved were destroyed when Willis' homestead in Secane was destroyed by fire. Though he made his mark as a prominent publisher, he also achieved notoriety as a farmer, cow breeder, horseman, author, and historian, before turning to land development. In 1854, he wrote a novel treatise on horseback riding for females, *Lady's Equestrian Manual*. The book seems elementary by today's standards, but it undoubtedly filled a need of the day. His introduction of the subject displayed a touch of coyness, perhaps an artifact of his genteel Southern upbringing: "He accordingly flatters himself, that at a time when riding has become so eminently fashionable an exercise for ladies, and when the road daily displays so many elegant women on horseback, his work will ensure security, ease, and grace of the riders." As an historian, Hazard co-authored a substantial volume on the history of Philadelphia published in 1842, *Annals of Philadelphia and Pennsylvania in the Olden Time*.

It is not known exactly how he made his way to the Olde Wyncote tract, but several connections may have provided opportunities to become familiar with the area. In his 1879 book, *How to Select a Cow,* (a more serious topic then than strikes our ears now) Hazard uses Charles L. Sharpless' prize Jersey cow, Tiberia, as a case study. His text implies a visit to Sharpless' farm in Chelten Hills. In addition, one of Hazard's customers in the prize cow business was Wayne MacVeigh, the Attorney General of the United States, a Philadelphian who was a close political confidant of Wharton Barker.

Upon purchasing the land, Hazard immediately went to work developing the tract by selling individual lots to builders and to other developers. His first client was a new land development firm in Hatboro by the name of Evans and Garner, to which he sold eleven sites. The local Newspaper, *Public Spirit,* followed the progress of the tract:

-May 9, 1885: "Joseph W. Hunter has surveyed the streets at the Kent property at the station and laid them out. Hugh O'Donell will grade and open them, so those who have purchased lots can go on and build."

-July 11, 1885: "The work of opening the new avenue through the Kent property is progressing rapidly. A number of lot owners will build shortly."

-August 22, 1885: "Hon. I.N. Evans and S. J. Garner, Hatboro Capitalists, have purchased some half dozen more lots near the station."

-September 19, 1885: "Thomas Nicholson, the popular coal and lumber dealer at the station, has the contract for the lumber on the Evans and Garner houses. He will have a sale of firewood on Saturday a week, on the old Kent property. Here is a chance for a supply of firewood."

-January 23, 1886: "Garner & Evans' new houses at the station are nearing completion. The plastering was delayed by the cold, it being necessary to wait for the heaters. The houses will be furnished with gas, hot and cold water and all other modern conveniences."

-June 26, 1886: Hon. I. N. Evans and wife and S. J. Garner and family of Hatboro were down here on Sunday looking over their new houses on Beechwood Heights which are now completed.

The local paper was not unaware of the financial benefits of Hazard's venture.

- July 18, 1885: "Mr. Hazzard [*sic*] of Chester County who owns the Kent Woods tract has made a good thing of it. He paid $15,000 for the 25 acres of woods and sold half of it for $13,000."

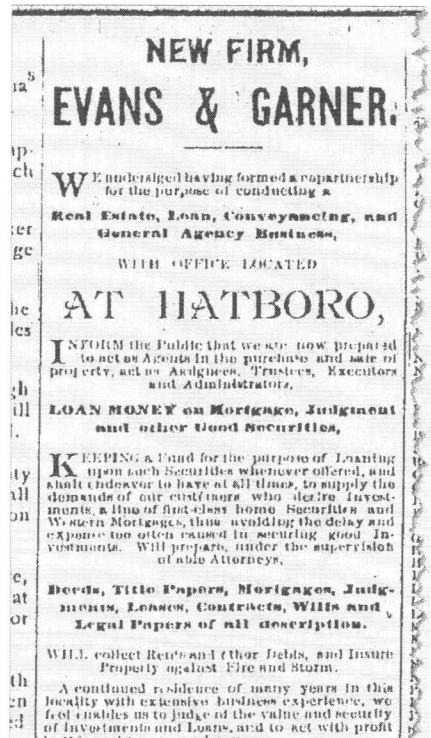

Evans & Garner Advertisement
Public Spirit, February 19, 1887

At a purchase price of $600 per acre, he was well on his way of turning a profit of about 43% in just a year. Kent's heirs also didn't do badly for a long-term investment: he had originally purchased the property for $201 per acre thirty-one years earlier.

Evans and Garner would build many of the houses themselves and rent them out (as many other owners also did) to city folk as summer residences or to test out the environment for possible permanent residency. While so doing, the renters would also be reviewed by existing residents for suitability as neighbors, thus leading to the nickname of "probationary hill" for the Kent tract.

Another client of Hazard's was Dr. J. Elwood Peters of Jenkintown. A practicing physician, Peters graduated from

Hahnemann Medical College in Philadelphia in 1875 and he was thirty-one years old at the time of his purchase. Peters obtained six lots in 1886, including a most valuable lot at the corner of Greenwood and Glenside Avenues. By June, Peters had a store with an overhead residence under construction and under lease to a young Jenkintown businessman, Thomas Buckman Harper. Harper had worked for several years in his father's store at the corner of West Avenue and York Road in Jenkintown. The newspaper, recognizing the growing need for a commercial operation opined that the store "will be a great convenience to the locality." In October, the *Public Spirit* noted the progress of Peters' first two homes opposite Evans & Garner's on Beechwood Heights and in November lauded the busy doctor as "one of our most enterprising citizens." His activities did not come without complications, however, as that same November saw a lawsuit against Dr. Peters by a Timothy O'Brien who sued the busy Dr. Peters for "malpractice on the part of the doctor in permitting the death of O'Brien's wife." The newspaper noted that Dr. Peters is a "man of large practice and is prepared to make a strong defense."

1886: Martin Luther Kohler

Another active developer, Martin Luther Kohler, had two ventures in Wyncote, while in-between developing property in Jenkintown and Glenside. Kohler, born in 1852, was from Lancaster County and received two degrees in law from the University of Pennsylvania in 1874 and 1877. After graduation he moved back to Trappe to practice law where he married and began a family. Moving to Jenkintown in 1881, Kohler was elected Burgess in 1884 and was enamored by the development opportunities evident in the area. He erected several houses on the new Hillside Avenue in Jenkintown and then in September of 1886, he purchased a ten-acre property from H. H. Lippincott just above the Greenwood Avenue and Glenside Avenue intersection. Lippincott, concerned about the adjoining and growing quarry operation, specified in the deed that, "no stone be quarried" and then carefully added that no building could be erected that would be used for the "manufacture or sale of

spirituous liquors." Kohler built several houses along
Greenwood Avenue in 1887 and opened a road up the hill
from Greenwood Avenue called Fernbrook Avenue that
curved at the top of the hill to form Helion Avenue and
arrayed his plots on both sides. He made twenty-eight sales
in the village between 1887 and 1890. In order to facilitate
his sales activities, Kohler constructed a small office at the
railroad station, next to Harper's Restaurant. The historian
Rev. S. F. Hotchkins noted it in his visit to the village in
1892: "His office is in the tasteful one story parti-colored
shingled building at the station." The *Public Spirit* reported
that "business is brisk" for the desirable homes in the Kohler
tract, with three new buildings underway within two months
of opening the office in September.

By 1887, he also owned a large parcel of land in Glenside
that had been part of the Heist farm along the west side of
Easton Road (between Waverly and Glenside Avenue) and
began developing that area, moving his family to one of his
new homes at Lismore and Glenside Avenue. He is credited
with inventing the name of Glenside and promoting that
appellation for the post office and the train station. In 1900,
his attention turned back to Wyncote and Jenkintown. He
partnered with Joseph Hunter, Jenkintown magistrate and
surveyor, and W. W. Frazier and other influential
businessmen to form what was locally known as "the
Syndicate" to develop the tract of land east of Greenwood
Avenue in Jenkintown. Much of this land had previously been
owned by Kent, E. T. Stotesbury, and Heacock and, though he
advertised under the name of "Jenkintown," his marketing
booklet included numerous views of his properties in the new
village of Wyncote, just across the tracks.

Kohler's last land operation was the Pardee estate in
Wyncote in 1916 where he opened a short road named
Pardee Lane. In a tragic mishap, Kohler was killed that year
when he was returning from a trip to Easton to pick up his
daughter. On narrow Route 611 five miles below Easton, he
attempted to pass another car and went over the
embankment into the canal. Riding that little-changed
stretch of road even today, it is easy to imagine such a
calamity. His convertible provided scant protection from the
impact and he did not survive. Ironically, rescuers were
already on the scene as they were in the process of removing

the body of a trucker who had a similar accident just an hour before. His daughter, Ruth "Bobbie" Bates, was rescued and though seriously injured, went on to take over his business and conclude the development of the Pardee estate. Ruth Kohler Bates continued to be involved in real estate along Serpentine and Pardee Lanes through the 1930's.

Kohler was a very private man and consequently little is known of his personal and business life; he threatened to sue newspapers that published his name in any way. This belligerent or obstinate streak is evident in the lawsuit that Jenkintown filed against its former leader in 1908 to recoup expenses in repairing the curb and sidewalk in front of Kohler's Jenkintown property, repairs which Kohler had declined to undertake. Nonetheless he was hailed in a *Times Chronicle* obituary as in "the forefront of all civic movements of moment for the community's good" and a person who "did more for the up-building of the immediate vicinity than any other man." Among other efforts, Kohler served as one of the instigators and president of the Jenkintown Water Company that had its pumping station in Wyncote and provided fresh water for the new village. Kohler served in a similar capacity for the new electric company that would serve the area, thus leveraging his own investment in land.

1886: Joseph Heacock, Jr.

In May of 1886, Joseph Heacock, seeing the future or perhaps just having discarded farming for his booming florist business, decided to capitalize on the development boom and engaged "Squire Hunter," the Jenkintown magistrate and surveyor, to lay out building lots on the farm. Heacock announced his plan in September of 1886, began subdividing the perimeter, and sold his first properties along Washington Lane beginning in 1887. He then created a loop, first developing properties along the new Mather Avenue and finally developing Webster Avenue in 1893 leading from Glenside Avenue up to his service road, Maple Avenue. However, he preserved ownership of his greenhouses, the old homestead, and his own home on Glenside Avenue. On

The Heacock Land Rush
Notice of the sale of farmland near the train station prompted a large crowd of buyers to attend. Twenty-four of the lots offered for sale were sold on that day.

Saturday, May 5, 1888, Heacock's agent, B. F. Glenn & Son of Philadelphia, held a public sale of lots on site. Twenty-four of the thirty-six lots offered were sold on that day for an average price of $1,200 testifying to the attractiveness of the location and the offer. A fresh and crisp spring day in the open fields of the old farm must have made for a pleasant event – for the customers. If he had any reservations about the process, it is likely that the pragmatic Joseph Heacock would not have shown them, but it is easy to imagine that his sisters would have been devastated by the loss of their home grounds, or, as it was called then, the "improvement of the land." He completed his sales by 1906.

1887: William A. Selser

An individual purchase in 1887 resulted in a new road that instigated further development up the hill on the east side of Greenwood Avenue. A Philadelphia businessman, William A. Selser, purchased a three-acre estate adjoining Greenwood Avenue from H. H. Lippincott in May. The deed listed the twenty-eight year old Selser as a "merchant": he was a partner in the firm of Selser, Meurer & Company of Philadelphia, manufacturer of fine morocco leather. Philadelphia was the center of this type of industry in the late 19th century and the company was conducting about a million dollars in business by that time. Shortly after purchasing the home, he married Pauline Hallowell of the extensive Abington Hallowell family. Two of Selser's partners, Theodore Glentworth and Charles Meurer, moved out to Wyncote with Selser and were among Kohler's first customers. Tragically, Theodore Glentworth died in his sleep next to his wife at the age of 28 shortly after moving in. Lippincott, now landlocked as a result of the sale, required Selser to guarantee access to Greenwood Avenue along a twenty-foot strip from the top of the hill to Greenwood Avenue. As a result, Selser collaborated with M. L. Kohler, holder of the neighboring property on the northeast, to construct a road along the right-of-way utilizing an equal strip from Kohler's property. The road connected to Helion Avenue and thus formed a loop off of Greenwood Avenue. The ever prudent and vigilant Lippincott, perhaps suspicious of Selser's occupation, added other onerous restrictions to the deed, specifying "that his building to be erected thereon shall at [no] time thereafter be used for the manufacture of soap, candles, glue, starch, Lamp Black, White lead, or gunpowder, or as a bone boiling establishment or for any other offensive purpose or occupation whatsoever, and no spirituous liquors shall ever be sold on the said premises."

Perhaps to exact revenge for Lippincott's picayune codicils, Selser named the new road Curacoa Avenue after his company's specialty product. Curacoa, a fine goat leather, was used for kid gloves and other articles of high end clothing.

William A. Selser Figural Honey Bottle
This bottle was discovered in an October, 2008, archeological dig in a privy pit in Catasauqua, Pennsylvania.
Photos: Courtesy of Rick Weiner, Allentown, PA

Top: Selser Advertisement
Public Spirit, July 29, 1895
Bottom: Selser Illustration
From The apiarist's "cyclopedia" by A. I. Root, 1917. Note the supply of figural bottles on the right similar to the one shown on the previous page.

Lippincott did not think of proscribing honey. Selser was an amateur apiarist, that is, a bee keeper, and apparently turned to that hobby to make a living about the time he moved to Wyncote. He became a knowledgeable and skilled apiarist with a scientific bent and a national reputation, and was later known as Philadelphia's "honey-man." Selser honey even appeared in the inventory of the larder of nearby Beechwood Hotel. As his career blossomed, he conducted research for the Academy of Natural Sciences of Philadelphia in 1894, and published an article in the 1904 edition of the *Journal of Pharmacy* deliciously entitled "The Origin and Formation of Honey, and its Relation to the Polariscope." His reputation spread as far as New Orleans as he was featured in a front-page April 20, 1906 article in *L'Abeille De La Nouvelle-Orleans* for his proposed cure for Rheumatism by bee sting. The article noted: "William A. Selser, who owns one of the largest bee farms or apiaries in the vicinity of Philadelphia, is acquiring a fortune from extracting the stingers of his honey bees." As a member of the National Bee Keepers Association, he was charged in 1904 with counteracting an article in *Ladies Home Journal* that claimed that artificial honey was as good as the real thing. His assignment was to contact the publisher to clarify the matter: one suspects that his colleagues knew he could capitalize on being a neighbor of the *Journal's* publisher, Cyrus Curtis.

Women in this era rarely received any notice, but an article in the February 1, 1899, newsletter of the Bee Keepers organization, *Gleanings in Bee Culture,* noted that Mrs. Selser, besides being responsible for labeling all Selser honey bottles, was a consummate hostess: "Those of us who had the honor and privilege of being entertained at Mr. Selser's home realized that his 'better half' is not only a queen in a bee-keeper's home, but a royal entertainer." The annual convention of the Bee Keepers that was held in Philadelphia in the fall of 1899 resulted in a visit to the hospitable Selser's home. After the last meeting of the day, Selser gathered together his guests and, one of them, the editor of the *American Bee Journal*, described the event:

We all took the 10-mile [train] ride out to the beautiful suburb of Philadelphia where he lives. It was perhaps 11 o'clock when we arrived, and then met Mr. Selser's charming wife, who was 'keeping a light in the window,' as it were, for her beloved and his friends. And more than that, everything was ready for us all to sit down to the table and partake of a luscious water-melon and lemonade before retiring. (American Bee Journal, 1899)

To enhance his supply of honey, Selser maintained an apiary on the grounds of Abington Friends School in nearby Jenkintown and at Mt. Airy on the edge of the city. Selser associated himself with the A. I. Root Company in Medina, Ohio, the largest and most innovative of the nation's bee keepers and he opened an office at #10 Vine Street in Philadelphia to represent the company. Root continues in business today as the largest supplier of beeswax liturgical candles in the United States.

Selser's sense of humor must have been unappreciated by the staid citizens of Wyncote as the name of his road was changed soon after his departure. Curacao was renamed to match Heacock's considerably less exotic-named Maple Avenue that was reached by a crooked cut-through that connected the top of Heacock's loop with the top of the Kohler loop. Such delicacy and propriety was a hallmark of many facets of life in the new village that, as one resident noted, never even had a saloon.

1887: John Wanamaker

The versatile Willis P. Hazard was also a smart flash-in-the-pan. In March of 1887, John Wanamaker stepped into the fray and purchased all of Hazard's unsold property, including the site of the Mather millpond. He paid $1200 per acre for the land. For less than two years of brokerage activity, Hazard therefore realized a spectacular gain of 100% on his remaining land. The man who came from across the Delaware Valley to initiate the building frenzy in Wyncote disappeared as fast and completely as he came. The following May, as his first contribution to the improvement of the new village, Wanamaker put a four-horse team and ten men with wheelbarrows to work at the millpond to dredge the "foul-muck" of the "malerial pond" and, in the words of the fawning newspaper, "make the pond a sightly

TIMES CHRONICLE, August 13, 1904

A JENKINTOWN INDUSTRY

———

THE NEW CURE FOR RHEUMATISM AND LUMBAGO

———

Formic Acid Produced from the Stingers' of Honey Bee – More than 1,000,000 Bees in W. A. Selser's Apiaries – His Discovery as to the Best Mode of Extracting the Insects' Stingers Which are Worth $8 or $9 per 1,000.

Since the discovery a few months ago that formic acid from bees' stingers is a sure cure for rheumatism and lumbago, the demand for the stingers has leaped far in advance of the supply. Chemists and wholesale druggists are placing orders for all of them that can be had and apiarists are doing their utmost to supply the demand.

Experiments made at the H. K. Mulford laboratories, near Glenolden, Delaware County, this State, proved the efficacy of the bees' stingers as a cure for rheumatism and lumbago.

On the end of the stinger, which is about one-thirty-second of an inch long, is a tiny sac, containing a drop of formic acid. This sac the bee detaches with the stinger after the latter has been deposited in human flesh.

Formic acid neutralizes uric acid the presence of which in the system produces rheumatism and lumbago. Science has found a way to convert the stingers with their supply of formic acid into a serum which, used as anti-toxin or vaccine virus is used, effects a cure.

As the loss of the stinger does not interfere with the honey-producing capacity of the bees, the apiarists are finding fortune in the newly discovered cure and a great impetus has been given to bee cultivation. The stingers bring $8 or $9 a thousand.

William A. Selser, who has one of the largest apiaries about Philadelphia, located here in Jenkintown, finds himself wholly unable to keep up with his orders for stingers. At this apiary there are more than 1,000,000 bees under cultivation.

Mr. Selser has devised a regular system for extracting their stingers for market.

Bees, he has discovered do not like the odor of rubber, and when they detect it will attack the rubber in a frenzied manner. The gentleman has had made a soft rubber blanket or mat. This he places near his hives.

The bees smell the rubber, and, attacking the mat, deposit their stingers, pumping into the small sac more formic acid than they are wont to do when attacking a person or when not greatly excited.

After the bees have vented their fury upon the mat, it is removed and the stingers are extracted by means of small tweezers, care being taken not to destroy the formic acid pouch.

As the stingers are removed, they are placed in small bottles containing pulverized sugar. These in turn are sent to chemical laboratories, where the formic acid is extracted and reduced to a serum.

Other apiarists who are undertaking to supply the demand for bees' stingers pick up the bees, one at a time, with small tweezers, and with another pair of tweezers extract the stingers, afterward freeing the insects. This is a slower method than the use of the rubber mat, but apiarists are finding profitable.

Mr. Selser says bee cultivators in all parts of the country are working industriously to supply the demand for the new cure, as its efficacy is no longer in doubt.

He claims to have been cured of chronic lumbago by the repeated attacks of the bees among which he works.

lake where now it is offensive to the sight." Wanamaker's supervisor, Mr. Patterson, offered that "nothing is impossible to Mr. Wanamaker." Wanamaker subdivided the lots to the north of the millpond and became another of the seven major developers of Wyncote. He formally called his neighborhood "Beechwood Heights" and planned smaller lots with more modest homes than those in the rest of the growing village.

Another community effort of Wanamaker's will win sympathy from modern residents who have at some time looked over the park from the bend in Glenside Avenue above the station and said about West Avenue on the other side, "so close yet so far." It appeared that way to early residents as well. When Beechwood Avenue was ordered in 1887, the owner of Beechwood Hotel, Richard J. Dobbins, was awarded compensation of $2,500 for the loss of his property to the public road. Wanamaker offered a donation of $5,000 if Dobbins would contribute his award towards the construction of an iron pedestrian bridge that would connect the bend in Glenside Avenue with the dog-leg in Beechwood Avenue on the other side of the creek and tracks. (Unlike today, the land was private property and there was no footbridge connecting the two sides. The park would not be created until 1925.) The newspaper called "this grand connection between the hills" a "grand idea" and it met with wide public acclaim. Dobbins was not interested, however, and the idea was soon dismissed.

1890: Bradley Redfield

Another developer, Bradley Redfield, appeared on the scene. In 1890, he obtained a forty-five acre parcel which had been the Isaac Shoemaker farm fronting on Church Road between the Lippincott estate and Wharton Barker's former home. Another smaller plot, purchased from William Pancoast, extended his holdings adjacent to Wharton Barker with frontage on Greenwood Avenue. He immediately put in roads, Bend Road (the name would be changed in the new century to "Bent," probably out of constant mispronunciation) and Accomac Road, and started subdividing, eventually selling twenty-five lots. Not much is known about Redfield or what brought him to Wyncote. In the 1880's, Redfield was a prosperous nurseryman, dealing wholesale in fruits and vegetables in the area of Camden, New Jersey. He has been overshadowed by his son, Edward Willis Redfield, who was recognized at the beginning of the twentieth century as one of the foremost impressionist landscape painters in the United States. Edward led the development of New Hope in Bucks County as an enclave of artists. In 1890 just preceding his Wyncote venture, Bradley Redfield purchased *Edgewood,* a farm that is now part of the Holy Sepulchre Cemetery in the southwest part of Cheltenham Township. As of this writing, the old Redfield homestead, used most recently as Mueller's florist shop and greenhouses, is being razed for an expansion to the cemetery. Redfield's Wyncote development reflected the prevailing pressures to insure a well-to-do community by specifying in deeds minimum home prices of $7,500 – a substantial sum – and setbacks of at least 100 feet on minimum two-acre lots.

1890: William E. Weber

In a transaction that marked the end of William C. Kent's holdings in Wyncote in December of 1888, coal yard operator Thomas Nicholson obtained the block of land bounded by the railroad, Greenwood Avenue, Fernbrook, and Webster Avenue. This included the land under his yard, the quarry and the land on the Southwest corner of the Greenwood/Glenside intersection. No doubt it was the businesses that comprised his interest in the parcel as the other parts of the land lay fallow for eight years amidst the development swirling around.

Another developer, William E. Weber obtained random properties from Kohler beginning in 1890 and the Nicholson property West of Glenside Avenue in June of 1897. He immediately put a crew of twenty men to work filling in the old quarry to make it level with the street. His next task, during the winter of 1897 was to encase in a culvert the small stream, Barker Run, which flowed down the hill from the old Barker estate. The stream runs mostly underground today, except for an open stretch through Robinson Park, and empties into the Tookany just south of the Greenwood Avenue bridge. In 1898, he began a development of six twin homes in the lower part of the old abandoned quarry off of Greenwood Avenue, but only three of the twins were built by 1909. The street would eventually be named Cliff Terrace. Later, in 1909, he would construct a row of houses along the southeast side of Greenwood Avenue up to Fernbrook Avenue. He declined to plan for the construction of any stores on the very visible corner that already had commercial establishments on the northwest side, a decision that was noted approvingly by the *Times Chronicle* on August 7, 1909: "Few stores suffice for a suburban community, as much of the shopping is done in the city." He ruled off plots in the large quarry as well, but for unknown reasons, that property was never developed and he later sold the inactive quarry to Thomas B. Harper.

Two final developments of the 19th century, involving the estate of James Nile and the holdings of Wharton Barker, would occur closer to the end of the century.

The work of the developers could not be completed without builders and architects. A major builder of the period was W. John Stevens. Stevens was a carpenter from Jenkintown who had started building for other developers around 1885. He operated out of the old Rice's Mill on the far western corner of the Olde Wyncote tract. In 1909, he incorporated with E. Allen Reeves and Albert V. Willett and constructed a modern, large woodworking shop and office along the stretch of commercial buildings on the West side of Greenwood Avenue, just below L. I. Bean's livery stable. That building is now part of the ATD-American complex. By the turn of the century, several other large builders were active in the village including James Pickwell, Michael E. Hauser, Burke & Dolhenty, and S. L. Schively. Homes cost between $3,500 and $7,500, with mansions of the more wealthy residents reaching $50,000. The homes constructed in this period reflected the popular styles of architecture, particularly the Queen Anne style, such as those on Woodland Avenue and Fernbrook Avenue. More expensive homes adopted Tudor and Colonial Revival styles. Most property owners contracted with individual architects to design their homes, thus avoiding the cookie-cutter style of today's developments, and, befitting their wealth and status, the architects were often accomplished and well-known figures. Frank Furness and Horace Trumbauer are the most familiar of those architects. Furness had achieved fame for his buildings of modernist Gothic-Victorian style including mansions on Rittenhouse Square, the Pennsylvania railroad's Broad Street Station, and the Pennsylvania Academy of the Fine Arts. Trumbauer worked in Wyncote in his early phase before turning to more extravagant styles for the very wealthy and became known for many important buildings such as the Philadelphia Art Museum, Harvard's Widener Library, and the Free Library of Philadelphia. He also constructed distinguished and extravagant local mansions for P. A. B. Widener (Lynnewood Hall), William Elkins (Elstowe), E. T. Stotesbury (Whitemarsh Hall), and William Welsh Harrison (Grey Towers). Angus S. Wade's homes on Fernbrook Avenue were featured in an 1894 illustration in *Scientific American* magazine. He had previously achieved fame for his Rittenhouse Square mansions and many hotels, such as the Hotel Rittenhouse. He moved to the new village and died on a trip to Florida in 1932. Local architect, J. Linden Heacock, and his firm, Heacock and Hokanson, are also represented in the village. The homes in the core of Wyncote Village were honored as the Wyncote Historic District with placement on the National Register of Historic Places in 1986 led by the pioneering effort of preservationist Doreen Foust of Wyncote.

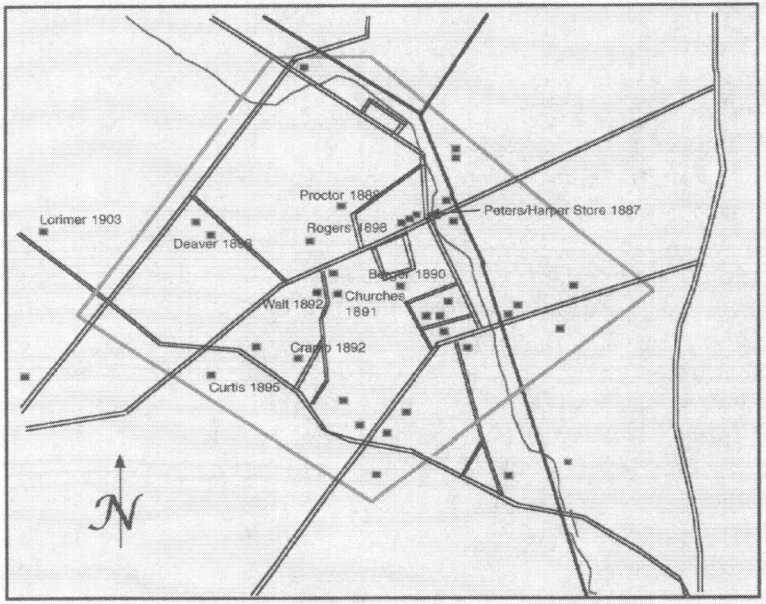

The Age of Community

The opening of a general store marked the beginning of a busy thirteen year period to the end of the century when the community was defined.

Chapter 7

COMMUNITY

*The banker, the merchant and the manufacturer who step from
the afternoon trains on the North Penn Road, hurrying to the
calm contentment and restful influences of country homes amid
the picturesque jumble of streams and rolling hills and stretches
of high level woodland around here, feel that here indeed is the
atmosphere where the honey is to be found that is an
andidote [sic] for the city's gall.*
(Chelten Hills, 1888)

1887: The General Store and a Name for the Village

An important enhancement to a growing community is a
place to buy food and other household goods. With the
opening of Harper's general store in the Peters building at
the corner of Greenwood and Glenside Avenues in 1887, the
Olde Wyncote tract had its first store. But the store offered
something even more important. As the store was preparing
to open, the transplanted Jenkintown businessman, Thomas
Buckman Harper, had received authorization from
Washington, D.C., to open a post office in the center of the
growing village. In its edition of Saturday, February 12,
1887, the *Public Spirit* newspaper, in a pithy article typical
of local journalism of the day, announced the prospective
opening of a new post office complete with a snide editorial
comment. "Hon. I.N. Evans has succeeded in having a post-
office established at Jenkintown Station and Thomas Harper

159

Peters/Harper Building
The first commercial building in Wyncote stood at the Northwest corner of Greenwood and Glenside Avenues. The photograph was probably taken early in 1888 just after the post office had moved in and Harper started his store. One of the first houses on Woodland Avenue looms above the store but construction on the Kent tract has not yet decimated Kent's woods. The store building stood alone, an outpost of civilization, until a new commercial building was constructed to the left in 1893. The sign post at the bottom left corner of the photo indicates the direction of Shoemakertown, Edge Hill, Jenkintown, and Limekiln Pike. There is a sign tacked on the post below the directional signs that appears to have the headline "Reward." Perhaps someone was already looking for a lost cat.
Courtesy of OYRHS

is the new postmaster. The new post office . . . is in [*sic*] to be called Beechwood Heights. . . . No such plebian cognomen as Jenkintown, Thank you." The new post office indeed opened on February 14, 1887, but with the name "Wyncote," as noted by the newspaper in the next weekly edition. The unique identity of the new village was finally established. The application for the post office clearly indicates it was intended to be located in the Peters building, but construction may not have been completed in time to

Porch Detail
This detail of the photograph of the Peters/Harper store shows the sign indicating that it is also the site of the Wyncote Post Office. Typical dry goods can be seen in the window and porch. The man is not identified, but it may be Mr. Harper. His appearance is very similar to other photographs of the young postmaster and storekeeper.

accommodate it, so it opened in the Jenkintown railroad station just across the Tookany Creek and moved to the store later in the year. This was the first of five locations in one hundred and twenty-two years. Located in the old "shack with a newsstand" that had served as the first railroad station, the new post office was burglarized in its first week of operation. "Squire Kohler" received the first letter at the Wyncote Post Office. The Post Office was robbed again in its new location in the store on April 22, 1899. William Croasdale, the barber, living upstairs from his shop next door, heard noises at 3:00 a.m. and discovered a gang of men had broken into the post office. He grabbed his shotgun and fired several volleys at the now-fleeing men. An investigation found burglar tools and drills left behind, the door of the safe drilled off, and all the money and stamps missing. "They were undoubtedly experts," the newspaper opined.

The old Jenkintown nomenclature died hard. For many editions after the naming of the post office, the *Public Spirit* still referred to events in the new village by the traditional name. In a typical piece, the paper welcomed a new resident in the edition of March 5, 1887, not as a resident of Wyncote, but of Jenkintown:

Lewis C. Leidy, assistant cashier in the U. S. Mint, Philadelphia, is about to become a permanent resident of Jenkintown. A handsome new three story residence is now nearing completion on Beechwood Heights and will be ready for occupancy in the early Spring. Mr. Leidy will be welcomed as a new resident of our enterprising borough.

The paper stretched the ambiguous nomenclature even further as Leidy's house was actually constructed on the corner of Helion and Curacoa, rather than in the Kent or Wanamaker tracts that went by the name of Beechwood Heights. It wasn't until three months later that the paper referred to an event as occurring in "Wyncote," and only sporadically for months thereafter. In contrast to the attention paid to Gilded Age residents, the newspaper almost turned its back on events in nearby Cheltenham and much detail about daily life went unrecorded. The situation did not change until the *Times Chronicle* was founded in 1896 and offered a regular column entitled "Wyncote Whispers."

1889: Presidential Visit

Lawyer and Civil War hero Benjamin Harrison, the "Gilded Age" president, was elected the twenty-third president of the United States in 1888. His conservative Republican positions appealed to John Wanamaker and Wharton Barker and both found their way into his retinue.

Wanamaker was Harrison's campaign manager (more accurately, one of several managers) in 1888 and succeeded in raising over $400,000 for the campaign including his own $10,000 donation, unheard of amounts in those days. *Harper's Weekly* magazine accused him of strong-arming his manufacturing and business associates to contribute by raising the fear of decreasing protective tariffs on their businesses if Harrison's opponent were to be elected. Despite his lack of experience in national politics, Wanamaker's success as a strategist and fund-raiser earned him an appointment in Harrison's cabinet as Postmaster General. Harrison's rationale was that he favored experienced businessmen and successful managers for a task such as the leading the raucous Post Office department. Wanamaker served four years in that capacity, not without some controversy, but generally to acclaim for his progressive innovations.

The new village of Wyncote had Wanamaker to thank for the establishment of home delivery of mail in the new century, although many residents complained about the demise of the custom of meeting one's neighbors at the post office on the corner regularly while collecting their mail. Wanamaker's new system was tested in the borough of Jenkintown in 1891 and met with a "gratifying" response. The carrier made two deliveries per day and his expenses were more than covered by the drastic increase in the number of stamps sold at the post office. The test in Jenkintown included the innovation of installing drop boxes for mail at ten locations. The effectiveness of Wanamaker's stewardship of the Post Office Department is evident in the Heacock file of letters that are part of the Carl Gatter collection at the University of Pennsylvania. One typical letter addressed to Joseph Heacock bears an outgoing postmark of Brooklyn, New York, at 10:00 pm on September 10, 1900, and an incoming postmark of Wyncote, Pa., on September 11, 1900, at 7:00 am. It is doubtful any of us in the twenty-first century have experienced such effective delivery of our correspondence, except by email.

Wharton Barker's association with Harrison went back even further than Wanamaker's. In his only foray into national politics before the 1888 election, Barker had successfully engineered the nomination of James A. Garfield

President Harrison Meets with John Wanamaker, 1889
In this photo taken at *Lindenhurst*, President Harrison is seated in the center. His wife is on his right. John Wanamaker is with the cane seated at the far left. Harrison visited Wanamaker in September while visiting Hatboro for the anniversary celebration of the Log College.
Photo: Courtesy of The Historical Society of Pennsylvania

as the Republican candidate for president at the convention in Chicago in 1880. Barker met Harrison at the convention where Harrison also supported Garfield. After Garfield's election, Harrison was approached about a cabinet appointment, but declined in order to assume the Senate seat to which he was elected. Barker had seen a potential presidential candidate in Harrison, kept in touch in succeeding years, and suggested his candidacy for president in 1887 at the end of Harrison's senatorial term.

After Harrison's election, politics confused and delayed the appointment of the cabinet, much to the consternation of the press that began to ridicule Harrison's election and Wanamaker's role in financing it. Barker had lobbied his friend, Harrison, for the appointment as Secretary of Treasury, for which he had ample qualifications. However,

Barker's candidacy was opposed by the powerful Chairman of the Republican National Committee, Philadelphian Matthew Quay. Barker had crossed paths and swords with Quay many times before 1888. An exact opposite to Barker in terms of mentality and political experience, the wily Quay feared a threat to his power from a fellow Philadelphian. Bowing to Quay's influence, Harrison offered the Treasury position to Senator William Windom of Minnesota. Besides, Harrison seemed to appoint only Presbyterians and the Quaker Barker did not fit that mold. It would mark the end of Barker's friendship with Harrison and the beginning of Barker's disaffection with the Republican Party. That disappointment would lead to Barker's nomination by the Populist Party for the presidency in the 1900 election. He is, to date, the only person from Wyncote to run for the highest office in the land.

On September 4, 1889, President Harrison visited his Postmaster General while on his way to Hatboro to participate in the celebration of the founding of William Tennent's "Log College." Arriving that evening at the Jenkintown station, he was met by a crowd of hundreds who "cheered lustily for every member of the party" as they stepped down from the train, according to a newspaper account of the visit. Wanamaker's carriages picked up the presidential party at the station and carried them through the estate gates just on the other side of Greenwood Avenue to *Lindenhurst*. A gala dinner was held that evening which included the Mayor of Philadelphia, Edwin H. Fitler, and the Governor of Pennsylvania, James A. Beaver.

The dinner party was serenaded by the Jenkintown Band, twenty-strong.The next morning, the presidential party set out from Wanamaker's along the Old York Road to Dr. Isaac Newton Evans' home in Hatboro. Evans was the Republican Congressman representing the 7th district that covered Hatboro all the way to Wyncote. A long procession of carriages fell in behind the lead barouche carrying Harrison and Wanamaker. According to the *Public Spirit* article, "there rolled landaus, Victorians, phaetons, surreys, buggies, road carts, and market wagons. . . .Along the miles of country from the Wanamaker mansion, Harrison was tendered one continuous ovation." (Log College, 1889) The

In the News

The Trouble With Horses

Mr. Charles Hewett and wife met with an accident on Thursday last, while driving on Washington Lane near Chelten Hills station. They were coming down the hill on the West side of the railroad when they were signalled that a train was approaching, and Mr. Hewett pulled up suddenly just opposite the road leading to Jenkintown station. The horses either became frightened or misunderstood Mr. Hewett and turned short around into the road to Jenkintown station, upsetting the carriage and throwing the occupants out. Mr. Hewett escaped injury, while Mrs. Hewett was prostrated with fright and had her arm very badly bruised. The carriage was completely demolished.
Public Spirit, October 14, 1882

Thomas Brannan, our stage driver, came near meeting with a serious accident last Saturday. A wagon belonging to Charles Wilson, the grocer, in attempting to drive over the railroad track at Jenkintown station behind the train that was about stopping, the horse became frightened and in crossing started up the station road at full speed. As it neared the wagon in which Mr. Brannan was in he attempted to clear it, but it struck, throwing him violently to the ground, striking his chin and doing him other injury. His horse ran some distance, but was fortunately stopped before any damage was done. Mr. Wilson's wagon was upturned, the horse was also thrown, and when found the driver was lying on the side of the wagon inside. The wagon was somewhat demolished. Moral, don't attempt to drive across the track until the cars have stopped.
Public Spirit, August 9, 1884

The town is just now greatly excited over a singular case that is being investigated by the authorities. Last Friday evening, Dr. Cross, a well-known physician, drove up in front of the residence of Cashier A. H. Baker and stepped into the house to see a patient. While the Doctor was in the house his horse suddenly dropped to the ground dead. It is alleged by the Doctor that death was caused by a shock received from a ground wire running down the light pole to which the horse was hitched. The Jenkintown Electric Light Company had just turned on the current in the wires for the night.
Public Spirit, March 28, 1891

George Kohl met with a painful accident while out driving on Monday. On coming down a hill the harness broke letting the wagon come against the horse. The animal kicked the dashboard which cut Mr. Kohl quite badly on the knee.
Public Spirit, November 7, 1891

On Wednesday an accident took place at Beechwood. A party of three ladies started for a drive, one holding the lines. As they descended the hill drive towards the gate the horse began to kick and ran off the road into a clump of trees, throwing the driver out and breaking up the carriage. The other ladies were badly shaken up and frightened. The driver fainted and was carried up to the house.
Public Spirit, January 8, 1893

Wyncote was in great excitement Monday morning when one of L.M. Bean's horses geared to a cart loaded with flue pipe started from the station running towards the store at the bridge the keystaff was lost, the cart dumped and threw the driver out backward, the horse continued his running, the noise of which started another of Mr. Bean's horses, which has been in use to C. M. Case's delivery wagon. Mr. Case's wagon was torn to pieces by striking an electric pole which stands out in the road now that the road is widened.
Times Chronicle, June 20, 1896

On Thursday while Mr. Jenning's team was standing in front of Mr. Cases's store, the horse became uneasy and started off. The wagon struck something and the horse began to run. In a mysterious way about half a dozen teams escaped being struck on the road, but when the horse was caught on Bend Road, the wagon was a complete wreck.
Times Chronicle, October 3, 1896

On Monday morning, Lukens Shoemaker was at Thomas Nicholson's coal yard with his four-horse team, getting a load of coal. He had detached the leaders and was holding them as a train came by and alarmed them. They started to run and threw the owner to one side. The horses tried to go on both sides of the shed over the scales. One was thrown violently down on the scales and the other got away by the breaking of the harness. The shed was torn away. The large roof 14x16 feet came tumbling down to the ground. While one horse lay dead on the scales the other was stopped on the platform at the station before getting into the waiting room.
Public Spirit, November 19, 1897

Mr. and Mrs. Harry K. Walt, of Wyncote, were badly injured in a runaway accident Sunday afternoon. The horse became frightened at an automobile at Greenwood avenue and Church road, Wyncote, upset the carriage and dragged both the occupants for quite a distance. Mr. and Mrs. Walt were badly lacerated and bruised about their heads and bodies. The horse was horribly injured and may have to be killed.
Pennsburg Town and Country, November 26, 1904

procession so long that it took a half-hour to pass left a cloud of chalky dust that soon covered everyone. Young Ellwood Parry of Wyncote, residing in the old Mather homestead across the street from Wanamaker, recorded the event in his diary.

A fine day. Thermometer 80 degrees. After getting dressed, we hung a large flag across the road, opposite the stone house, on the other side. I also stuck a number of flags in the lawn in proper places. About 10:30, music was heard. A dozen mounted guards came in sight immediately followed by the band, then came some foot soldiers., from the same post as the cavalry, and then the Presidential party. (Parry, 1889)

Despite his long friendship and his active campaign for Harrison, and despite the efforts of Barker's three sons who organized the Harrison and Morton Marching Club during the campaign, Barker was conspicuously absent from the celebration.

1890: Train Station Renovation

The growth of the neighborhood brought increased traffic to the Jenkintown Station, rendering the 1872 facilities not only too small but too humble. An article in the local paper complained of the undignified atmosphere of the small station house.

At most railroad stations there are two waiting rooms. The one, for "ladies only" is clean, tidy, and more or less comfortable and homelike. The company evidently does something to make it worthy of its female tenants, who, to their credit be it spoken, do not defile the floors or the walls as do some of the other sex. To the "Ladies Waiting Room," that of the men presents an abrupt contrast. The paint is dirty, the floor is dirty, dirty spittoons are scattered around, dirty lamps and disorderly boys fill the seats. (*Public Spirit, 12/27/1884*)

In November of 1890, the railroad announced plans for major renovations to the increasingly important station on its growing system. The Reading not only had local development on its mind, but also knew that the completion of the attractive Reading Terminal would unleash new demand for its services once patrons could ride directly into the heart of the city. The inconvenient and uncomfortable horse-trolley rides from the Berks Street terminus would be forever abolished. The veteran Jenkintown quarrymen and contractors, Felix O'Neil and Son, were hired for the job that was budgeted at $10,000, a sum that the Reading touted would make the station "one of the most complete stations on the road." The improvements included raising the roof to increase interior space, extending the roof to provide outside shelter for riders, the construction of two pavilions on either side of the old waiting room so that there would be a separate "Ladies Waiting Room," and the best innovation of all, "complete toilet rooms" for the use of patrons. The improvements included the construction of a new building on the outbound platform to house a baggage room and a covered shelter for passengers. Shortly after opening, the railroad added safety gates to the Greenwood Avenue crossing to reduce, hopefully, the number of accidents caused by spooked horses and inattentive pedestrians. A final amenity came in February of 1892. It was a pole, installed on the roof of the station by the "signal bureau" on which would be mounted flags depicting the weather forecast for the day.

The earnest efforts of the railroad were not completely successful, however. Riders complained of the open "cave" or "bear pit" that served as the waiting room on the outbound side, demanding that it be enclosed and equipped with a stove. Alas, that amenity did not materialize until Trumbauer's 1932 reconstruction. Also, the horses apparently were persuaded to respect the tracks but the humans were not. The railroad installed a wrought iron fence between the tracks in 1896 to prevent crossing in the path of trains. This prompted an outcry by riders who now had no choice but to cross at Greenwood Avenue where there was no boardwalk (forcing them to "wade through the snow, slush, or mud"), or skirt the fence at the end of the baggage platform (forcing them to navigate "all kinds of miscellaneous freight, boxes, and barrels"). The railroad met their concerns by constructing an iron bridge that connected the Wyncote side with the outbound platform and Beechwood Avenue, the bridge of "size and sighs." The

Top: Jenkintown Station, 1888
The 1872 station is pictured just before renovations to expand the station.
Courtesy of The Historical Society of Montgomery County
Bottom: After Renovations, 1890
The station is pictured just after construction of the new station buildings.
Courtesy of the Library of Congress

failure of that solution was admitted in 1904 with the construction of a tunnel connecting the outbound and inbound platforms. The renovated station included extensive flower beds that cheered riders and passers-by. The *Public Spirit* lamented in October of 1891, "The flower beds are at their best just before the frost, how sorry we will all be to see them wilt away."

1891: The last of the Gilded Age

The world imploded on the esteemed banker, Abraham Barker, on Thursday, November 20, 1890. The failure of the Barker Brothers Bank necessitated Extra editions the next day from all of Philadelphia's newspapers as they spread the news of the unthinkable and embarrassing failure. *The Daily Evening Telegraph* noted that "Abraham Barker, the venerable founder of the bank, seemed overwhelmed by the catastrophe which had befallen it." The cause of the failure was an almost perfect storm of financial woes coming from three directions. Internationally, the large and prestigious Barings Bank of London, itself in distress, called in several loans from corresponding companies, which included Barker Brothers, its American representative. Nationally, the Barker Bank was heavily invested in several railroads that were struggling, including the Reading, and personally, Wharton Barker's extensive investments in the proposed telephone and railroad infrastructure in China were becoming unraveled. Abraham Barker's personal statement, printed by the *Telegraph* that day, made it sound very simple: "People who owed us money, and upon whom we depended, did not pay us. We expected that they would do so, but they failed to meet their engagements, and now we have failed to meet ours."

The sums of money involved must have been gigantic to precipitate such a disaster on the experienced company that had survived so many other trials through the years. The personal effect on Abraham was almost immediate as he vacated his treasured estate in Wyncote and moved back to the city: he had lost almost everything. His assignee, Edward Mellor, also his son-in-law, took charge of managing his assets including his and Wharton's Wyncote properties.

In December of 1897, Wharton Barker's property along Greenwood Avenue was cleared for auction and sixteen lots were sold, making the former Barker holdings inadvertently the last major development of 19th century Wyncote. The sale raised $56,660 for his creditors.

Abraham Barker's mansion did not stay vacant for long. One of the last moguls of the Gilded Age was climbing the ladder in Philadelphia and was seeking a country home. He was Cyrus Hermann Kotzschmar Curtis. Curtis had founded a newspaper in his hometown of Portland, Maine, but, after a disastrous fire that destroyed his business, decided that better opportunities existed in Philadelphia. He moved to that city in 1876 and founded a newspaper, *Tribune and Farmer,* in 1879, a four-page weekly that catered to the rural farming community. The magazine prospered but a chance feature led to even greater success. That feature was a one-page supplement on women's issues that Curtis published in 1883 for an issue that was short on articles. The feature was an immediate hit, so successful that Curtis allowed the column to evolve within a year to a new magazine, the *Ladies Home Journal.* Aimed at middle-class homemakers, Curtis recognized the important shifts in attitudes toward women and honed-in on their needs and interests. Curtis appointed the writer of the original column to be the editor of the new publication. Her name was Louisa Knapp Curtis, Cyrus' wife. In just five years, it became the largest circulation periodical in the world.

His growing prowess in the publishing field, led by the success of the *Journal,* resulted in the incorporation of the Curtis Publishing Company in 1891, and a move to Wyncote. Renting the vacant *Lyndon* from Barker (through Edward Mellor and his agent, Angelo Freedly, who now owned the Barker deeds), Curtis tested the waters of the burgeoning village, as so many others were doing up on "probationary hill." By February 1893, Curtis purchased the mansion part of the property. In May of 1895, he purchased the remainder of Barker's estate and announced that he would build a new home on the site. He invested a reported two million dollars demolishing Barker's modest old homestead, building a Renaissance Revival mansion, and hiring noted landscape architect Frederick Law Olmstead to turn the Barker farm into a parkland of lawns, ponds, and gardens. The home was completed in the summer of 1896.

Curtis kept busy. In 1897, he purchased a venerable but failing magazine, *The Saturday Evening Post,* for just one thousand dollars. Later, he added several newspapers including Wanamaker's paper and the *Philadelphia Inquirer.* In 1898, Curtis hired George Horace Lorimer to work as literary editor for the *Post* and under Lorimer's leadership, it shortly superseded the *Ladies Home Journal* as the largest circulation magazine in the world. The young Lorimer must have been very persuasive to land the job since his credentials were quite thin. Lorimer had only one year of experience as a reporter for a Boston newspaper at the time he was hired. Before that, he had only one year of college and seven years of experience as a meat packer for the Philip Armour Company before turning to Journalism. Nonetheless, Curtis was so impressed with the hard-working Lorimer that he promoted him to editor-in-chief of the *Post* the next year.

He was an immediate success. Curtis coaxed him to live in Wyncote in 1903, as he would do later to his daughter who married the *Journal* editor, Edward Bok, and his step-son-in-law, making just another extended "family compound" in Wyncote. Lorimer purchased the most recent estate of Wharton Barker, who had vacated due to his own financial decline, and constructed *Belgraeme.* That mansion has survived and is now the main building of Wyncote's Ancillae-Assumpta Academy. *Lyndon* was not so fortunate. After Curtis' death in 1933, his daughter preserved the music room but demolished the house to save taxes, sparing only The music room and potting shed. She donated those facilities and the remaining 47 acres to Cheltenham Township in 1937 for a park that now bears the Curtis name. The luxurious mansion had lasted barely thirty-seven years. The landscaped ponds, rolling hillsides, stone wall, ornate gates, and two buildings, are all products of Curtis' residency as Barker lived far more modestly, enjoying the natural beauty of the countryside and using the grounds as a farm.

Many other notable professional and business leaders of the late Nineteenth Century also found homes in Wyncote, though the extent of their success and size of their homes would not match the proportions of Curtis and his gilded age predecessors.

CYRUS H. K. CURTIS
The Publisher

GEORGE HORACE LORIMER
The Editor

Cyrus H. K. Curtis and George Horace Lorimer
This view shows the jaunty publishers aboard Curtis' yacht, *Lyndonia,* circa 1925. The photograph appeared in *A Short History of The Saturday Evening Post* published by the Curtis Publishing Company in 1936. Curtis was an avid sailor and served as the Commodore and benefactor of the Camden Yacht Club.
Photo: Courtesy of the University of Pennsylvania, Gatter Research Collection on Ezra Pound, Rare Book & Manuscript Library

Josiah Kendall Proctor, *Oak Shade,* November 1888: Also known as Joseph Proctor, he moved his family to Philadelphia from Massachusetts and founded the Philadelphia Textile Machinery Company in 1885. The company specialized in processing machines to support the large textile industry in Philadelphia. At forty years old, he purchased one of the new houses on Woodland Avenue soon after the founding of Wyncote. His company eventually merged with the Silex Corporation to form Proctor-Silex, best known today for its coffee machines.

William H. Berger, *Fairview*, November 1890: Berger founded Berger Brothers in 1874 and produced tinners' supplies for roofers. He purchased five acres from Henry Lippincott for his mansion after being forced out of his property near John Wanamaker's mansion due to Wanamaker's expansion. There were accusations that Wanamaker wanted to free himself "from proximity to goat and pig farms." Berger's stately mansion on top of the hill cost $15,000. The company evolved and grew through mergers and acquisitions and still operates today as a unit of Berger Holdings, a conglomerate of building materials companies. His mansion was donated to the German Reformed Church in 1928 and became a nursing home. Expansion of the home enveloped the mansion until it was demolished in 1968 for another addition.

Henry K. Walt, *Bend Terrace,* April 1892: Walt purchased a nine acre tract from Bradley Redfield and engaged Horace Trumbauer to build a French-Norman residence overlooking a park. The property was one of those featured in Kohler's "Jenkintown" booklet for his building syndicate in 1900. Walt was president of the Jenkintown National Bank, founded in 1875 by a group of local businessmen and farmers. The successful local bank, when founded was capitalized at $50,000. For comparison, consider that Wharton Barker's bank at the same time was capitalized at five million dollars. Walt was an influential figure in developing the infrastructure for Wyncote and Jenkintown at the end of the 19th century. The house still stands overlooking the township's Robinson Park.

In the News

Wyncote Wildlife

Wharton Barker's son Samuel killed a rattlesnake three feet long this week on his father's farm near Wyncote. It is to be sent to the Pennsylvania University.
Public Spirit, March 24, 1888

A dog, said to be worth $150, and belonging to John Wanamaker was killed by a stranger near Chelten Hill station, the other evening. The dog was out in the road running about when the man drew a revolver and shot it, he then quickly boarded a train and was off.
Public Spirit, July 8,, 1890

One of Wanamaker's lakes was drained on Tuesday. Several hundred carp and other varieties of fish were taken by the local fishermen. Mr. Wanamaker will stock the yard with black bass, and supply water from an artesian well.
Public Spirit, August 17, 1890

Two German Carp were caught in the creek back of the station on Wednesday. One weighed eight and the other five pounds.
Public Spirit, July 4, 1896

John Plunkett of Chelten Hills has been acquitted of unjudiciously shooting a stork on the premises of John Wanamaker.
Public Spirit, December 19, 1896

M. J. Slifer caught an eel two feet 8 inches long in back of the station on Thursday.
Public Spirit, October 30, 1897

Henry H. Cramp, May 1892: Cramp was the Secretary and
Treasurer of the shipyard bearing his father's name, William
Cramp and Sons. Henry's older brother, Charles, became
president following William's death in 1879. At the time that
Henry purchased his summer home on Bent Road in
Wyncote, Cramp Shipyard was the largest concern of its kind
in the United States and had constructed famous ships for
commercial use as well as military vessels for the United
States and other countries. In 1878, Cramp had produced
four modern warships for the Czar of Russia under Wharton
Barker's direction. Cramp purchased his home from Bradley
Redfield and brought his young nephew out to Wyncote with
him. Courtland D. Cramp was the son of Charles, and he and
Henry signed for their properties on the same day. The
Cramps entertained numerous foreign customers at their
summer home, each visit dutifully reported in the local
newspapers.

John I. Rogers, *Dunluce,* February 1898: Rogers read law in
Philadelphia under Charles Ingersoll, famed Philadelphia
jurist and congressman, and was admitted to the bar in 1865.
He achieved the rank of Colonel in the First City Troop and
was called upon by the governor of Pennsylvania to serve as
judge advocate general. He developed a code of military
justice that became a model for the rest of the nation. He was
a visitor to Beechwood Inn who became enamored with
Wyncote and purchased a sixteen-acre estate from the
assignees of the bankrupt Wharton Barker across Greenwood
Avenue from the schoolhouse. Rogers, an avid baseball fan,
purchased the Worcester Brown Stockings of the National
League in 1883 and moved them to Philadelphia. He renamed
them the "Phillies" to sound more local, and the team hs
survived as the oldest continuous franchise in the National
League.   Rogers was later a co-founder of the National
Football League with his friend and nemesis, Ben Shibe,
owner of the Philadelphia Athletics. After his death in 1910,
the house was owned by Max and Jennie Sladkin, who
manufactured the Black Beauty bicycle and the Ace
Motorcycle. Sladkin renamed the estate *King Fox Ranch* and
raised foxes on the site. Many neighbors still remember the
pungent atmosphere surrounding that enterprise.

In The News

HOLDUP IN WYNCOTE

KARL ROGERS SHOT, BUT WHIPS FOOTPAD

Gets Highwayman's Revolver in Struggle on
Greenwood Avenue, But Assailant Makes Escape –
Wound Not a Serious One

Battling with a highwayman in the dark of an unlighted street in Wyncote Tuesday night, Karl Rogers, third son of Col John I. Rogers, former owner of the Philadelphia National League Base Ball Club, was shot through the thigh,

Wounded though he was, Rogers forced his assailant to drop the weapon, won in the struggle for its possession, and drove the footpad off. The latter escaped. His victim's wound is not serious.

The attack took place near the Rogers residence, "Dunluce," which wiles about a quarter of a mile from the Wyncote Station, on Greenwood avenue. Mr. Rogers was on his way home from a call in the neighborhood. The time was about 11.15 o'clock.

The scene of the hold-up was near a lane that leads into the grounds about the residence of J. Wesley Pullman, next to the Rogers place. Just before the lane is reached in the direction Rogers was going the road curves about two big trees, and it was behind them that the footpad lay in wait.

There are electric light poles along the road, but the lamps were not burning. As Rogers stepped abreast of the two trees, the highwayman slipped out swiftly and thrust a revolver in his face.

"Hands up," he said curtly.

Rogers lacks only an inch of six feet, and is built in proportion. When he left the University of Pennsylvania about a year or two ago, he was a member of the swimming team, and for about a year he has been in the lumber business in Tennessee. His condition hasn't suffered since he left college.

The Highwayman was slightly shorter than Rogers. The latter looked him over swiftly, and decided that, revolver or no revolver, he would make the hold-up one of the liveliest the man in front of him ever mixed in.

He raised his arms, but he dropped them as swiftly as he raised them, and the footpad found himself in a struggle with a trained athlete, who had all his nerve in commission. Rogers got a grip on the other man's pistol arm, and forced the weapon downward.

The two swayed and struggled, Rogers seeking to wrest the revolver from the other's grip, the footpad striving to free the weapon for use on his victim. In some way the trigger was pulled, and the bullet tore clear through the fleshy part of Rogers' thigh. Rogers gathered his strength and fought with increased energy. He slammed the footpad around until the weapon dropped to the road, and then the two of them fought to reach it.

Rogers won. He flung the robber off and snatched up the revolver. When he straightened up the footpad was running down the road. Rogers saw him turn up the Pullman lane, and followed him. He flashed into sight near a tree up the lane, and Rogers stopped to shoot. The pistol missed fire three times, and by the time Rogers realized that it was useless the footpad disappeared in the darkness.

The young man was growing weak from the loss of blood and the shock of the bullet wound by that time, and he decided that he had better get home as fast as he could. The wound began to pain him, and he made slow progress to the house. The residence is on a high terrace and his journey up the steps increased the pain from the injury.

He made the house finally, and the family was aroused. Colonel Rogers sent for Dr. M. K. Neiffer, who lives nearby, and the physician reached the house quickly. He relieved the agitated parents of the young man with an assurance that the wound, though painful, was not dangerous.

The police of Abington and Cheltenham townships, in which Wyncote lies, were notified and police were sent out to scour the country about the scene of the hold-up. They got no trace of the robber. Rogers could give only a meager description of him. The darkness prevented him seeing his assailant plainly, and all that he could tell the police was that the footpad was a little shorter than himself, inclined to stoutness, and wore something over his face.

Colonel Rogers was indignant over the lack of light on the street. He said that the streets of the neighborhood were frequently in darkness because there was not current enough to give service to both house and highways. Had the lights on Greenwood avenue been up Tuesday night young Rogers would probably have seen the footpad and been prepared for his attack, declared his father.

It was probably lucky for the hold-up man that his weapon, a cheap .22 calibre revolver, did not work when Rogers pulled the trigger. The young man, like his two brothers, John and Frank, is an expert revolver shot. The brothers have spent a good deal of their time at home practicing on all sorts of targets. All of them usually carry revolvers when they expect to remain out late, but Tuesday night Karl did not have his in his pocket.

"Anybody would have done it, I guess," he said. "A man doesn't like to stand still and let another fellow put it all over him when he can put up a fight."

He came downstairs early, and didn't look much the worse for his encounter. The wound is expected to heal quickly, although it will hurt for a while.

Dunluce
On a hillside overlooking Greenwood Avenue, John I. Rogers' estate kept
watch over central Wyncote. The house consisted of thirty rooms, five
bathrooms, and a conservatory. The basement contained a full-sized
bowling alley. The water tank and windmill apparently provided a copious
supply of fresh water for the house.
Photo: Courtesy of Robert M. Skaler, Elkins Park

John B. Deaver, April 1898: Dr. Deaver was surgeon-in-
chief of the German Hospital (today's Lankenau, originally
in North Philadelphia) and professor of surgery at the
University of Pennsylvania. He is the father of the
appendectomy and pioneered other surgical techniques,
inventing a surgical retractor that bears his name today. He
rented J. W. Brock's home on Wyncote Lane (today's Deaver
Road) in 1897 and purchased it a year later. The home
stands today. An obituary in *Time* Magazine of October 5,
1931, indicated that he could manipulate the scalpel equally
well with either hand. A medical journal memoir described
his work habit of as many as twenty-five operations in an
afternoon, eschewing assistance from his residents except
for the final suture. He was the author of many books and
monographs on surgery. Dr. Deaver declined all invitations
to participate in professional organizations indicating that
he did not wish to spend his time listening to discussions

"better understood by himself than by the speaker" or learning about something "he did not care to learn."

<u>Harry C. Deaver</u>, *Sunnymede,* April 1898: John's younger brother, Dr. Harry Deaver, lived on the estate next door to John. Dr. Deaver was a professor at Women's Medical College and surgeon-in-chief at the Episcopal Hospital and the Kensington Hospital.

The brothers and their families were inadvertently drawn into a local version of the future Lindbergh case a decade after moving to Wyncote. As the *New York Times* reported on January 27, 1913, a trio of "foreigners," kidnapped the nephew of Dr. Harry Deaver's caretaker in a bungled attempt to kidnap Dr. John B. Deaver's son, Montgomery. Young John Twin reported that three rough Italians grabbed him after pulling their covered wagon into the driveway of the Deaver estate on Wyncote Lane. Blindfolded and thrown into the wagon, Twin was driven to a house in nearby Edge Hill. He finally persuaded his captors that he was not Dr. Deaver's son and suggested that it was safer to let him go than kill him as they threatened. He escaped after an altercation among the kidnappers over whether to release him or execute him. Arriving home and telling his story precipitated a thirty-six hour search for the foreigners by a "posse" of constables and neighbors. Armed watchmen were hired to guard the two Deaver estates for the next two days amid frayed nerves on the part of all the parents involved. Fortunately no Italians were caught – because they did not exist. Young Twin finally admitted two days later that he invented the story to cover his late arrival home after an afternoon of galavanting in the woods with friends. No record was kept of what discipline may have been administered to the fourteen year-old for his costly deception.

1891: Two Churches

As the community developed, the desire to have close access to a place of worship became pressing. A group of new residents of the village organized a Sunday School in January of 1891 and proceeded to raise money for the construction of a chapel. Among the organizers were Charles Meurer, Lewis Leidy, Prof. Robert Ellis Thompson, and William H. Berger. Their efforts were quickly successful and they purchased a parcel on the corner of Greenwood and Fernbrook Avenues from William E. Weber for $2,000. The plot, just 180 feet by 160 feet, was intended to hold a temporary structure pending further decisions on forming a new congregation. The 260-seat building, designed by Angus Wade, was completed in time to host an Easter Celebration on March 29, 1891, perhaps the first formal religious service in Wyncote. In April of the next year, a petition signed by thirty residents was presented to the Presbytery of Philadelphia North and, on May 20, 1892, the Committee on Home Mission met in the small wooden chapel and approved the formation of the Calvary Presbyterian Church of Wyncote.

In 1893, land was purchased at the top of the hill on Bent Road in what was still the "Shoemaker tract" as a site for a permanent church. The old chapel was moved during the two middle weeks of September by a struggling team of horses to the new site and in April 1894, ground was broken for a manse located on the newly extended Fernbrook Avenue. In 1886, a building fund committee was authorized. A June Fete on the lawn of the Waddingham estate in 1897 helped raise six thousand dollars that year. For the festive event, the new electric company ran special wires to the house and the evening activities on the lawn were lit by "arc lights which were augmented by hundreds of small incandescents artistically arranged about the trunks and limbs of the trees." The *Public Spirit* article of June 19th went on to note that "the full light from all this electricity was plainly visible for miles around." This indeed must have been a spectacular and festive event in a time just before electricity was provided to individual houses. The success of the effort was fully realized on February 5, 1899, when the first service was held in the new church. Rev. Carlos T. Chester was the founding pastor.

Another group of residents who were attending the Episcopalian Church of Our Saviour in Jenkintown also sought to form a mission in Wyncote. The rector, Rev. Roberts Coles, entertained a request from Jenkintown residents C. B. Newbold and John W. Pepper along with new

Wyncote residents M. L. Kohler, W. W. Frazier, and William C. Kent II to establish a mission. W. W. Frazier volunteered his home at the corner of Greenwood and Curacao in March of 1891 for a chapel and hosted the first devotional meeting, a Prayer Book Service, on March 27, 1891, with the Rev. Coles presiding.

Later, the new congregation purchased another property one block south at the corner of Greenwood and Bent Road. The property was part of the Redfield tract and sold through M. L. Kohler. A small frame chapel was established on the property next to Greenwood Avenue in 1892 and in 1893 the mission committee added Cyrus Curtis and Charles Hewett to the vestry and the name of "All Hallows Mission" was adopted. Plans for a permanent church were authorized that year from the Furness and Evans company at an anticipated cost of $12,300. Furness was well established at the time, unlike Horace Trumbauer who was honing his skills in the new village. After three years of planning and fund-raising, the church was constructed in 1896-7. A principal feature of the church was an organ donated by, Cyrus Curtis and a stained-glass memorial window constructed by Tiffany and Company of New York was installed after the turn of the century. On Friday, February 12, 1897, the new church was consecrated by Bishop O. W. Whitaker. Rev. Alfred J. P. McClure was the founding pastor. The All Hallows mission church became an independent parish in 1909.

1894: Beechwood Inn

If Richard J. Dobbins ever had a year he wished he could trade away, it would have been 1891. His troubles started in 1887 when illness set in. The papers described his illness as Rheumatism, and he escaped frequently to his North Jersey beach home to recuperate. The newspaper dutifully noted his return each time with good wishes for his condition.

R. J. Dobbins returned home from his cottage at Long Branch on Tuesday last. The New York Express stopped at Ashbourne at four o'clock pm, and Mr. Dobbins arrived home. His eight carriages arrived on Wednesday. We hope Mr. Dobbins is in improved health. (*Public Spirit,* October 8, 1887)

In the News

The Tramps

Tramps are appearing among the country seats about here. People cannot be too careful not to leave their premises unguarded when they go to church. A dog in the kitchen saved the premises of Charles Hewitt, Esq., near the station from plunder on Sunday last.
Public Spirit, June 13, 1885

Special Officer Bates, in company with a number of Reading Railroad detectives, made a raid on the tramps of this vicinity on Saturday night, and another on Sunday last. About a dozen tramps were caught in their dragnet between Chelten Hills and Glenside stations.
Public Spirit, June 16, 1894

The Reading railroad officers on Friday night, caught, at Jenkintown station, two tramps and a sporty looking young fellow with patent leather shoes and the latest style clothes. A complete kit of burglars' tools was found on the dude when searched.
Public Spirit, June 16, 1894

The tramp resort down at the old Rice dam should be broken up.
Public Spirit, July 28, 1894

Reading railroad special policemen made a midnight trip along the North Penn on Monday night. At Chelten Hills, the station had been broken open by three men who were snugly ensconced around the red-hot stove. When the train stopped, the men made a break for the hills, but were captured after a short chase.
Public Spirit, December 7, 1895

News reports seemed to show him still personally engaged in his business activities at first, but decreasingly so as the next years went by. Yet his health must have been a major concern even then as he announced that he was putting Beechwood Hotel up for sale. The asking price was $140,000. The newspaper deemed it "a very valuable property."

In the middle of the summer season of 1888, further disruption plagued the hotel. The construction of the new Beechwood Avenue, which Dobbins had unsuccessfully fought for two years, reached the lawn in front of the hotel, parallel to the railroad tracks. The construction necessitated a deep cut in the lawn, and the construction of a stone retaining wall, spewing dust, debris, and commotion across the grounds of the busy hotel for most of the summer. By the next summer, the asking price was $125,000 and the newspaper noted the enticement of choice building lots that came with the property that could sell for a purported $5,000 per acre – probably referring to Dobbins' new development on recently cleared Florence Avenue across the back yard. Still, no buyers came forward as the venerable resort took another step toward losing its sylvan setting.

Things seemed back to normal in 1890 with "a very successful season" according to the *Public Spirit*. Unfortunately, at the end of that season, his dependable and successful manager, R. W. Farr, tendered his resignation in order to take on a new challenge in Savannah, Georgia. Mr. Dobbins hired a replacement in February, 1891, Mrs. H. B. Markland. It is a choice that the street-savvy Dobbins no doubt wished he had never made. In April of 1891, at the start of the summer booking season, Mrs. Markland announced that she would no longer accept guest bookings from Jews. The newspaper dryly noted that "in previous summers, the Hebrews have been plentiful." Besides the shocking social nature of her decision, as a business decision it seemed to doom the enterprise and the new season indeed suffered a drop in patronage.

Dobbins' next concern would have been the fact that his new manager failed to forward any of her rent payments since taking control. By the end of the summer, the situation had become critical and intolerable. There was serious friction between the manager and the staff, and the baker, the cook, and the head-waiter went to Norristown - the county seat - to sue for back pay. A Constable was sent to the Hotel with an attachment order and inventoried the contents of the kitchen. An attorney for Mrs. Markland went to Norristown the next Wednesday to protest the filing, but no doubt upon hearing the evidence and estimating the tenor of the court, her attorney persuaded her to drop her protest. By the twelfth of September, Mr. Dobbins filed an additional suit to remove Mrs. Markland. The *Public Spirit* described the scene:

The exciting muddle at Beechwood, the fashionable summer resort here, had a stir of [sic] two Friday afternoon when the Sheriff of Norristown and his posse made a second descent on the place, ordered the proprietress to vacate immediately, discharged the servants, gave the guests twenty-four hours' notice to leave and left things in charge of an employe [sic] of the owner of the property. It appears that the inn as a resort has been a financial failure this season. (*Public Spirit, September 12, 1891*)

The paper could have added that the hotel was a potential business and social failure as well. By the next week, Mrs. Markland had failed to leave and Sheriff Clinton Rorer and his deputies returned to the Hotel to forcibly evict her, collect all room keys, and take an inventory of furniture and equipment. Mr. Dobbins then assigned several employees to clean and repair the hotel. They found it "in a bad state: dishes on the table from the last meal and beds unmade from their last occupation." Little is known of the manager's qualifications and mentality, but, at seventy-seven years old, one wonders if she was up to the demands of managing the large enterprise, although she was perspicacious enough to advertise the hotel in a logical location that year: a resort supplement in a national medical journal. She remained a resident of Wyncote after her Beechwood experience and in 1894 was thrown from her sleigh on a cold February day after her horse was spooked and ran uncontrolled through the countryside for several miles. Her serious injuries led to her death, but one has to admire the fortitude of an eighty-year-old to be out and traveling under such circumstances.

In failing health, Richard Dobbins, accompanied by his wife, four sons and daughters, and three servants left

Philadelphia in late October by private rail car for Southern California. He would never return. Dobbins found a new manager in April of 1892 in the person of one Mr. Raymond Hamilton about whom little is known. He apparently accomplished the clean-up that the hotel desperately needed and had a successful summer according to an article in the *Public Spirit* after the 1892 season ended in September. Although he expressed his intention to manage the following summer, his tenure was short-lived and he moved on to manage the Hotel Wopsononock near Altoona in the Allegheny mountains. Unfortunately, Dobbins' health continued to decline and on January 8, 1893, Dobbins died at his winter home in Pasadena, California, bringing to an end an important Philadelphia and suburban enterprise. His heirs and business associates quickly recruited a new and experienced manager for the hotel.

It was announced on January 21, 1893, that Shimer B. Hillman and his wife Hattie had been awarded a five-year lease on the hotel. They were serving as the proprietors of Highland Inn in Secane, Delaware County, about eighteen miles south of Philadelphia. The thirty-eight year old Shimer originally was employed by John Wanamaker in Philadelphia, but left retail work to enter the hotel business. Their neice, Josephine Curry, relates their adventurous arrival at Beechwood on a cold February night after traveling from Secane all day by horse and sleigh. Curry herself lived at Beechwood as a child and recalls the rolling setting: "in the summer this hilly side was a mass of daisies, cornflowers, wild carrot, and buttercups. Under [the trees] grew the softest moss, cool to walk on in bare feet on a hot day." (Curry, 1992)

The Hillmans apparently were swift and sure in their resurrection of the hotel, producing a successful season in 1893. On first of November of 1893, Wilhemina, Richard's widow and executor, sold the hotel, grounds, and adjoining property to the east, to Hillman for the sum of $115,000. There must have been some interesting politics involved in the disposition of the property. It is not clear how Hillman, essentially a working man and not apparently independently wealthy, could have afforded the purchase. There was no mortgage involved in the sale. In an unusual transaction,

Beechwood Inn Ad
The ad appeared in the 1891 issue of the *Medical Record,* Vol. 39.

Hillman turned the property around in less than a week and sold the hotel to Beauveau Borie for a like amount.

Borie, a Jenkintown resident and civic activist, was a wealthy banker in Philadelphia. Borie, in his turn, just a few weeks later sold the Beechwood to a new company, The Beechwood Improvement Company, on December 12, 1893. The Improvement concern was incorporated on November 20, so Borie was no doubt a place-holder for the property during the company's formation. Additionally, Borie was a member of the Improvement Company syndicate, a very distinguished party. Besides Borie, it included W. W. Frazier (another important land developer and Philadelphia sugar magnate), the peripatetic Joseph W. Hunter, Clement

Newbold (stock-broker and Jenkintown resident), W. W. Harrison (of Grey Towers, a sugar magnate), Martin Luther Kohler, and Cyrus Curtis. Borie's sale price was only forty-seven thousand dollars indicating that Borie retained a majority interest in the enterprise. Nonetheless, the lean amount of Borie's compensation and the role of Hillman in the affair remain issues cloaked in mystery.

The Beechwood Improvement Company undertook immediate improvements to the property, investing $175,000 in new furnishings and exterior improvements to the buildings. A public sale of the old furniture on December 7 drew large crowds. The date, before the syndicate's purchase, is further indication of Borie's intentions and level of involvement. The five-day owner, Shimer B. Hillman and his wife, were kept on as managers and architect Horace Trumbauer was engaged to update the appearance of the building. He joined the two structures that had to-date comprised the hotel, added decorative trim to integrate the appearance of the now "L" shaped complex, and constructed an entrance portecochere on the East and parapets on either end. The old stable behind the hotel was auctioned and a new stable for forty horses was constructed on the other side of Beechwood Avenue. Amenities of the new inn included "swift-running" elevators, forty new bathrooms, a bowling alley and a billiard hall. The staff of ninety-eight catered to every need of the 300 guests. Imagine the excitement of arriving for your vacation on a fine early summer day:

The main entrance opened into a very large Exchange at the junction of the two wings, and onto this main floor opened all of the principal rooms for the use of the guests. The Exchange was oak-beamed and paneled. Three large oak columns, circled with electric lights, supported the high ceiling. At the windows facing the porch were window seats. A huge fireplace that could hold five-foot logs had a decorative mantel above it. Heavy red velvet rugs covered the floor, and the same color runner led down the corridor to the ballroom. To one side of the broad oak staircase was a platformed space with benches for uniformed bellboys. (Curry, 1992)

In the News

Life and Death in 1901: Remembering Ella

Death came to Ella Cannally Friday morning in a violent form. Walking along the Reading tracks, a flying express overtook her just south of Glenside station. She was on her way to Beechwood Inn, Jenkintown, where she was employed in the laundry. She had just left her home in Edge Hill.

Miss Cannally was bridesmaid at her brother David's marriage on Wednesday night. She herself was to wear white and orange blossoms in August, becoming the bride of John Mitchell, a baker. Agnes Jackson stopped for Ella at six o'clock. Both worked at Beechwood Inn, and were in the habit of walking the two miles to Jenkintown along the railway. At Glenside Miss Jackson entered a grocery store on the crossing corner to make a purchase and Ella continued slowly down the track.

Rushing behind came the Buffalo express, due at Glenside at 6:30, but six minutes behind time, and with full speed up. Swinging around the curve above the station, the engineer saw the brown-clad figure ahead. He blew his whistle. There was time to warn, but no time to stop a 50-mile-an-hour express.

But the girl either didn't hear or was slow to realize her peril. A local train had just slipped by on the northbound track and may have bewildered her. She did step aside, but too late. The high cylinder had struck her and the lifeless body was picked up 30 feet farther on, lying across the adjoining track. The dead girl worked at the Windsor hotel during the winter. There she met Mitchell, the baker, to whom she was to be married. The funeral was held Monday morning.
Ambler Gazette, June 27, 1901.

Under Hillman's direction, and with the new name of "Beechwood Inn," the hotel prospered as a focus of recreation and social events for another eighteen years. It was an astonishing feat to accomplish such extensive renovations in less than six months and new furniture was still being moved in the week before the June 1 opening.

Hillman left Beechwood after the 1895 season, and the lure of the area as a country retreat gradually faded as development covered the adjoining hills and consumed the open property encompassing the Inn. In 1912, the resort business came to an end. The facilities were operated by new owners as the Beechwood School for Young Ladies, then purchased in 1925 by Beaver College. When Beaver College consolidated its campus on the nearby estate of W. W. Harrison in 1962, the old hotel complex was demolished for the Beaver Hill Apartments that stand on the site today.

1894: Public School

In the spring of 1894, the Cheltenham School Board authorized the establishment of a new elementary school in Wyncote village. The Board purchased a one-acre plot from Henry and Mary Walt on Greenwood Avenue and began construction. The cost of the land was $3,500 indicating the exploding land values in the new village. The school itself actually started in a private home that had been recently constructed at the corner of Greenwood and Fernbrook Avenues. Classes met for the first time on September 17, 1894, but were forced to immediately take a week-long break as there were inadequate supplies for the unexpectedly large group of students who presented themselves. The new construction was completed in time for the beginning of the school year in 1895. The cost of the two-story stone building was $10, 261, a handsome sum even in the late nineteenth century. Florence Ridpath, formerly of the Jenkintown School, was appointed the first principal and teacher. A long-time resident recalls the beginning of the school day:

The Beechwood Inn
An old post card shows the Inn around 1900 after the Trumbauer renovations. *Courtesy of the Old York Road Historical Society*

South Porch of the Beechwood Inn, circa 1900
The porch is ready to accommodate guests.   The proprietor's niece described the setting overlooking the Tookany valley: "It was a sedentary life for some of the ladies who had been coming to the inn year after year. They took proprietary interest in certain chairs and places on the porch where they always spent their mornings, rocking down their breakfasts and engaging in some form of needlework. And woe be to the boy who moved these chairs to another spot when the porches were washed in the morning. Younger sports-inclined women were off soon after breakfast, but the young married women and newly-weds seemed very sedate." (Curry, 1992) *Photo: Courtesy of OYRHS*

When school started in the morning, all the classes met in the hall. The fifth and sixth grade students were lined up on the stairway and the other three in front of their respective rooms, all facing the center of the school. The lines were arranged by height and since I was always one of the shortest, I was either second or third in line. Daily we recited the Pledge of Allegiance to the Flag which was followed by a Bible reading and recitation of the Lord's Prayer. It didn't hurt us any, but I doubt if any of us gave any thought to what we were doing. I also don't recall anyone objecting. (Heinemann, 2008)

The school served the community for fifty-three years until a new building was erected on the former Schoble estate at the corner of Barker and Rices Mill Road in 1948.
1894: Commercial Buildings

Dr. J. E. Peters, slowly divesting himself of his investments in the new village, sold his corner store property to Horace Hale in January, 1892, for $8,500, who then sold to J. E. Luskin in July for $9,900. Harper had left the general store to tend to his growing well-drilling business, and grocer C. M. Case from Jenkintown took over the store in July of that year. Peters then sold the property adjacent to his first store in 1893. The purchaser was James Nile, an aspiring businessman and a resident of Wyncote who had a home on Greenwood Avenue. Nile was the long-time gardener for Abraham Barker and obviously managed his income well. Nile hired Horace Trumbauer to design the building and he produced a stone and frame building with two stores on the first floor and a residence above. The initial commercial occupants were Howard S. Eckels, who operated a pharmacy, and Harry Croasdale, a popular barber for the Barkers and the Beechwood Inn, who followed his friend Nile and opened his own shop. Eckels, who resided on Bend Road at Accomac, was trained as a pharmaceutical chemist and was engaged in the manufacture of "patent" medicines. He also was an expert in the use of disinfectants and antiseptics that included the use of formaldehyde. He put this expertise to work in the founding of the Eckels School of Mortuary Science in Philadelphia in 1895 and in 1899 took over the former Harper's restaurant building at the station for his medicine operation. Unfortunately James Nile died in 1894 and the newly completed store was resold to James F. Walsh.

Peters sold the third property above the corner in 1894 to Walsh who desired to open his own business. Ground was broken in March, 1897, for another two-store building designed by local architect, J. Linden Heacock. Signifying the growth of the community, it was operated as a grocery by Walsh. The other store in the new building was rented to "a Chinaman," who operated the Celestial laundry. Both buildings were purposefully designed in a colonial style to fit into the residential atmosphere of the neighborhood with subdued storefronts and residences on the second floor. On New Years Day at the start of 1897, Case suffered a fire in his store that destroyed his stock and caused a suspension of business for several months. After a brief comeback selling "notions," the Case store finally closed in June, 1898. The vacated store on the corner became the offices of the new Jenkintown Electric Company and later in 1898, Case and Walsh formed a partnership, operating a "fancy" grocery and meat market out of the Walsh store.

Another commercial building was established on the fourth Peters property in late 1894. A squat building with a wild-west flavor was constructed by Edwin Tyson, who operated a hardware and plumbing business ("agent for the Iron Turbine and Columbia Steel Wind Mills") to serve the booming construction industry. Upon the death of James Nile, Tyson became a developer as well, purchasing the Nile estate, laying out a short new road – Greenwood Place – and surveying ten lots. The houses and plots were the most modest yet in the village and some of them suggest an Arts and Crafts influence, the only such samples of the period.

Tyson's building survived well into the end of the twentieth century as the headquarters of John J. O'Donnell plumbing. It was demolished for a parking lot for the ATD complex in 1985. The Nile building was demolished in 1968 to expand the gas station that had replaced the original Peters/Harper building in 1935 and so, of the first four buildings, only the Walsh/Heacock building survives today. A final commercial establishment was the construction of the L. M. Bean livery stables in 1897 which provided local transportation services to the neighborhood still in the horse

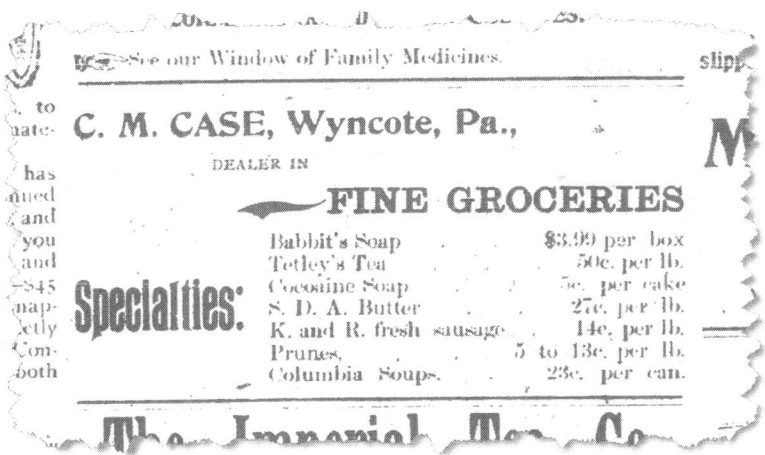

C. M. Case Grocery Store Ad
From: Public Sprit, 2/8/1896

C. M. Case Grocery Store
Thomas Harper left his general store in 1892 as the building changed ownership. C. M. Case was the new renter and he opened a grocery store in the building. It looks like a thriving business. Case added a new barn behind the store that can be seen on the right. This photograph must have been taken just after Case opened as the Nile building (1894) has not yet been constructed to the left.
Courtesy of the Old York Road Historical Society

and buggy era as well as hauling. This building later served as the J. Barton Benton foundry and a lumberyard, before its rebirth in 1979 as an office complex of ATD American, an institutional furniture wholesaler.

1896: Township Line Road

The initial colonial roads in the Olde Wyncote tract that helped define it on three sides were all thoroughfares: that is, roads designed to move people from one place to another through the tract. The first road built for residential purposes, The Serpentine, was constructed in 1854 and was

The Wyncote Business Strip, 1898
This view along Glenside Avenue to the Greenwood Avenue intersection shows the nascent business district of Wyncote. The Peters/Harper building, now eleven years old, is the dark barely visible structure in the right center of the picture. Its new barn is the lighter structure hovering over its right shoulder. The Nile building and the Walsh building are lined up on the left, followed by the Tyson plumbing store and another dark building, the Bean stable. The fallow ground of the Weber property in the foreground was used as a tennis club. Woodland Avenue above the business strip appears fully developed.
Courtesy of the Old York Road Historical Society

not followed by other residential roads until the building boom initiated by Hazard's construction of Woodland Avenue in 1885. The final boundary-road of the tract was conceived in 1893 when a road was proposed to connect Greenwood Avenue with Washington Lane along the long-invisible township line, the fourth border of the Olde Wyncote tract. The road had an odd genesis: it was born out of a proposal to <u>eliminate</u> an existing road.

When John Wanamaker purchased land from Isaac Mather in 1880 to expand his estate, it bordered an old unnamed road that connected the Old York Road with Washington Lane. The road had been in existence since 1804, perhaps a product of the original Isaac Mather's construction of a home for his son, John, which stood where the township dividing line crossed Washington Lane. In February of 1893, John Wanamaker petitioned the Montgomery County Court to close the road. A jury of locals, including Joseph Shoemaker, Hugh O'Neill and Joseph W. Hunter, was appointed and quickly issued a ruling favorable to Wanamaker by dividing the property on which the road stood to the two owners of the route, Wanamaker and Isaac Mather (the grandson). The decision appears to have been unpopular, to say the least. In November of 1893, a group of citizens from Jenkintown, Abington, and Cheltenham filed a petition with the court to establish a public road that would connect Greenwood Avenue, "opposite the entrance to Beechwood Inn," through the old road, crossing the Old York Road to the Meeting House road in Abington. A new jury was appointed that appears to have been less politically connected locally than the first. The Jenkintown Council endorsed the proposal and a hearing was held in April of 1894. Wanamaker may have been surprised by the opposition that lined-up against him at the hearing. Led by Isaac Mather himself, the jury heard testimony from a group of local luminaries: Joshua W. Lippincott, Thomas Williams, Joseph Heacock, Martin Luther Kohler, and others. Faced with such opposition, the jury vacated the previous order closing the existing road and ordered that the proposed extended road on the township line should be built.

The idea percolated for a year, as even some of those in favor of the project debated the problem of crossing the quarry, now owned by the Beechwood syndicate, that stood along the proposed path of the road just a hundred yards above the station. It was still a working quarry complete with a new steam drill to increase output. To construct a road, it was estimated that fill up to twenty-four feet in depth would be required to provide an acceptable level of roadway. At a hearing on September 20, 1896, W.W. Frazier, a land developer who was a part owner of the land on the north of the route (by virtue of his partnership in the Beechwood Improvement Company), stepped forward to propose a solution. Noting that Jenkintown would only allocate $500 to the project – and Cheltenham nothing - Frazier offered to accept all costs of the project above the five-hundred dollar allocation. His proposal was accepted, much to the acclaim of the people of the area. Of course, Frazier's motives were probably not entirely charitable as he was busy forming another syndicate to develop the land north of the proposed road along with Martin Luther Kohler, the "Jenkintown Syndicate," and an access road would greatly enhance the value of the project. Jenkintown sued Cheltenham to obtain its participation and road construction started later in the year. By this time in the development frenzy, officials and developers must have run out of prosaic names as the resulting road was called simply "Township Line Road."

1899: The Bridges

The old rickety wood-beam bridge over the Tookany creek did not stand up well to the traffic of a growing community. The *Public* Spirit termed it a "miserable ramshackle" bridge after an accident in 1886. On July 22, a coal wagon driven by Mr. Heist of Glenside had a collision on the narrow bridge with a carriage from the Beechwood Hotel carrying guests on an outing. Nobody was hurt, but the newspaper asked: "Does Cheltenham own the bridge? Then, let us have a better one." Another problem resulted from the declivity on both sides to the valley of the Tookany Creek. During heavy rains, the downpour drained to the swollen creek, in many cases submerging the bridge. Such an event occurred on May 28, 1894. As the "valleys were afloat with flood of the overflowing streams," the old low-lying Greenwood Avenue plank bridge became submerged. A large crowd gathered during the rush hour and could not cross to the station or to continue their journey on the other side. Many people missed their trains or, getting off the train, were forced to wait hours to continue their walk home. The township petitioned the county for relief, and in 1899, County Bridge #53 was constructed to span the creek. A small stone arch bridge, it was connected to a stone retaining wall that propped up Glenside Avenue that was the 1891 handiwork of Felix O'Neil, the quarryman and contractor. The stone retaining wall remains today, but the bridge was swallowed-up in 1929 by an expanded concrete structure that provided for both the original route of Greenwood Avenue and the approach to a new bridge over the railroad.

Bridge Over Tookany Creek, 1899
This stone bridge took Greenwood Avenue over the Tookany Creek. The control tower at Jenkintown Station is visible above the bridge in the upper right. A portion of the fence demarking Glenside Avenue is visible in the lower left corner, and just above the pole holding the pipe, Glenside Avenue climbs the hill.
Photo: Courtesy of the Montgomery County Department of Bridges and Highways

Similarly, the railroad crossing was increasingly problematic. Accidents were frequent as horses were spooked by the trains while their drivers were attempting to guide them across the tracks. Travelers were regularly delayed by freight trains that stopped on the crossing while delivering freight cars to Nicholson's coal yard or the freight yard around the bend at the foot of Beechwood Avenue. By 1899, a jury was appointed to discuss a new route over the tracks. Their proposal was to close the Greenwood Avenue crossing. Reminiscent of a thirteen-year-old proposal by John Wanamaker, the jury proposed that a new bridge be constructed that would extend Beechwood Avenue over the tracks and connect with Glenside Avenue at the Woodland Avenue bend above Wanamaker's pond.

On May 24, 1900, the jury heard testimony from residents in the "building where the old drug store used to be." A "who's who" list of prominent citizens demanded to be heard, including Dr. J. E. Peters, Beauveau Borie, Clement B. Newbold, Wharton Barker, Joseph Hunter, Joseph Heacock, Thomas B. Harper, Hugh O'Neill, and others. The predominant opinion was that Greenwood Avenue could not possibly be closed without causing great harm to the residents and business people of the neighborhood.

The matter was taken under advisement, apparently abandoned, until the jury reconvened in the old store a year later on April 30, 1901, for further deliberation and testimony. A similar outpouring of opposition was evident, with Jenkintown Borough Council offering the opinion that assigning two watchmen to the crossing day and night would insure adequate safety. Exposing their political bias, they further testified that, should a bridge over the tracks at Greenwood Avenue should be constructed instead, the cost should be borne by the railroad and the Jenkintown Development Syndicate which would greatly profit from the access to the old Greenwood Avenue route. Maurice J. Hoover, real-estate tycoon and heir to the Jacob Reed clothing fortune, testified that a bridge would be more dangerous than the crossing because a horse spooked at the top of the bridge would engage in a dangerous flight down the steep slope to the other side.

The railroad stepped in to offer to pay the cost of a bridge at Greenwood Avenue (but excluding the cost of the approaches to the bridge). Bending to popular opinion, the Beechwood Avenue route was abandoned and the jury ordered a bridge to be constructed. Joseph W. Hunter surveyed the property in July of 1902 and construction began in September. The bridge was completed in the spring of 1903 with a plank roadway supported by a heavy timber superstructure.

Thomas Nicholson continued his opposition from the beginning as the bridge was built almost entirely on his property. Complications of the decision were not resolved until June, 1903, when Thomas Nicholson, the coal dealer, sued for damages as the new bridge blocked the former Greenwood Avenue access to his coal yard. The compensation for his loss was $7,500, considerably less than the $20,000 he demanded and some estimates of worth of $30,000.

Although an artifact of the horse and buggy age, the bridge became an obvious necessity as the automobile age and development of the area greatly increased traffic over the site in the years immediately following construction.

Through the end of the nineteenth century, Wyncote was emerging as an integral community with the infrastructure and all of the necessary amenities necessary to accommodate year-round residency in comfort and style. But the Gilded Age left its mark in one segment of the population that still valued the community for its resort qualities. There were two distinct life styles among residents: the seasonal residents who moved in for the summer and moved back downtown with the onset of winter, and the permanent residents who lived in the village all winter but vacationed during the summer. Of course, that usually meant going to the shore, even then. The latter rented their houses to city-dwellers during the summer absences. The former never rented. By 1900, the village offered churches for worship, community groups for civic action, socializing, and entertainment, a livery that provided transportation around town, and stores that provided an amazing array of goods and services. One could walk to the center of the village at Greenwood and Glenside Avenues, pick up the mail; dine in a restaurant or snack in an Oyster bar; buy a windmill, bicycle, furnace, kitchen sink, animal feed or paint; purchase medicine; replace your violin and mandolin strings; play billiards and get a haircut; and shop for the week's food. It finally was a community.

Greenwood Avenue Bridge, 1905
The new bridge over the tracks at Greenwood Avenue is viewed from today 's Morgan Park. The bridge sits on wood pilings and the dirt embankment for the approach on the Wyncote side is just visible on the right of the picture. The waterway is the old millrace for the Mather Mill that exited the pond just a few feet north of the waterfall over the dam where the creek continued its southerly course.
Courtesy of the Old York Road Historical Society

Train at Jenkintown
This handsome Gilded Age locomotive of the North Pennsylvania Rail Road sits on the siding just north of the station in 1888. In the background in front of the locomotive can be seen a herd of cows on the Baeder farm. The site now is occupied by two office buildings at the foot of West Avenue.
Photo: Courtesy of the Old York Road Historical Society

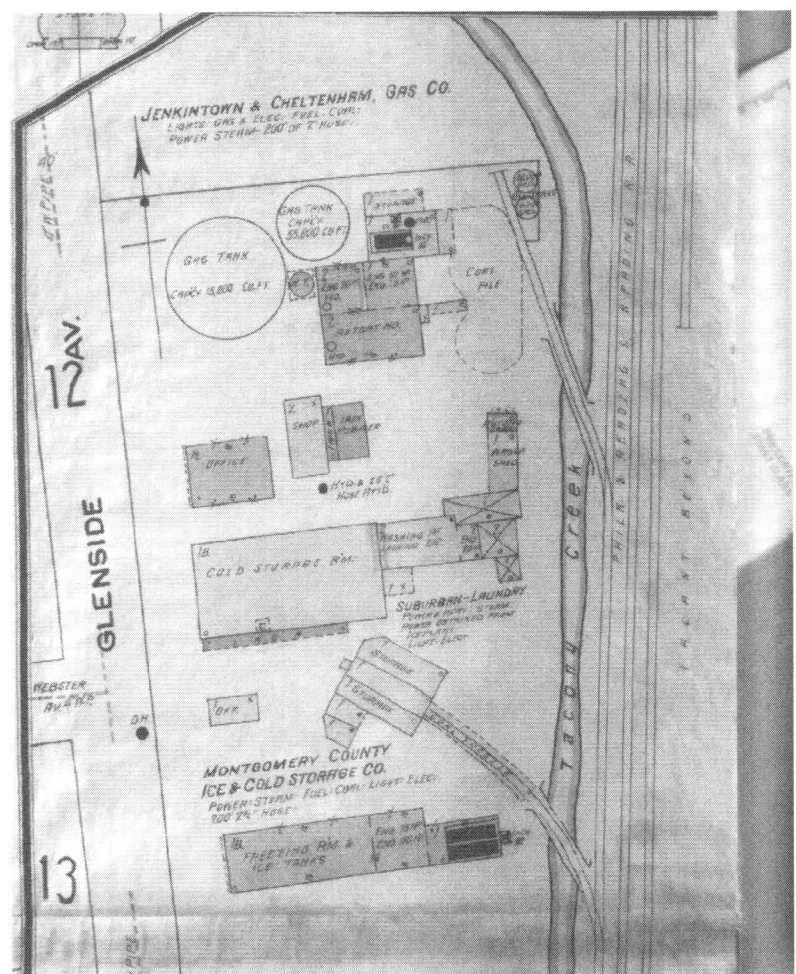

Glenside Avenue Industrial Complex
This 1902 map shows the entire industrial complex along former Heacock
pasture land in Wyncote. Today's post office is just at the location of the
notation at the top of the map, overlooking the gas tanks. Remnants of
the railroad siding bridge abutments were visible until remediation
construction in 2007.
Courtesy of the OYRHS, Sanborn Map, 1902

Chapter 8

Infrastructure

The works end of the plant will abut the railway. The buildings will be of stone quarried on the premises and involve the expenditure of quite $100,000. The establishment of the gas company will be a source of satisfaction to all those residing along its mains.
(Times Chronicle, *April 16, 1898)*

For 200 years, the residents of the Olde Wyncote tract managed their existence in the same manner from decade to decade. They drew their water from wells outside of their kitchen door; nearby was a hole in the ground covered by the outhouse that served as a toilet, and perishable food was kept cool in a springhouse or cold cellar. Their roads, consisting of compacted soil deeply rutted, turned into a quagmire when it rained and spewed clouds of irritating dust in the dry periods of the summer months. Municipal services as we know them today were unheard of and unexpected. Residents took care of their own trash: a culture of re-use and repair left relatively little to discard and the wide open spaces of the countryside afforded hidden locations for disposal of the occasional unwanted materials. Neighborhood security was a function of neighborly cooperation and winter heating depended on the scavenging of firewood or the latest coal delivery. Oil and then kerosene lamps moderated the darkness at the cost of their sooty residue and persistent chemical odor – and the occasional devastating house fire.

Even ordinary household chores required Herculean efforts. One author provided this charming description of the steps necessary to do the laundry in a late nineteenth century home:

On Sunday evenings, a housewife soaked clothing in tubs of warm water. When she woke up the next morning, she had to scrub the laundry on a rough washboard and rub it with soap made from lye, which severely irritated her hands. Next, she placed the laundry in big vats of boiling water and stirred the clothes about with a long pole to prevent the clothes from developing yellow spots. Then she lifted the clothes out of the vats with a washstick, rinsed the clothes twice, once in plain water and once with bluing, wrung the clothes out and hung them out to dry. At this point, clothes would be pressed with heavy flatirons and collars would be stiffened with starch. (Mintz, 2008)

As the nineteenth century drew to a close, affluence, development, and novel technological implements and applications drastically changed how people lived in the new village of Wyncote. In most cases, the pattern was the same. Without large networks of pipes and wires that we take for granted today, local businessmen started small companies to provide utilities to their own communities. Thus it was no accident that the first companies had "Jenkintown," or "Wyncote" in their name and the founders and officers of the companies formed what could be called an "interlocking directorate" in classic business terms. Martin L. Kohler - Wyncote developer and burgess of Jenkintown, J. Wesley Pullman - industrialist, W. W. Frazier – industrialist and developer, and H.K. Walt, banker, were some of the area names that were common to the operations of these companies. Within a few short years, amalgamation would occur and the large regional utility combines that we know today were formed.

In this way, important steps in the modernization of life in the village occurred within a stunningly short period of time in the twenty years surrounding the turn of the twentieth century.

Written Communications

An important precursor to the changes that would occur was the influence of popular periodicals such as the publications of Wyncote's Cyrus Curtis. They reached the homes of the burgeoning middle class, not only providing a new source of household advice, but also encouraging a new level of expectation for comfort in daily life.

Spurred on by inexpensive postal rates established by Congress in 1879, magazines such as *Ladies' Home Journal* and *Saturday Evening Post* soon had circulations that exceeded half a million. These popular periodicals, though not blatantly propagandistic, nevertheless presented a particular perspective that proved to be a major influence in shaping domestic life in the United States. Particularly after 1899, under the editorship of George Horace Lorimer, the *Saturday Evening Post* became a major vehicle of mass culture in the United States. (Jowett and O'Donnell, 2006)

Locally, before there was a Jenkintown *Times Chronicle*, - the local commercial newspaper founded in January of 1896 - the first means of organized communication among members of the village community occurred under the auspices of the Calvary Presbyterian Church. Pastor Carlos T. Chester, on behalf of the church, inaugurated a quarterly "newspaper," *Wyncote Outlines*, and served as its editor. Journalism must have been in his blood as the Rev. Chester had been serving as the editor of Philadelphia's *Sunday School Times* at the time of his appointment and had previously worked on the *Daily Saratogan* in upstate New York and subsequently as editor of the *Book Lover's Magazine*. He indicated his community-wide mission in the first issue in January of 1893: "There is a sincere desire in the editor's heart to use this little paper for encouraging every good thing in Wyncote." (Wyncote Outlines, 1893) The paper continued for six years to transmit information not only about church activities, but also news about the community at-large that was developing around it. Chester went on to promise that the paper would operate "without subscriptions or advertisements," a pledge that did not long survive the realities of a wealthy but small-village environment.

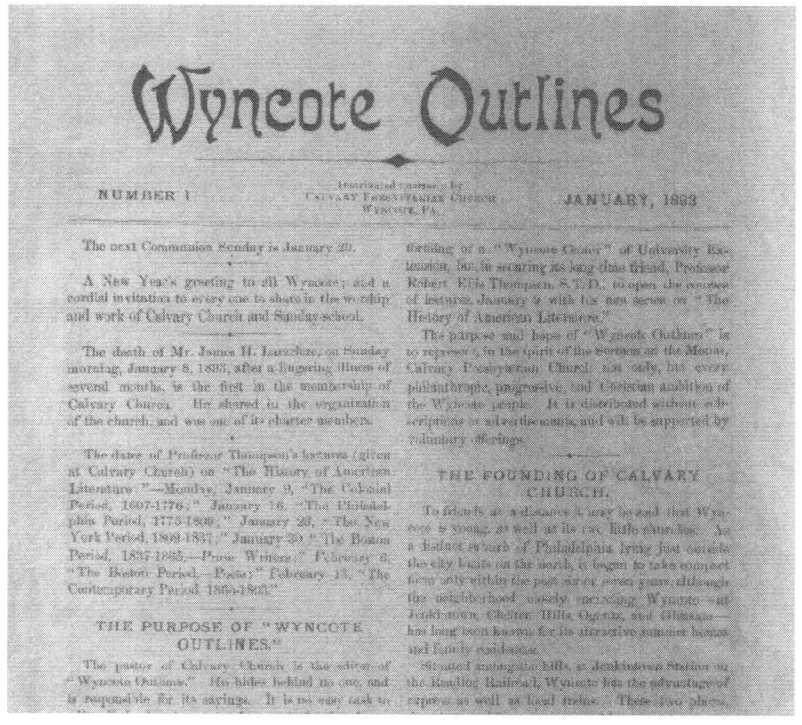

Wyncote Outlines, First Edition
The first edition of the newspaper was issued in January, 1893. And
contained a statement of the purpose of the publication.
Courtesy of the Calvary Presbyterian Church

Community Organizations

The first formal assembly of citizens for the purpose of
promoting the common good of the burgeoning community
occurred on June 22, 1893. Despite a fierce early-summer
thunderstorm, twenty-two men trudged through the wet and
muddy lanes to meet in the Calvary chapel to discuss the
welfare of their village. The result was the founding of the
"Village Improvement Association." The first issue
addressed was an infrastructure problem and the assembled
men appointed a committee to discuss the "cost of removing
garbage and sprinkling the streets." Without paving, the dirt
streets baked in dry periods and, particularly in the summer,

spewed thick clouds of dust with each passing horse and wagon.

By the next meeting of June 29, several of ladies of the neighborhood also attended. Neighbors had determined that the hundred properties of the village had produced a tax benefit of $7,000 for the township in the previous year, but only $1,000 had been spent improving the village infrastructure. The proposed solution was to establish the village as a separate borough. A committee was appointed to conduct a survey of the populace to determine the prevailing sentiment on the issue.

At the meeting of September 1893, the committee was able to report back to the Association that the citizenry had strong feelings about the incorporation proposal, but that the feelings were equally divided on both sides of the issue. The Association, no doubt wary of stepping into a maelstrom at the beginning of its existence tabled the report and suspended the work of the committee until such time as members were able "to perfect this temporary organization."

By the meeting of November 20, 1893, attendance at meetings outgrew the homey chapel and the assembly moved to the "audience room" of Mrs. Heacock's school on Mather Avenue. At that meeting, residents agreed to assume responsibility for administering contracts to provide electric lighting in the community, "that there might be one scheme for the whole village."

Seeking to sharpen the identity of the emerging community, the association, meeting on December 11, 1893, authorized a committee "to endeavor to have the telegraph and railroad companies give 'Wyncote' a place on their lists so that strangers and foreigners may find out where it is." Eighty years later, a successor organization would be engaged in the same quest.

On January 9th, 1894, it was determined that efforts should be made to secure the services of a night watchman and fire protection services. Thus, the organization was formally incorporated on May 8, 1894, as the "Wyncote Improvement and Protective Association" and continued to function until 1919 when it morphed into the more modern "Wyncote Civic Association." By that year, the growing township government took over several of the infrastructure functions previously managed by the Association and the organization needed to redefine its mission to preserve its membership and influence. Several prominent citizens and officers of the former organization moved over to guide the new one, including William C. Kent, George Horace Lorimer, T. Ellwood Frame, John Martin, and others. Cyrus Curtis joined the effort to promote the new organization and the "Wyncote Civic Association" was incorporated in Norristown in November of 1919.

Activities of the Civic Association included concern about the construction of a milk station at the train station (May 1921), advising the township on the installation of a sewer system (November 1924), concern about the Chelten Hills Railroad crossing (November 1924), establishing a playground in Wyncote (March 1925), the placement of "Wyncote" in the timetables of the Reading Railroad (March 1925 and again in 1929), and the establishment of a zoning ordinance (April 1925).

The Civic Association, suffering from declining membership, did not meet again after its April meeting until May 7th, 1945, when it met one last time to turn over its "charter, record and funds" to the more active Wyncote Men's Club.

One organization that provided an uncommon service for the community went by the ponderous name of the "Wyncote Center of University Extension." An offshoot of the Improvement Association, the Center's initial season in the winter of 1893 offered regular lectures on "The History of American Literature" at the Calvary Church. The first-year schedule included:

-January 9 – "The Colonial Period – 1607 - 1776"
-January 16 – "The Philadelphia Period – 1775-1809"
-January 23 – "The New York Period – 1809 – 1837"
-January 30 – "The Boston Period, Prose – 1837 – 1865"
-February 6 – "The Boston Period, Poets"
-February 13 – "The Contemporary Period–1865 – 1893"

The lectures were conducted by a member of the church and Wyncote resident Professor Robert Ellis Thompson. Unfortunately no other record of these lectures by this eminent educator has come to light and, although well-attended, the series lasted only two years, no doubt for lack of a comparable luminary to carry on the ambitious schedule.

The ladies of Wyncote united to form their own organization in 1898. Incorporated as the Woman's Club of Wyncote, the purpose of the organization was to "form a reading club to improve their minds." Among the founders were Mrs. Cyrus Curtis, Mrs. Maurice Hoover, and Mrs. George Horace Lorimer. The club met in private homes until moving to the All Hallows Church about 1910, its official home today. Interests evolved to world affairs, and music and art became important components of their programs. The club celebrated 110 years of activity in 2008, making it the oldest continuous community organization in Wyncote.

On June 27, 1906, a group of Wyncote men met in the parish house of All Hallows Church to "organize a Men's Club for the promotion of good fellowship, sociability and interest in Church work generally." (Wyncote Men's Club Minutes, 1906) W.C. Kent, J.H.F. Dixon, E.W. Kemble, F. Cooper Pullman, and other prominent citizens were at the forefront of the new group. Dues were fixed at "one dollar per annum" and the club became known for its educational lectures and after-lecture cigars for the next eighty years. Attendance hovered around from fifty to one hundred and fifty for lectures such as:

-November 2, 1908 – "Travels Through Russia," Rev. F. A. MacMillen

-January 4, 1909 – "Immigration," Dr. Frank Julian Werne

-March 1, 1909 – "Handling the World's Freight," Dr. J. Russell Smith

-October 1, 1914 – "The Interstate Commerce Commission," Mr. R. L. Russell

-November 5, 1917 – "Nature and Worth of Wit and Humor, Dr. Frances Green

-October 6, 1930 – "Construction of the Conowingo Dam," Mr. Joseph Barnes

One of the few civic questions addressed by the organization occurred in 1935 when the Club voted to change the name of Mather Avenue to Heacock Avenue, discarding the suggestion of Kent Avenue, and voted to change the name of Glenside Avenue to Chelten Hills Drive. It is not known how Heacock "Avenue" became "Lane" or why the Glenside Avenue change did not find favor with the commissioners.

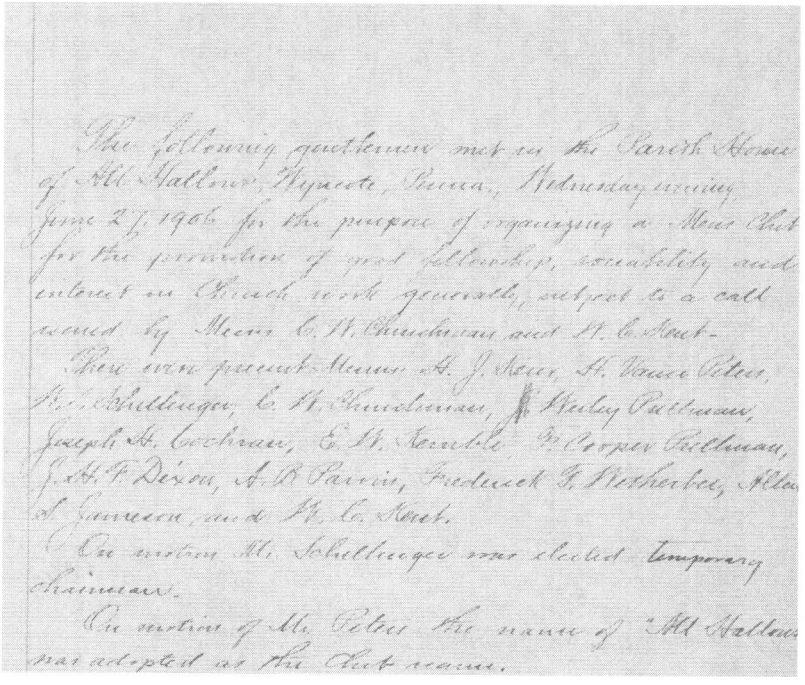

Minutes of the First Meeting of the Men's Club
The first page of the minute book of the Wyncote Men's Club indicates the attendance. It must have been a serious endeavor in order to attract the prominent men of the neighborhood who are listed.
Courtesy of the Cheltenham Township Historical Commission

The Wyncote Men's Club continued as a productive organization in the community in its 1920's format for almost seventy years. By 1990, declining membership forced a re-evaluation of the club's mission. It was felt that the old format of informative lectures was not as attractive in the television and Internet age and that the focus of the organization should be turned back to civic matters. For the 1990-91 season, the organization once again became the "Wyncote Civic Association."

Water

The first utility to be made available to the burgeoning population recognized the importance of clean and abundant water as a building block of civilization. The Jenkintown Water Company was formed in November of 1888 and chartered by the state in January of 1889. The company drilled their first wells at the headquarters site at the corner of Summit and Leedom Streets in downtown Jenkintown. Shortly thereafter, seeking additional supplies of water, the company purchased Wanamaker land in the Cheltenham settlement then still known as Beechwood Heights. A well and pumping plant, still standing today, was constructed near the intersection of North Avenue and Paxson Avenue just north of the Jenkintown train station in 1893. The station was opened on May 1, 1894 and consisted of two wells, 220 feet in depth. A semaphore system atop the station enabled the attendants of the Beechwood Heights plant to communicate with the engineers at Jenkintown and increase or decrease the pumping rate as necessary. Widespread availability of water in Wyncote had to wait until later with the incorporation of the Wyncote Water Company, which quickly became an adjunct of the Jenkintown Company. Water pipes were laid through the various developments in the village beginning by the late 1890's. The Pennsylvania State Treasurer reported taxes received from the company as early as 1904. The amount was two dollars and fifty cents.

But even the addition of the Wyncote well near the creek and unseen water table beneath was not enough to slake the thirst of the growing village. In 1909, the water company purchased land in Moreland next to the Pennypack creek and near Welsh Road to provide additional water to its customers.

Manufactured Gas

During the summer and fall of 2007, visitors to the Wyncote Post Office on Glenside Avenue could not ignore the mess in the field east of the post office building. Essentially, the park (officially part of the Edward Hicks

Parry Bird Sanctuary) was gone! The trees lining the creek bed that shielded the railroad tracks from Wyncote's view had disappeared, exposing the once far away office building and high rise apartment building on the other side of the tracks. Like lurking goblins eyeing the quiet residential neighborhood below, the structures looked so close and hulking without the natural buffer of the trees to soften their impact.

Surrounded by a chain link fence, a dozen heavy machines toiled for months digging the field down to creek level. Mountains of dirt at the top of the incline nearest Glenside Avenue were covered with tarps to prevent run off, construction trailers crowded a piece of the plot about mid-block, and the creek was even diverted for several weeks around the site.

Just as disturbing as the sight of the excavation work on former parkland was the smell. Neighbors encountered at the post office could be seen pursing their noses at the olfactory assault. "What is that?" was a common greeting for several months at the end of a typically hot and steamy summer that seemed to foster the propagation of foul organic odors. The malodorous vapors emanated from the lowest part of the excavation, a hole the size of a basketball court that filled with storm water as the months went by. The sludge-like debris pulled from the waste dump was a black, oily, mass that created the offensive vapors. The smell had a petroleum-like base, like old tar, with a sickly sweet overtone of rotting organic material. Forgotten for years, the encapsulated black mass sat beneath the surface, covered by the product of a decade of the township's fall leaf collections that were dumped on the site. In the fifties and early sixties, at the height of the leaf disposal era, winter would bring a Martian landscape of miniature steam vents that left a fog over the field as the organic mass below rotted and decayed.

This was Wyncote's closest cousin to a superfund site cleanup. Actually, it was an "environmental remediation" in the diplomatic words of PECO to clean up the byproducts of a turn-of-the-century (19th to 20th, that is) coal gasification plant.

The Jenkintown and Cheltenham Gas Company was incorporated in April, 1896, for the purpose of supplying gas for light, heating, and cooking to nearby customers. The first plant of the company was built on land purchased from Joseph Heacock along the Reading Railroad tracks and Glenside Avenue. It became operational on March 4 of 1899 when, as the *Public Spirit* announced on March 11, "illuminating gas was turned into about 15 miles of mains through Jenkintown and Wyncote on Saturday." "Formal exercises" were held to mark the event. Gas was a better-known substance than electricity and its introduction into the community in the face of electricity's arrival seemed not a bad bet. One resident saw a benefit in the competition that the new franchise would provide as a way of lighting his house "independent of the high priced [electric] light company." (*The Times Chronicle*, 10/10/1896) The newspaper, in an article in the April 16, 1898, edition that sounded almost like a marketing screed by the company, extolled the virtues of water gas as well as the economic benefits of locating their "attractive" plant in the vicinity. The enthusiastic paper promised that "this operation is conducted in closed vessels and is clean, quick, and inoffensive. Nothing escapes." It would take a hundred years to prove the inaccuracy of that statement. The paper also asserted that using the gas not only for lighting, but also for cooking was far superior to using coal. "No fuel to carry, no ashes, no clinkers, no dust, no waste, no getting up to make the fire at the time one dislikes to most. A turn of a valve and a match and full heat is had at once." In this case, they were right and customers lined up for the service as soon as the pipes were buried in their neighborhood.

Such plants were commonly used in the early to mid-1900s in many U.S. cities and towns. The site of such a plant required access to a rail line so that large amounts of coal could be imported, and the Wyncote site indeed had its own siding off of the Reading Railroad line. In a coal gasification plant, coal was heated in the presence of steam and mixed with vaporized oil. This so-called water gas, also known as coal gas or blue gas, was piped to residences, businesses, and street lamps in the immediate area before there were public utilities such as electric and natural gas. The process generated a lot of production waste, however, which was just buried in the backyard of the plant. It was this waste that the remediation effort was designed to eliminate. The expanded

Times Chronicle - **April 16, 1898**

A Gas Company for Jenkintown

Details of an important New Enterprise for this Vicinity

The Times Chronicle takes pleasure in herein giving to its readers the first public details regarding an important enterprise now shaping up in the vicinity, namely the formation of a local company for the distribution of illuminating gas.

Such an enterprise has for some time been on the minds of some of our citizens as a desirable thing to do, as well as in the minds of others familiar with gas matters but until the present time has never taken tangible shape, despite the fact that other suburban communities supporting water, electric lighting, and trolley companies have also supported a gas company to the advantage of the local residents. This is notably the case at Bryn Mawr where a gas company for some years has thrived in the supply of gas for lighting, heating and cooking to the dwellers along the line of the Pennsylvania R. R.

Some time ago, the United Gas Improvement Company of Philadelphia, well known as supplying gas in a large number of cities, took out a charter at Harrisburg for the supplying of gas in this vicinity, believing that the attractiveness of the country along the North Pennsylvania R. R., and its rapid growth quite equaled the Bryn Mawr section and would warrant the organization of a company here. For one reason or another however nothing was done in the matter until lately when other interests who had also investigated this section and believed in it made an offer for the existing charter resulting in an acceptance and its transfer from the United Gas improvement Company to the present owners. While the names of the new officers and directors have not yet been announced we are in a position to say that when they are made public it will be found that the men who will manage the company will be found to be experienced in the gas business, amply able to put the enterprise thorough and ones who believe that the best service known to the business will be none too good for those who will be their customers.

The corporate name is the "Jenkintown & Cheltenham Gas Company." Its charter permits it to operate in the three townships of Abington, Cheltenham, and Springfield and its principal office will be at the gas producing station in Jenkintown or immediately adjacent, although during the construction of the plant the company's office temporarily is in Philadelphia, No. 525 Drexel Building. The plant and distributing system will involve the expenditure of quite $100,000. Operations will be upon a considerable scale the plans calling for the laying of 10 miles of pipe at the very start, for while a large portion of the company's custom [sic] will be in this immediate vicinity it is equally intended that the pipes shall reach through Wyncote, Ogontz, Ashbourne, and Melrose, South to Oak Lane, as well as north to Glenside, Edge Hill, etc.

Active work has already commenced. Arrangements have been complete for an advantageous site adjacent to the railroad by the purchase of an acre of ground from Mr. Joseph Heacock, midway between Chelten Hills and Jenkintown stations. This lot is where the old quarry exists, adjoins the railroad yard property on the north and is centrally situated as regards the proposed pipe system. Contracts have been let for the gas producing machinery, as well as the storage and other vessels and the first shipment of pipe is on the way, if not already arrived. While a good start has thus been made it is obvious however, that completion of the plant will not come to pass before some time in the summer or fall, as the amount of work involved in the supply of all the necessary buildings, machinery, foundations, mains, service meters, etc. is very large. The works will be a model one of its kind, and the machinery of the most modern description to the end of making the best quality of gas, while the premises will be sightly and attractive.

The old style of gas works, such as at 23rd & Market streets in Philadelphia, is a thing of the past, due to the general adoption of the modern water gas system in lieu of the old coal gas process. The black volumes of smoke, the sulphur [*sic*], fumes, the tar and ammonia and smells of such works will have no place in the Jenkintown plant. In the water gas process no soft coal is used. Anthracite and steam form the bulk of the gas, enriched to a suitable illuminating value by a small amount of vaporized oil added. This operation is conducted in closed vessels and is clean, quick, and inoffensive. Nothing escapes, and excepting for the storage tank or gas holder there will be nothing to distinguish the works as a gas plant. A small boiler and steam engine and a few pumps will be the only parts visibly active. Owing to the quick producing capacity of the system day work only will ordinarily be necessary. At night and on Sundays the works will be shut down. On the street frontage on Glenside Avenue will be the entrance by suitable driveway, flanked by an attractive office building. The works end of the plant will abut the railway. Over in Bryn Mawr, the gas works is exceedingly attractive by virtue of a Queen Anne office, graded lawns and handsome Canna beds here and there, and we have a shrewd suspicion that the Superintendent of the Jenkintown plant will not let himself be surpassed in such things by any Pennsylvania R. R. mainline neighbors'. The principal buildings housing the gas machinery will be of stone, quarried on the premises. The gas holder, containing tank, will rest down in the old quarry bed and be almost concealed from street view. It may be added of the water gas process to be employed that it is the process now employed in all the principal cities – probably 75 per cent. of all the gas in this country being so made – the reason being that it produces the best quality of gas.

The establishment of the gas company will be a source of satisfaction to all those residing along its mains. There is no question but that a supply of good illuminating gas adds to the comfort of the public almost as much as a good water supply. For light it is one of the cheapest sources as well as the most convenient. It can be turned up or down much or little on. There is no smoking or chimneys to bother with as with lamps, and with the use of "Welsbash" burners it is quite as cheap as kerosene, one such burner in a living room affording as much light as a big lamp and throwing out nothing like as much heat.

Yet with it, one can heat a curling iron or cook the baby's food or heat hot water in a moment almost. Probably in the kitchen however is the place where the most comfort comes from having gas. Used for cooking in place of coal as in natural gas in Pittsburgh and the West, it is simply superb in its advantages over coal. No fuel to carry, no ashes, no clinkers, no dust, no waste, no getting up to make the fire at the time one dislikes to most. A turn of a valve and a match and full heat is had at once. When through with the gas it is turned off and all expense immediately ceases. And on top of all this it cooks better than coal for it has been repeatedly proven that gas cooked meats, for instance, are juicier, lose less in weight and are more savory when taken out of the gas oven that similar meats cooked by coal. The heat is more even – there is no bad side as in a coal fire. In the Bryn Mawr district about every other customer uses gas for cooking having discarded ranges, which proportion is pretty good evidence that it is advantageous so to do. For heating houses as a whole, gas is not cheaper than coal, but for heating single rooms, bath rooms, conservatories, and "taking the chill off" between seasons, quickly and easily it is

sufficiently cheap to be largely so used. The Jenkintown Company will carry a full line of convenient appliances for the use of gas and all that is known to the business that will give the cheapest and most satisfactory service to the user will be at his disposal for those in the gas company are firm believers that a "satisfied customer is one's best advertisement."

The advantage of a gas supply as an inducement to prospective residents here and purchasers of real estate is an important factor in this matter. Jenkintown and the district supplied by gas will be distinctively benefited in the strengthening of property values and their easier rental, by the advent of the company to say nothing of the large amount of money that will be spent here during the construction of the plant and the later payrolls of the company. We understand that due application has been made the Borough Council for a suitable ordinance granting the gas company the usual permission to lay its pipes in the streets.

and more-dependable use of electricity in the area in the 1920's brought the beginning of the end to the gasification industry and widespread use of natural gas was its final death knell in the early fifties. How ironic that, in the green-conscious 21st century, coal gasification, once abandoned as an obsolete technology, is being touted as one solution to our oil-dependency problems

The Wyncote plant ceased operations in 1916. Most structures were razed by 1928 as other utilities became available to the neighborhood.

Telephone

The Bell Telephone Company of Philadelphia was organized in November of 1879, shortly after Alexander Graham Bell's famous demonstration of his controversial invention at the Centennial exhibition in Philadelphia. Although it seems self-evident to the modern mind, one commentator found it necessary to explain how this company provided telephonic communications:

It located its central office at No. 400 Chestnut Street, for the purposes of an exchange. The wires used by the subscribers led from this place. Communications can be had with the office at any time, and every subscriber upon request is put in communication with any other subscriber which he may require by connecting the wires. By this means persons at each end of the terminus have direct speaking communication with each other. (Scharf, 1884)

A licensee, the Delaware and Atlantic Telephone Company, was commissioned by Jenkintown burgess (mayor) Thomas B. Harper to begin service in Jenkintown in 1902, although some influential residents had service out of Philadelphia earlier. The two companies merged in 1907 to form the Bell Telephone Company of Pennsylvania. It is hard to comprehend an age with a phone number in the single digits, but Cyrus Curtis, not surprisingly, obtained phone number 1 for his mansion off Church Road. John Wanamaker obtained phone number 2.

20   THE SUBURBAN DIRECTORY

Bell Phone call **Ogontz** Exchange   Keystone Phone call **Jenkintown** Exchange

Craft, Edmund, horseshoer, 507 Summit
Craven, Alonzo D, electrician, 316 Cedar   55 y �rž/
Craven, E Davis, blacksmith, 316 Cedar
Craven, Thomas B, blacksmith, 404 and h 402 Leedom   221 y △
                                                                                         11 x ☐
Crewson, Fannie R, tel operator, 414 Maple
Crewson, John M, laborer, 414 Maple
Crewson, John R, tel operator, 414 Maple
Cross, Hannah B, 418 York rd
Cross, Harold H, clerk, 418 York rd
Cross Helen M, 418 York rd
Cross, Surner H, Physician, 412 York rd   242 d △
Cross, William A, physician, 418 York rd   32 a △
Crowley, James, laborer, Switchville
Culver, Theodore B, v pres, Jenkintown Trust Co, h Florence   63 △
        c Greenwood
Curry, John, clerk, 514 W Greenwood
Curry, John H, clerk, 458 Leedom
Curtis, Cyrus H K, pub, Church rd c Greenwood   1 △

D

Daley, Peter, laborer, Switchville
Davis, Percy, printer, 200 Walnut   159 x △
Davison, Mary, housekeeper, 509 Summit

Curtis Phone Number
Cyrus Curtis was granted phone number one as shown in this 1902 phone directory. Note the two symbols on the right for Bell System phones and Keystone System phones. Both systems operated simultaneously at the beginning of the twentieth century but they did not afford interchangeability.
Courtesy of the OYRHS

While we may remember the war of survival between VHS and Betamax in the early days of home entertainment just a few years ago, such a conflict of competitive technological standards was not a new phenomenon. The Keystone Telephone Company which began service in Philadelphia on January 1, 1902 forced consumers in Wyncote to choose between the two incompatible systems – or choose to have one of each. Many doctors and businesses took the latter route to be sure of being available to the widest range of clients.

An opportunity for fame and fortune passed Wyncote by when this new device was invented. Alexander Graham Bell was in Philadelphia during the summer of 1876 to attend the Centennial Exhibition being conducted in Fairmount Park. His invention had just become functional in the months preceding his visit and he intended to demonstrate it at the Centennial. Upon seeing the demonstration of the strange device on June 25, Dom Pedro, the Emperor of Brazil, famously exclaimed "My God, it talks!" Bell, desperate for financial backing for his new enterprise, managed to capture the attention of the leading Philadelphia bankers while visiting the Centennial and was invited to Abraham Barker's country home to demonstrate his device. Bell strung a wire from *Lyndon*, across Church Road, to another phone located in Wharton Barker's home. Bell was up against an international standard for communication, the telegraph, and most businessmen saw no need to engage in long-distance verbal communication. Although the demonstration probably was successful, he failed to impress the assembled bankers with the value of his device, and he moved back to Boston where he once again depended upon the generosity and influence of his father-in-law to find funding.

Electricity

Public interest in electricity began as a concern for public safety: electricity was first seen as a means of improving lighting in the streets. Thus the first public use in Philadelphia was the lighting of Chestnut street east of City Hall in 1881 and in Jenkintown, the Jenkintown Light Company was incorporated for this purpose in 1890. The offices of the company were eventually located in the former Case store at Greenwood and Glenside Avenues in Wyncote. The company built a plant in Wyncote at the foot of "Electric Avenue" in Beechwood Heights, just north of the train station. Electric Avenue became Paxson Avenue in the 1930s. The *Philadelphia Ledger* described this plant in their edition of September 27th, 1890.

The new plant erected by the Jenkintown Electric Light Company was set in operation this week. The works are located a short distance north of Jenkintown Station. The building is a large stone structure, fitted out in the most complete manner for the purpose intended. There are two boilers of 100 horse power each, while the Wetherill Corliss engine has a capacity of 250 horse power. The fly-wheel is 18 feet in diameter, and weighs 14 tons. The dynamo is adapted for 1000 incandescent lights. Another machine, with the capacity of 2000 lights, is on the way and will soon be placed in position. The plant is built to run 8000 lights. (Hotchkin, 1892)

It's ironic to think that the power of the plant was just about equal to that of the neighbor's Ford Explorer – and just about as expensive at $40,000. This new amenity was notoriously undependable and dangerous at first. There were fires and electrocutions, even of a horse, and frequent outages. On the last day of July in 1894, "the whole town was left in darkness due to the breaking of the large belt at the electric light station. It did quite a lot of damage to the building."

The first house in Wyncote to be wired with public electricity was an event recorded in the newspaper: "The Electric Light Company has wired Mr. Joseph Heacock's house on Mather avenue for electric lights and bells." (*The Times Chronicle*, 5/23/1896)   But, privately, wealthy homeowners and businesses had been installing their own power plants to provide lighting in their homes and stores long before electricity became commercially available. The first use of electricity in Wyncote was the small dynamo powered by a 50 horsepower steam engine that John Wanamaker installed in the old Mather Mill in 1888. That plant provided electricity for his mansion, *Lindenhurst*, and his son Rodman's house, *Millrose*, across Washington Lane. Not coincidentally, Wanamaker had had a much larger power plant built at the site of his grand store on Market street in downtown Philadelphia in 1878, the first commercial building to be so equipped in that city, only adding to the growing list of "firsts" that marked the success of his enterprise. The event was described by the Electric Company's historian:

In his progressive way, he [John Wanamaker] became fascinated with electricity after seeing an experimental light at the Centennial fair. When the Franklin Institute accepted the superiority of the Brush arc lamp over others it tested in 1878, Wanamaker purchased a generating plant to supply twenty-eight Brush lamps for his Grand Depot. Installed in December 1878, these brilliant lamps made the store's interior almost as light as day and established the practicability of electric lighting in Philadelphia. (Wainwright, 1961)

Paving

Street paving, although taken for granted today, provided a major improvement in the life of residents. The original homes were built on dirt lanes, just twenty feet wide, which had been cleared of trees and stumps and leveled. The macerated street soil created by horses and carriages created clouds of choking dust in dry weather and, as Ralph Morgan noted, "as the number of automobiles increased the dust nuisance became very bad." (Morgan, 1933) Resident Frank Mayo recalls a walk along Greenwood Avenue while growing up in the early 1880s:

Greenwood Avenue west from the railroad was a first class dirt road, which heralded your approach in very dry weather with a cloud of dust or after rain with a spatter of mud. From Glenside Avenue to Church Road on the south side was only a post and rail fence and two small houses about opposite Wyncote lane, along the fence was a twelve inch wide plank walk, just who put it there, is beyond my ken, but him or they were real benefactors, for it rendered good service to those whose business or pleasure led them that way. (Mayo, 1932)

The clouds of chalky dust that inflicted President Harrison's parade were everyday facts of life for residents of the village. The Improvement and Civic associations addressed the problem early and their solution was to provide services to spray the streets regularly to keep the dust down. Water was first used and then light oil, which provided better adhesion and longer-lasting results. One can't help but wonder what the resulting pulverized mix did to the lungs.

The first type of paving, already typical in the growing borough of Jenkintown, was the construction of boardwalks along the major streets. Thomas Nicholson, operator of the coal yard at the station, organized the funding of the first boardwalk in Wyncote in the spring of 1884. It was finally accomplished in the spring of 1886 and stretched from the station to the bend in the road at "Mr. Pullman's gate," today's North Bent Road. The subscribers were, as could be expected, the residents who lived close-by and had the most to gain: Thomas Nicholson, Dr. Sinkler, Dr. Peters, Willis Hazard, and J. W. Brock. They contributed from $50 to $100 to Nicholson's subscription. Case and Walsh contributed a boardwalk in front of their stores. The builders who developed the Hazard tract installed boardwalks along Woodland Avenue, but most of the other developments did not provide that amenity. The "elegant" boardwalks, though cheap and easily constructed, were nonetheless easily damaged by carriages and flooding. The newspapers of those years frequently contained complaints about their condition, particularly after heavy July thunderstorms, which washed them away. In 1896, the paper noted the typical damage caused by deluges: the heavy rain on Thursday did considerable damage around here, washing the boardwalks on Greenwood Avenue out of place."

The initial efforts to pave the roads in the developed areas were accomplished by dumping cheap slag from stone works operations on the streets. The township let the first contract for hauling slag, and later plain stone, from the train station in the fall of 1885. Wharton Barker paid half the cost for the material. The *Public Spirit* approved of the plan. In an article on November 21, 1885, in a position that seems warped by today's standards, the paper stated that "this was a fair distribution if the cost of improving the roads were divided between the property benefited and the taxpayers." In May of 1886, Wharton Barker spent $3,000 on laying stone on Greenwood Avenue from the station to the bend in the road. The *Public Spirit* noted that it "will be a grand thing for people who use the station in the winter." In 1887, he continued the effort by macadamizing Church Road from Greenwood Avenue to the gate of his house and also Wyncote Lane which went from his back gate to the mill road.

Woodland Road, 1895
A snowy day but the boardwalk is clear.
Courtesy of the Old York Road Historical Society

The Commissioners of the township first voted to issue a bond for $80,000 to pave roads in April of 1892. They designated parts of Washington Lane and Church road to be paved with the new Macadam mixture and former commissioner Ralph Morgan proudly noted that the treatment lasted for over thirty years. Notwithstanding their efforts, the improvement of the roads remained a slow task and a prickly issue with the residents. The Wyncote Improvement and Protective Association hosted township supervisors Nagle and Evans on June 24, 1896, to discuss the matter. The commissioners not surprisingly sympathized with the residents but complained that the township did not have the funds to act, particularly in light of the "number of new roads to be opened" that year. Their solution was to offer a referendum to issue another bond for $50,000. The bond issue was passed and the $77,978 raised produced 4.32 miles of macadam paved roads, 18 feet wide. By 1910, the process of Macadamization became standard practice.

Other Improvements

One of the reasons that the "good ol' days" were not so good is the problem of sewage. With the increase in building and population, the traditional method of venting kitchen and toilet wastes to the street, backyard, or the cesspool, became problematic as the number of homes increased. The lovely little Tookany was turned into an open sewer, a condition that was accepted as a necessary part of life by new residents but decried by old-timers such as Lippincott and Heacock who remembered a more pristine setting. Typhoid was an everyday concern and occurrence. The typical scenario was represented by the development of Kohler's Jenkintown Syndicate tract in 1900. The eighty homes that were built emptied their waste into a small rivulet that exited the property on the south side of the tract. The stream ran through a meadow on Wanamaker's property before emptying into the Tookany where the creek turns just east of the Washington Lane bridge. (That meadow today is covered by the lower grounds of the apartment building and adjoining office building.) Conditions became so intolerable that Wanamaker sued the owners of the syndicate property to force them to install cesspools in their homes. In testimony, Wanamaker noted that "there were bad smells almost all of the time." The problem was exacerbated in storms when the stream overflowed its banks "scattering the filth and refuse over more than an acre of ground," the smell reaching the house, gardens, and tennis court. The Wanamakers prevailed, an outcome for which all residents should be thankful, although the owners of the Syndicate homes were faced with a large bill to install cesspools.

The problem was not more permanently solved for another quarter of a century. That modern taken-for-granted luxury, a sewer system, first discussed at the Civic Association meeting in 1924, became a reality in 1926 and 1927. The pact to connect with the Philadelphia system at the eastern end of the township cost the township a million dollars and the main line was buried beneath the lowest lying ground, the Tookany Creek. The neighborhood centering on Greenwood Avenue and Glenside Avenue was the first to be served. There are a few isolated streets today that still have not been connected due to the expense of cutting into dense rock formations.

The area around Jenkintown station was an issue for residents for many years, even after Wanamaker's attempt to improve the old millpond in 1897. On April 23, 1905, the *Times Chronicle* published a conversation with William Berger in which Berger complained about the condition of the grounds surrounding the station on the Wyncote side. "The traveler who comes [to the station] has a poor means of knowing of the beauty of the place by judging of the surroundings at Jenkintown Station." He proposed asking Mr. Wanamaker to beautify "the swamp" or if he would not, "let the people themselves take subscriptions and beautify the creek, level the ground off and make a handsome park where the present eyesore of a spot is to all who feel a pride in our lovely community." It was finally made a park by the township in 1925.

Preservation of food was a problem throughout the history of mankind. Besides the tried and true method of using nature's refrigerator, the spring house, which was mostly effective only for dairy products, early residents depended on the collection of ice from ponds during the winter to provide refrigeration during the warm season. Such ponds in the village included Wanamaker's pond and Heacock's pond along Glenside Avenue. A report in the *Public Spirit* of January 4, 1879, indicates how important a role this process played: "The work of ice cutting is progressing rapidly. The ice is in a splendid condition and the weather favorable in temperature. Most of the ice houses are full." Progress came in the form of The Montgomery County Ice and Cold Storage Company. Located just South of the gas plant on an acre purchased from Joseph Heacock in April of 1899, the plant produced "Hygeian Ice" which was widely distributed around the neighborhood. Shortly after opening, the plant was producing 900 tons of ice per month at "the splendid plant here, which is under the management of that forceful and up-to-date gentleman, L. R. Dutton." The oldest remnant of the complex was an office building that sat at the top of the hill on the edge of Glenside Avenue at the base of Webster Avenue. This building served as a residence through the early part of the 20th century and was the location of the first switchboard for the Bell

Telephone Ogontz telephone exchange that served the neighborhood. The exchange was moved to a larger facility in Jenkintown, across from the train station, in 1950, at which time the old building on Glenside Avenue was razed.

Times Chronicle, January 30, 1904

Legacy Voices

Heinz J. Heinemann
Formerly of Hewett Road, Wyncote
Now resident of Newtown

In this oral history, Heinz Heinemann talks about life in early Wyncote.

TW: Heinz, how did you discover Wyncote?
HH: My father, who came from Germany, bought a brand new house on the two hundred block of Hewett Road in 1927. We moved there when I was two years old. The house was built on an orchard. There were several old apple trees left on our property. Behind us, was a big field which was plowed by an African American named John Burgess who lived in the small tenant next to the creek on Rices Mill Road. There was a large barn to the right of the house and chicken coops. . . . A windmill pumped water from one of the springs in the field. It was rusted and probably not too safe, but we climbed to the top and had a view of a lifetime. I am sure my mother never knew that it was there or I would have been forbidden to climb it. The field was our second home.

TW: Do you remember the quarry across from the post office?
HH: Oh, yes, the Boy Scout cabin was in the quarry, troop #1. It was a one-story building with a small room, storage room, and an office and a big room where we met. There was an office for a drilling company in there also, to the right. [The Boy Scout Cabin] had a cast iron coal stove that had to be started when we met in the winter-time. There was a quarry at Greenwood and Woodland and the stone from that was used to build Thomas Williams school. Down the road, at ATD, was a quarry and the stone for the church was quarried there.

TW: Do you remember the ice plant?
HH: Yes, there were two buildings: one for making the ice and one for storing the ice. It was made on chains in stainless steel tanks and pulled out when frozen and pulled to the storage house on endless chains. The blocks of ice were huge, the size

of this card table. The horse drawn wagons backed up to the loading dock for the supply of ice. We kids were allowed to watch the operation from the outside and the workers would give us slivers of ice to suck on. Our house had a unique feature: the iceman could put the block of ice in our icebox through a door on the outside of the house, so he didn't have to come into the kitchen.

TW: Somebody told me there was a dump behind the houses on Hewett.

HH: There was a dump in the swamp at the dead-end street near the Waverly and Hewett intersection. We burned whatever we could. . . . The other dump I remember was at the foot of Glenview Avenue on Glenside Avenue. To the left of the entrance to the park there was a dump where everyone from Wyncote dumped their trash.

The full oral history can be found in the archives of the Old York Road Historical Society. HTTP://OYRHS.ORG

Ice and Cold Storage Plant
Top: One building in the plant at the foot of Webster Avenue, 1902.
Courtesy of the Old York Road Historical Society
Bottom: A view of the industrial complex, showing the building above,
from Washington Lane intersection, 1924.
Courtesy of the Hagley Museum and Library

Chapter 9

THE NAMING OF WYNCOTE

I have been at Wyncote. It is a great house, with wings in the Italian manner, and a fine fountain in the court.
(Hugh Wynne, 1897)

The Olde Wyncote tract was known by several names before the title of "Wyncote" was formally and permanently established in 1887. Determining the source of that name and how it got applied to the new village turns out to be an interesting and complicated story. The name does not have the transparent genesis enjoyed by our neighbors of Jenkintown to the north, Elkins Park to the east, and Glenside to the west.

There is one story that receives occasional traffic, but is not true. The similarity of Dr. Thomas Wynne's name (William Penn's physician) to that of Wyncote has created speculation that Wyncote is named after him. However, there appears to be no reasonable connection. Wynne's lifespan significantly preceded the naming of Wyncote and there is no involvement of Wynne in this part of the colony. Conversely, Wynnewood, in the western suburbs of Penn's green country town, where Dr. Wynne owned five thousand acres of land in the western wilderness, is connected. His residence became the estate of Colonel Owen Jones who named the site in perpetuation of Wynne's name.

"Wyncote" has a consonantal sound typical of Welsh

words that were widely bestowed on buildings and towns in the Philadelphia suburbs at the end of the 19th century. The use of Welsh place names was common in the history of the Philadelphia environs reflecting the strong representation of the Welsh among early settlers, and even Penn, though his immediate ancestors were English, deemed himself of Welsh extraction. It was also in fashion in the 19th century to bestow Welsh names on buildings and places. The most egregious example was the wholesale renaming of towns along the new Pennsylvania Railroad Main Line in the western suburbs of Philadelphia. From 1880-1897, George B. Roberts, the powerful president of the railroad replaced the names of stations and towns along the way with Welsh-sounding names to honor his Welsh heritage, whether for marketing reasons or as a whimsical exercise of his power. Closer to Wyncote, there are numerous examples of the Welsh influence including the village of Bryn Athyn and the Welsh Road in Abington.

The area of Olde Wyncote has gone through a succession of names. The first name, Chelten Hills, seems concurrent with the development of the North Penn Railroad through the area. The name probably was of long use, but it was at least formalized by Edward M. Davis. Davis formed a development company in 1854 that he named the "Chelten Hills Association." A later name was "Kent's woods" after the Philadelphia merchant William C. Kent and, by 1887, part of the area appeared on maps as "Beechwood Heights." The name likely was invented by the developer who had purchased large portions of the property for subdivision, although architect Frederick Platt attributes the name to John Wanamaker who ruled off lots prior to subdivision of his holdings west of Greenwood Avenue in 1891.

The vicinity was also widely known as Jenkintown through the first part of the 19th century. Curiously, Platt notes that Horace Trumbauer, the famous Philadelphia architect responsible for the Museum of Art among other buildings who honed his skills early in Wyncote, listed the location of his buildings in the village as "Jenkintown." This was not uncommon nomenclature at the time. A contemporary prospectus for the development of Kohler's "Jenkintown Syndicate" property northeast of the railroad shows several properties in Wyncote including All Hallows

Church and the Robinson estate. In fact, Wharton Barker was known as a Jenkintown resident. A Philadelphia directory by Gopsill in 1885 lists Wharton's house as located in Jenkintown and a contemporary biography by Donehoo, in 1926 lists his son, Folger, as born "at Jenkintown at his father's estate."

The most prominent explanation of the naming of Wyncote is contained in several modern publications. Let us call this the "Barker story" after resident Wharton Barker because the Barker story stipulates that the village was named by Wharton Barker. Secondly, the story notes that the choice of name caused considerable consternation among the citizens of the village. Finally, some of these sources indicate that Barker borrowed the name "Wyncote" from a book entitled *Hugh Wynne, Free Quaker*.

Because of the similarity of the stories and the contemporary timing of late 20th century production, it is likely that the common source of the story is the one-time resident and local historian Horace Mather Lippincott. Lippincott, a descendant of the early Mather family, lived from 1887 to 1967. As a contemporary of Abraham and Wharton Barker, therefore, he could have had first hand knowledge of the founding of the village. Writing all too briefly and discretely about the subject in 1938, he stated that Wharton Barker "fastened the wholly inappropriate name of 'Wyncote' upon our beloved Chelten Hills about 1885." (Lippincott, 1938)

When the *Public Spirit* newspaper announced the opening of the post office on February 12, 1887, it got the name wrong, relating the name as "Beechwood Heights" rather than "Wyncote." The error in reporting the name is curious. Perhaps the name was unexpected by the populace either because of a misunderstanding, or more likely because the public was afforded no role in its formation and naming. But, officially at least, there was no secret in naming the post office. The United States Post Office Department application for the post office dated October 28, 1886, clearly states the name as "Wyncote." The application was signed by Thomas Buckman Harper who was also listed as the first postmaster. This is the same Harper who had obtained the lease on the commercial building under construction at the corner of Greenwood and Glenside Avenues.

Thomas Buckman Harper
Photo: Courtesy of the State Library of Pennsylvania, Harrisburg

If the impetus for the establishment of the post office with the Wyncote name was Wharton Barker, it is difficult to see a direct connection to Thomas B. Harper. Thomas Buckman Harper was but twenty-seven years old when he signed the application for the new post office. He was the son of a successful Jenkintown merchant, Charles, whose store on York Road was hailed as one of the largest and most popular general stores in the area. Young Thomas had concluded working for his father as a clerk in the family store and had begun a well-drilling business in 1886 at the time that he became postmaster of Wyncote. Thomas apparently struggled in the family business as indicated by one of his eulogists, Joseph Heacock. Heacock noted that Thomas "went early into his father's store, . . . but was not successful." (Heacock, 1911) In fact, his major accomplishment may have been the installation of the first public telephone in Jenkintown in 1884 in his father's store, with which, he "proposes executing his orders with more promptness." However, future accomplishments suggest that Thomas was ambitious and politically active at the time the post office was founded. These accomplishments include election to the office of burgess (mayor) of Jenkintown in 1890, and election as a state senator in 1908. He was a state senator upon his untimely death in 1910. Other eventual distinctions in Jenkintown include his appointment as a trustee of Grace Presbyterian Church in Jenkintown in 1890, election to the Jenkins Town Lyceum in 1900, and election as a director of the new Jenkintown National Bank in 1905. While Charles Harper was a successful merchant in a small country town, it is doubtful in a socially conscious age that he or his son would have associated with the wealthy class of Philadelphia bankers represented by the Barkers. The depth of this divide can be detected in a subtle remark in a eulogy upon Thomas' death that referred to his success "in the conduct of a useful business," an apparent reference to his well-drilling service. (McIlhenney, 1911)

What was the motivation for forming a post office in the new village? The population did not seem to justify such a facility at that time, and the process would have needed powerful political support in Washington to push the idea through a sluggish bureaucracy. The Hopkins property atlas published in 1886 (but showing data for 1884-1885) displays only thirteen homes and the Nicholson Coal and Lumber yard within the Olde Wyncote tract, hardly enough to justify the effort, although the application listed service to 500 people. But development loomed on the immediate horizon. That development was evident in the person of the investor Willis P. Hazard who had purchased part of the land called Beechwood Heights and began development of the neighborhood by May of 1885. Hazard also worked directly with Harper on a proposal from Harper and a friend named Joseph Stoddard – a builder in Jenkintown - to rent Hazard's property on the southwest corner of Glenside Avenue and Greenwood Avenue in order to construct a "large general store." That building opened in late 1886 with Harper's store as its "anchor" and it was the eventual home of the post office.

Harper would have had valuable assistance in filing the "location paper" for the new post office from his father who had served as postmaster at Jenkintown from 1871 to 1885. Thomas took over briefly in 1885, but was replaced in October of that year. His assistant, a man named Hastings, took the trouble to travel to Washington, D.C., in order to lodge a complaint against Harper regarding "irregularities" in the conduct of the Jenkintown Post Office. It is not known what became of those complaints, but it did not stop Harper from receiving the appointment at Wyncote. Postal Service appears to have run in the family for Anna Griscom, Thomas' sister, served as postmaster of Jenkintown starting in 1889. Certainly it was not the most attractive job. Long hours for postal workers was a common fact of postal life and the postmaster typically received a commission based on sales as part of his or her pay. In a place like Wyncote, this could not have been much of a livelihood and the postal service was notoriously politicized. Indeed, one local historian places Harper's salary at a mere $111 per year. In addition, the postmaster was responsible for obtaining, managing, and paying for the office space. Patronage ruled and positions, particularly as postmaster, only went to those who were politically active or connected.

What emerges is a portrait of an ambitious young man in 1886 intent on finding a career, possibly in politics, and, in that case, willing to pay his dues as a political neophyte and functionary. Harper's front page obituary in the Jenkintown newspaper on May 21, 1910, reviews his many political accomplishments but says not a word about his involvement in Wyncote.

The figure of the Hon. I.N. Evans hovers in the background. Evans was cited for his support of the new post office in the February 12 newspaper article previously mentioned. He was referred to as "Hon." because he represented the Jenkintown area as a Congressman (7th district) in the 45th, 48th, and 49th Congresses. Isaac Newton Evans was born in West Chester and was 59 years old at the time the post office was created. He was a physician, having graduated from Jefferson Medical College in 1852. He practiced in Hatboro. Was the public thanks he received in the newspaper simply a formality due to the usual attention a Congressman would have paid to affairs impacting his district or was there another reason for his interest? His Congressional biography notes that he was involved in the real estate business and in banking. Although apparently a practicing physician, he managed the time to found and serve as president of the Hatboro Fire Company in 1893 and was previously a founder of the Hatboro National Bank in 1875. A personal Wyncote connection therefore does not seem likely except for the fact that Rev. S. F. Hotchkin, in his history of the York Road area, states that "The Hon. I. Newton Evans and Samuel J. Garner built the first two houses" on the new Hazard track in 1885. (Hotchkin, 1892) Newspaper accounts of the day are replete with Evans and Garner's activities in the Beechwood Heights tract and a review of the Cheltenham Township tax ledgers for 1885 list several adjacent properties owned by "Evans and Garner." In fact, Hazard's own plot plan lists about a dozen properties earmarked for Evans and Garner. Conversely, Evans is recorded as entertaining President Benjamin Harrison "in his home" in Hatboro in 1889, thus casting doubt on the possibility that he ever resided in Wyncote. If it is not likely that Evans actually lived in Wyncote, it is evident that he had at a significant business interest in the village.

Isaac Newton Evans (1827 – 1901)
Two-time Congressman and Physician from Hatboro. As a banker and real-estate broker, he was an early and influential investor in the new village of Wyncote.
Courtesy of the Library of Congress

The third part of the "Barker Story" attributes the name to a book entitled *Hugh Wynne, Free Quaker*. This book, written by a prominent Philadelphia physician, Dr. Silas Weir Mitchell, was a historical novel about the Revolutionary War, told from the perspective of one Hugh Wynne, a fictional grandson of Dr. Thomas Wynne. Apparently the book was so accurate that it was used for many years as a textbook on the history of that era. The story includes a passage in which the protagonist Wynne reflects on his childhood and his ancestral estate in Wales.

In my father's bedroom, over the fireplace, hung a pretty picture done in oils, by whom I know not. It is now in my library. It represents a pleasant park and on a rise of land a gray Jacobean house with at either side low wings curved forward, so as to embrace a courtyard shut in by railings and gilded gates. There is also a terrace with urns and flowers.

Later, Wynne recalls a guest saying:

When thou art a man, my lad, thou shoulds't go and see where thy people came from in Wales. I have been at Wyncote. It is a great house, with wings in the Italian manner, and a fine fountain in the court, and gates which were gilded when Charles II came to see the squire. We lost Wyncote for the love of free air. (Mitchell, 1896)

Dr. Mitchell was a unique individual, an American renaissance man. Sociologist E. Digby Baltzell called him the "most versatile American since Franklin and probably a genius too." He graduated early from the Jefferson Medical College in 1850 at the age of 21. As an internationally known scientist and physician, he hobnobbed with such world scientific figures as John Shaw Billings and Michael Faraday. As a physician, he pioneered in neurology and the treatment of nerve diseases, particularly in women, hypothesized the connection between eyestrain and headaches, and developed an antidote for snakebite. As a socialite, he associated with Carnegie, Drexel, Stotesbury, and the rest of Philadelphia's elite society. As a Civil War surgeon, he modernized the treatment of gunshot wounds. He traveled extensively and at the age of fifty embarked on a literary career that produced at least seven novels including *Hugh Wynne*. Unlike Harper, he traveled in the kind of circles patronized by Wharton Barker. The 1900 census lists a household with three live-in servants and his diary for 1895 lists such dinner guests such as "Drexels," "Roosevelt and son," "Cadwalader," "Wharton," "Biddle," "Cabot Lodge," and "Harrison."

Alas, the connection of the *Hugh Wynne* story to the naming of the village of Wyncote is very problematic if not impossible due to the fact that the book was published in 1896, a full ten years <u>after</u> the post office was named by Thomas B. Harper.

If the *Hugh Wynne* part of the Barker Story is indeed incorrect, several intriguing coincidences nonetheless seem to surround Mitchell's role. Mitchell entered medical school in 1848 with Isaac Newton Evans (though, as a prodigy, he graduated earlier than Evans), the future congressman and Wyncote property owner, whom he therefore certainly must have known. He was a frequent lecturer at the University of Pennsylvania Medical School in the late 19th century, where coincidentally, Sarah Wharton Barker (Mrs. Abraham Barker) served on the board of trustees. Also, coincidentally, Wynne's genealogy includes, as heirs to the house of Wynne Hall in Wales, one Hugh Wynne and one Isobel Weir who married into the family. There is also linkage to Wharton Barker through his friend and patient, the Philadelphia publisher and historian Henry Charles Lea. In 1890, Lea worked with Barker to successfully elect Robert Pattison as the governor of Pennsylvania and Lea, Mitchell, and Barker were members of the elite National Republican League that met just five blocks from Mitchell's house on Walnut Street. Mitchell was also a literary associate of Harrison S. Morris, the author and publisher, who had a farm in Wyncote. Finally, Mitchell's next door neighbor and fellow physician on Walnut Street in Philadelphia was Dr. John B. Deaver, who established an estate in the developing Wyncote village and for whom a local road is named.

Is it possible that the name was created earlier than the book and somehow made its way through social intercourse to Wharton Barker? It does not seem likely that Mitchell had been considering that particular book, let alone the minor detail of the protagonist's estate's name earlier than 1895. He had published several other books in the years immediately preceding *Hugh Wynne* that would have occupied his time. In his personal diary of July 21, 1895, Mitchell entered the following notation: "At home busy to get underweigh [sic] Hugh Wynne." The following dates of the 22nd to the 28th all contain the simple notation "Hugh Wynne." (Mitchell, 1895)   Intriguingly, Mitchell's own literary notebook for *Hugh Wynne*, written in 1895 and early 1896, indicates that the fictional name of Hugh Wynne's estate in Wales was to be "Wynne Hall," the same as the historical home of the Wynne family in Wales. When and why did the name change for publication within the year? The answer may be that the naming part of the Barker story is backwards: that Mitchell named the estate in his book on a whim to honor the elite country village of Wyncote that figured, although peripherally to be sure, into his life through his friends.

As previously noted, there is one more historic location with the name "Wyncote." This was an estate named *Wyncote* in England, demolished only in 1960, the property now part of the playing fields of the University of Liverpool.

The estate was constructed in 1840 for physician Dr. William Reynolds who presumably named the estate. Reynolds apparently shortly lost the house to his bank and ownership was assumed by Sir William Brown, principal of the bank that held the mortgage. Brown in turn rented the home to Joseph Shipley. Shipley, a native of Delaware, had moved to Liverpool to manage the affairs of Brown, a principle with his brothers in a Liverpool Bank, Brown Brothers and Company. Shipley never married and dedicated his life to the success of the bank becoming a partner in the Liverpool bank in 1826 and of all affiliated companies in 1836. This included the branch office that Brown Brothers had established in Philadelphia in 1818. The bank survives today as Brown Brothers Harriman of New York. When Shipley left Brown's employ in Liverpool, he moved back to Wilmington and commissioned the architect of *Wyncote*, George Williams, to design an updated version for his residence in Wilmington. That mansion, named *Rockwood*, is similar in style and construction to *Wyncote* and is operated today as a museum. One could assume that, as members of the Philadelphia banking fraternity, Shipley and Barker (Abraham at least) would have known each other. Alas no evidence in identified sources has come to light to support that connection. One reason could be the loss of records of the Brown bank. John Crosby Brown, grandson of the founder in his history of the bank, notes that most records were destroyed at the turn of the century when the attic of the building which housed the bank became too crowded to contain any more paperwork. (Brown, 1909)

Wyncote House, Liverpool
The home of banker Joseph Shipley, Wyncote was demolished by the University of Liverpool in 1960 and the grounds are now part of the university's athletic complex. The complex bears the Wyncote name and, coincidentally, it is located on Mather Avenue in Liverpool.
Courtesy of the University of Liverpool Library, D821/4/1

The Wyncote name has a long memory in British history. Aston Cantlow Parish in the County of Warwick records property granted to John de Wyncote in 1315 and Little Rissington in County Gloucester records "a manor and four yardlands" sold to Thomas Wyncote in 1619.

Wharton Barker's most notable home was an estate west of Greenwood Avenue on the north side of Church Road that he had purchased about 1891 from his old friend and collaborator, Penn professor Robert Ellis Thompson. Barker concluded his residency in Wyncote about 1897 for reasons not clearly known and moved back into Philadelphia. His intense activities to secure the candidacy for president may have led him to locate closer to the politicians who would make this effort a reality. In addition, growing financial and legal problems with his banks and other investments may have led to financial pressure, and he may have wished to be close to his father, now back in Philadelphia, after giving up his estate after his bankruptcy. After Barker's exit, the property was sold to George H. Lorimer, Cyrus Curtis' new editor of the *Saturday Evening Post,* who renamed the estate *Belgraeme.* Curtis had just purchased Abraham Barker's estate. The brief obituary in the local paper makes this estate his home of record:

Wharton Barker, financier and publicist and Populist candidate for President of the United States in 1900, died at 1 am Monday, at his home, Wall Garden, Roxborough. He would have been seventy-five years old on May 1. Mr. Barker was a former resident of Wyncote, having lived for many years on the beautiful estate now owned by Mr. George H. Lorimer. (*Times Chronicle,* 1921)

But this was not Barker's first Wyncote home. Abraham Barker began to buy property in Cheltenham in 1854, owning the property south of Church Road that was to become the site of his mansion, and the property on the north side of Church Road almost all the way to the Jenkintown train station. Wharton's name does not appear on any property in the area until 1877 when he purchased several properties throughout the area. However, a new house was built on Abraham's property immediately north and across Church Road from the entrance to Abraham's estate about 1877. This property eventually bore Wharton Barker's name but not until the mid-1880's. A visitor in 1882 provided this description of a visit to Wharton Barker's estate:

If you leave Jenkintown from the station, on the west side of the track, and follow the road that leads off on the right for say, perhaps, eight or ten minutes, . . . and turning once more to the left, taking your choice of avenues which lead through handsome woods, you come very speedily to a cosily nestled house set upon a hill, amid an abundance of trees, a sufficiency of flower beds, and the ordinary accompaniment of barns, outhouses, walks, *et id genus omne.* The house is a fairly artistic two-story and a half wooden structure, domesticated in this Jenkintown wood . . . (Balch, 1882)

The naming of estates was a popular affectation among the area's wealthy inhabitants. The Hopkins and Mueller maps both show names for most of the estates that were neighbors to Barker. Despite the proclivity for Welsh sounding names in parts of the Philadelphia area, Wyncote reflected its English roots. Pastoral or whimsical names were popular such as Oliver's *Sunnymede*, Pullman's *Dogwood*, Sinkler's *Berkeley*, and Starr's *The Orchard*, and Wharton's father had named his estate on Church Road *Lyndon*. Perhaps the adoption of the Welsh mode in an otherwise Anglo-named community was, at least partly, one source of Lippincott's ire when he called the name "wholly inappropriate." Wharton Barker's estate is notable in the absence of an assigned name on these maps or in the literature. But remember Lippincott's statement, previously noted, that Barker came up with the name in 1885. Was this merely an error in memory by Lippincott, or does it in fact indicate use of the name prior to the founding of the post office? Fortunately, Barker's papers in the Library of Congress contain a letter written on Barker's personal embossed letterhead. The letter, dated in 1884, shows a header: "Wyncote, Jenkintown P.O.." An even earlier letter to Barker at the same address shows a date of November 18, 1882. It is evident, therefore, that Barker did name his estate "Wyncote" prior to the founding of the post office in 1887 and that must have been his home east of Greenwood Avenue.

Where did the Wyncote name come from, who named Wyncote, and why?

Clearly the name for the village came directly from Barker's estate. But, where did that name come from? Unfortunately, the source of the word "Wyncote" remains the most hidden part of the story. The *Hugh Wynne* part of the Barker Story although a tidy solution is a red-herring, established through repeated use over the years from an unknown source. The answer must lie elsewhere. Perhaps an unidentified relationship existed between the Barkers and Shipley or other later residents of Wyncote House in Liverpool. Wharton Barker certainly had numerous opportunities to learn of Wyncote House. As fellow prominent Philadelphia bankers and industrialists, the Barkers and Shipley would have had the opportunity to

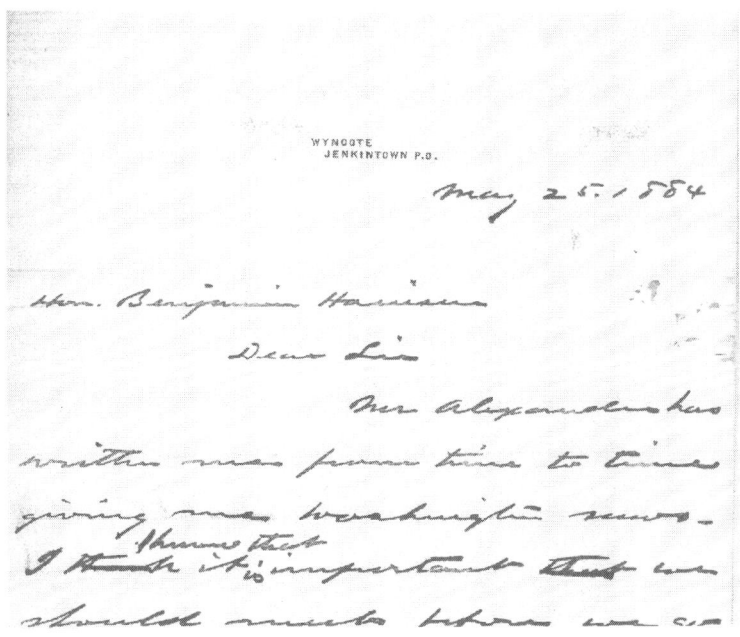

Wyncote Letterhead
This letter, to Barker's friend Benjamin Harrison, displays the name of
Barker's estate, Wyncote, three years before the name became the official
name of the village.
Courtesy of the Library of Congress

know each other, and Barings and Brown Brothers were the
two major banks in England in terms of Anglo-American
business. Further, as a frequent world traveler, (business
visits to Barings in London, European meetings sponsored
by prominent banks to discuss bimetallism, agent for the
Russian government) Barker made several trips to Europe
and easily would have learned of the Wyncote name. He
made at least four trips directly to Liverpool, which gave him
the opportunity to learn of Shipley's estate, *Wyncote*,
although his exact activities there are not known.

Who named Wyncote? Technically, Thomas Buckman
Harper is the person of record who gave Wyncote its legal
name and processed the federal paperwork creating the post
office. Yet, Harper, having no apparent reason for

independently appropriating the name and forming the post office, was surely working on someone else's behalf. Lippincott's recollection in which he claims that Barker "fastened" the name on the village has been taken to mean that he also was the behind-the-scenes force who founded the post office. For this presumption to be true, one would assume that the heavy-handed application of a "wholly inappropriate name" reflects the hubris of a wealthy resident who disregarded local history and public sensitivities in deciding a new name and found the means to do so. This presumed connection does not seem to correspond well with Barker's life, temperament, and activities, particularly at the time the post office was founded.

Why the name? The role of I.N. Evans bears further scrutiny. As a Member of Congress and a political activist, he had the means to secure a political factotum to pursue the mechanics of founding a post office and he personally had the opportunity to push the paperwork through the appropriate bureaucratic hurdles. In terms of motivation, Evans was a practical man who invested substantially in the nascent village. He understood that the financial viability of the area might depend on establishing not only a new identity, but in providing amenities such as convenient postal services. Home delivery of mail was an innovation that would await the turn of the century. In Barker's time, a postal address was simply a matter of personal affinity rather than bureaucratic assignment. If a resident wanted to obtain mail, he or she would tell correspondents to address him or her at a certain post office where the resident would check periodically for any mail. By establishing a new post office within the village, an attractive alternative to climbing the hill to Jenkintown was provided for prospective residents of the new village. Evans was in a position to see the creation of the small post office through the balky federal bureaucracy, and was congratulated for doing so by the local newspaper. It must have been the "capitalist" Evans, working perhaps in concert with Hazard, who recruited a local political newcomer and social climber, Thomas Buckman Harper, to serve as the functionary who would do the paperwork of establishment and serve as the initial postmaster.

Although Barker applied the name *Wyncote* to his estate as early as 1882, all evidence indicates that it was Evans who appropriated a premier local name and applied the name to the new post office through Harper. There simply was nothing in it for Barker, but everything at stake for Evans, Hazard, and Harper. Nonetheless, the authority of Lippincott weighs heavily and is not easily dismissed, but there is little other legacy evidence contemporary with Lippincott and Barker that provide support for the Lippincott view. Descendents of the early families have understood the story for years that Barker is to blame for applying the name. The only other contemporary comment comes from Annie Heacock. In a handwritten notation on the first photograph of students at the Chelten Hills School dated 1857, Annie wrote in 1935: Chelten Hills is now called Wyncote, a ridiculous and inappropriate name." But, the object of her scorn is not evident, and in her *Reminiscences,* she states, again ambiguously, that the name is "a relic of the Wharton Barker times."

Whatever the source, the life of the "fair village" named Wyncote was well underway.

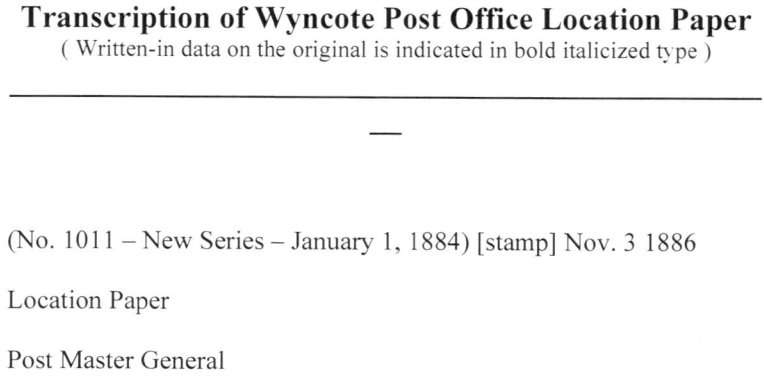

Transcription of Wyncote Post Office Location Paper
(Written-in data on the original is indicated in bold italicized type)

—

(No. 1011 – New Series – January 1, 1884) [stamp] Nov. 3 1886

Location Paper

Post Master General

Post Office Department

Office of the First Assistant P.M. General
Washington, D.C., *Oct. 28ᵗʰ, 1886*

Sir: Before the Postmaster General decides upon the application for the establishment of a post office at
Wyncote   , County of *Montgomery,*
State of *Penna*   ., it will be necessary for you to carefully answer the subjoined questions, get a neighboring postmaster to certify to the correctness of the answers, and return the location paper to the Department, addressed to me. If the site selected for the proposed office should not be on any mail route now under contract, only a "Special Office" can be established there, to be supplied with mail from some convenient point on the nearest mail route by a special carrier, for which service a sum equal to two-thirds of the amount of the salary of the postmaster as such office will be paid.

You should inform the contractor, or person performing service for him, of this application, and require him to execute the inclosed certificate as to the practicability of supplying the proposed office with mail, and return the same to the Department.

Very respectfully,
K. E. Stevenson
First Assistant Postmaster General

To Mr. *Thos. B. Harper*   .
care of the Postmaster of *Jenkintown*, who will please forward to him.

STATEMENT

The proposed office to be called
                          Wyncote,
   **Select a short name for the proposed office, which, when written,
will not resemble the name of any other post office in the State.**
It will be situation in the _____ quarter of Section ***Cheltenham***
Township, _____ (North or South)
Range _____ (East or West) _____ in the county of
Montgomery, State of ***Penna***.
It will be on or near route No. ***69197***, being the route from
Jenkintown Station
To ***Jenkintown***, on which the mail is now carried ***daily 4 times except
Sunday***
The contractor's name is ***Leon Hay***
Will it be directly on this route? – Ans. ***No***
If not, how far from and on which side of it? – Ans. ***About 400 feet –
West of Present Route***
How much will it increase the travel of the mail one way each trip? –
Ans. ***About 400 feet***
Where will the mail leave the present route to supply the proposed
office? Ans. ***Jenkintown Station***
Where intersect the route again? – Ans. ***Jenkintown Station***
What post office will be left out by this change? – Ans. ***None***
If not on any route, is a "Special Office" wanted? – Ans. ***No***
To be supplied from ***Mail Agent on Rail Road***
The name of the nearest office to the proposed one on the same route
is ***Jenkintown***
Its distance is ¾ ***of a*** miles in a ***n Easterly*** direction from the
proposed office.
The name of the nearest office on the same route on the other side is

_____
Its distance is _____ miles in a _____ direction from the
proposed office.
The name of the nearest office to this proposed one not on this route is
Germantown Philadelphia
Distance by the most direct road ***four*** miles in a ***Westerly*** direction
from the proposed office.
The name of the most prominent river near it is ***Schuylkill***
The name of the nearest creek is ***Tacony***
The proposed office will be ***Seven*** miles from said river on the ***West***

Side of it and will be ***Seventy five feet*** miles from said nearest creek on the ***West*** side of it.

The name of the nearest railroad is ***North Pennsylvania R.R,***

If on the line or near a railroad, on which side will the office be located: how far from the track and what is or will be the name of the station? – Ans ***West – about 400 feet – Jenkintown Station***

What will be the distance from the proposed site to the nearest flag station? – Ans. _____

State name of station: _____

What will be the distance from the proposed site to the nearest station at which mail trains make regular

st

ops? Ans. ***About 400 feet***

State name of station? ***Jenkintown***

If it be a village, state the number of inhabitants – Ans_____

Also, the population to be supplied by the proposed office – Ans. ***500 or more***

A diagram or sketch from a map showing the position of the proposed new office with neighboring river or creek, roads, and other post offices, towns, or villages near it, will be useful and is therefore desired.

A correct map of the locality might be furnished by the county surveyor, but this must be without expense to the Post Office Department.

All of which I certify to be correct and true according to the best of my knowledge and belief this _____ day of _____, 188_.

(S

ign full name) ***Thomas Buckman Harper,*** proposed P.M.

I certify that I have examined the foregoing statement and that it is correct an true, to the best of my knowledge and belief.

[undecipherable signature]

Postmaster at ***Weldon, Pa***

About ½ mile from proposed office.

Chapter 10

LITERARY AND ARTISTIC WYNCOTE

I [can still see] the last load of hay coming up the lane in the twilight and tired men walking beside the eager horses wanting to be home.
(Lippincott, 1938)

This story of Wyncote has thus far focused on leaders of business and industry who found the tranquil countryside a suitable retreat from the tribulations of big city business and politics. The business and manufacturing prowess of the great city nearby afforded a strong community of businessmen in the Olde Wyncote tract. The refined taste and attendance to culture that their unusual wealth and education afforded them also engendered a nurturing setting for persons of literary and artistic attainment. The institutions that created a vibrant city of commerce were matched by equally great cultural institutions that supported talented writers and artists. Many of them came to Wyncote for the same reasons as their business counterparts: serenity and beauty that supported their artistic endeavors. The case of Walter Damrosch may have been archetypical. The quiet charms of the Beechwood Inn and its neighborhood were the motivation for the legendary New York Symphony conductor and composer to reside at the Inn during his summer stints at Willow Grove Park. He moved his family and his piano to a large suite at the beginning of the 1897 season and may have found inspiration for his compositions while enjoying the countryside around the inn. Other artists, musicians, and authors followed.

Christopher Morley (1890 - 1957)

Christopher Morley was born in Haverford, Pennsylvania, in 1890. His father was a mathematics professor at Haverford College and his mother was a musician and poet. Young Christopher attended Haverford College, studying drama and writing. His brother would be appointed the president of Haverford in 1940 after winning the first Pulitzer Prize for the *Washington Post,* completing the family love affair with Haverford. As an early twentieth century man of letters, he achieved wide respect as a humorist, essayist, author, editor, poet and playwright.

A post with the *Ladies Home Journal* brought him back to Philadelphia after studying in England and the Journal's owner, Cyrus Curtis, probably induced him to live in Wyncote, where Curtis had his estate and several other members of his publishing "family" found homes. He described his circumstances as living "in Wyncote, Pa., ten miles from Philadelphia on the Cinder and Bloodshot. Commutation, $6.88 per month. Plumbers' bills, ditto per week." Finding a place on Fernbrook Avenue, he was at the center of the community and turned his critical eye on the life around him, although he complained that the realtor placed him in a "queer 'desirable residence' near the gas tanks at Marathon." [Referring to the coal-gas plant on Glenside Avenue.] Morley wrote about the village in his book *Mince Pie* that was published in 1920. No doubt seeking to insulate himself from the potential disapproving eye of his neighbors, he euphemistically called his hometown "Marathon": he noted that, in the town, it was a "worse sin to have our lawn uncut than to have your hair uncut." He was not so reticent to use the name in his novel *The Ironing Board*: but in that case, Wyncote is a character in his story. One biographer credits Morley's stay in Philadelphia and Wyncote with incubating his distinctive style: "good natured, whimsical, and being somewhat disengaged from the period's progressive literary movements, ultimately middle browed." (Kalfus, 1990)

Morley did not miss the village's natural beauty, noting: "The landscape around Marathon is lovely, but it has itself well in hand. The hills pretend to be gentle declivities.

There is a beautiful little sheet of water, reflecting the trailery of willows, a green salute to the eye." He also described the wide use of stone walls with vertical stone features on the top to "discourage the sedentary." Look over the stone wall on Greenwood Avenue at Robinson Park today, and you will enjoy the same rustic scene. Morley also noted the sophisticated underpinnings of the culture in the village:

Marathon is a suburban Xanadu gently caressed by the train service of the Cinder and Bloodshot. It may be recognized as an aristocratic and patrician stronghold by the fact that while luxuries are readily available (for instance, banana splits or the latest novel by Enoch A. Bennett), necessaries are had only by prayer and advowson. The drug store will deliver ice cream to your refrigerator, but it is impossible to get your garbage collected. . . . Another proof that Marathon is patrician at heart is that nothing is known by its right name! The drug store is a "pharmacy," Sunday is "the Sabbath," a house is a "residence," a girl's school is a "young ladies's seminary." (Morley, 1920)

There was one amenity in particular that Marathon dangerously lacked in Morley's opinion. He complained: "I hardly know whether Marathon is a safe place to bring up a child. How can he learn the horrors of drink in a village where there is no saloon?"

Mary Elizabeth Hallock Greenewalt (1871 – 1950)

Mary Elizabeth Hallock was born in Beirut, Syria in 1871, where her father was serving as the United States consul. Her mother, Sara Tabet Hallock, became ill while abroad and was sent back to the United States for treatment. She died shortly thereafter at age twenty-eight in Massachusetts. Mary's father, Samuel, then sent the four children back to the States for education in boarding schools. The two boys went to Massachusetts where there were relatives and the

In the News

Miss Mary E. Hallock, the Philadelphia pianist, who was a graduate of the Chelten Hills Preparatory School, and who not long since delivered her lecture on "The Pulse Origin of Rhythm" in the hall of Miss Martin's school here, appears to be winning both recognition and fame. On Thursday of last week she played at Colorado Springs, and on Wednesday afternoon of this week she gave her lecture at the Drexel Institute of Technology in West Philadelphia. The matter presented by this talented young lady, of whom and of whose growing fame the principal and students of the Chelten Hills School feel very proud, represents original research and contains a mass of proof bearing upon her contention that rhythm in music depends upon arterial impulse, and that it has its analogy in the entire animal world. Her use of the metronome to illustrate her subject is both ingenious and pleasing, and her splendid gift of mastery of the piano gives extreme pleasure to all lovers of music "who are once privileged to hear her interesting lecture.
Times Chronicle, January 30, 1904

two girls, Mary and her younger sister Ethel, were sent to the Heacock School in Chelten Hills. It is difficult to imagine the emotional state of the children faced with such tumultuous changes in their early lives. Mary received her primary and secondary education at the Chelten Hills School, where she lived with the Heacocks, graduating at the top of her class in 1888. Annie Heacock noted her varied talents, particularly in mathematics and piano and called Mary her most talented student. In recognition of her potential, Annie accompanied Mary to the convention of the National Music Teachers' Association which was held at the Continental Hotel in Philadelphia in 1889. Mary studied piano and received a degree at the Philadelphia Conservatory of Music, which, through a series of mergers, has become the University of

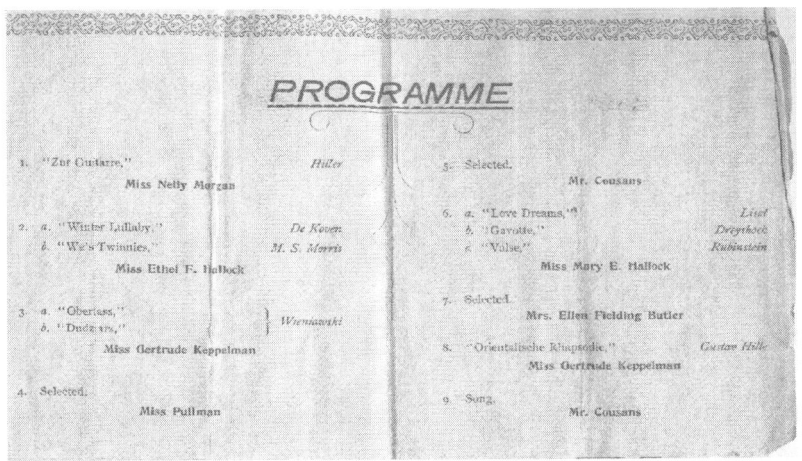

PROGRAMME

Chelten Hills School Concert
The program for a concert at the School in 1888 indicates that Mary
Elizabeth Hallock and her sister, Ethel, both performed.
Courtesy of the Old York Road Historical Society

the Arts. She honed her piano skills by playing numerous
concerts in her old neighborhood at the Chelten Hills School
and the Beechwood Inn. In 1898, she married Dr. Frank
Linsday Greenewalt, the chief physician at Girard College.
As her career advanced, Mary Hallock Greenewalt toured
with the Philadelphia Orchestra and the Pittsburgh
Symphony, performing throughout the United States. She
was internationally recognized for her interpretation of
Chopin and was an early recording artist for Columbia
records in 1919 and 1920.

Mary Elizabeth also was an inventor and author. She was
a pioneer in the use of light and colors to enhance music and
received nine patents for her musical lighting device, the
"Sarabet" (named in honor of her mother). Her first
performance with the instrument was at the Bellvue-
Stratford Hotel in Philadelphia to a conference of electrical
engineers and she later performed at the Wanamaker stores
in Philadelphia and New York. General Electric infringed on
her patent and she sued, despite opposition from many who
were skeptical that a woman could have created such

Mary Elizabeth Hallock Greenewalt at her Light Organ
Mrs. Greenewalt is shown at her electric light color organ about 1925. It was developed at Longwood in Wilmington with the support of duPont. *Courtesy of the Library of Congress*

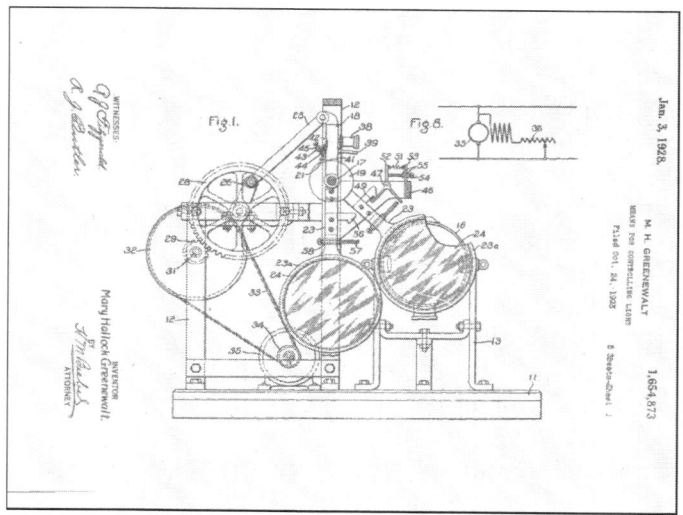

Greenewalt Patent 1,654,873
"Means for Controlling Light." *Courtesy of the United States Patent Office*

technical devices, or at the very least should not be in that field of endeavor. Despite her misgivings and dismay when she learned that her attorney was also on retainer with General Electric, she won her lawsuits and published a book on her art entitled *Nourathar: The Fine Art of Light-Color Playing*. The technology Web site *Techman* calls her an "early Woman-Geek," a compliment that only a modern person might understand, but one that Mrs. Greenewalt might have appreciated.

Mary's sister Ethel (and fellow Chelten Hills student) married Pierre duPont's brother, William, connecting her family with that Delaware dynasty which supported Mary's work. Mary and her husband Frank had only one child,

Crawford Hallock Greenewalt. He inherited his father's interest in science and nature and his mother's inventiveness, inquisitiveness and energy. He was chemical engineer who invented nylon for DuPont and then went on to become the President of that company. During World War II, he was a major figure in the Manhattan Project that developed the Atomic Bomb and was present at Stagg Field in Chicago in 1942 when Enrico Fermi activated the first nuclear reactor. As a hobby, he became an expert in hummingbirds. It was said that his extensive work on the birds would have earned him tenure at any university.

Harrison S. Morris (1856 - 1948) and Anna Wharton Morris (1868 – 1957)

This couple gives new meaning to the phrase "prolific authors." Harrison S. Morris was born in Philadelphia in 1856. He was educated in the "common schools" of Philadelphia and, being the only son, he went to work at the age of sixteen at the Reading Coal & Iron Company to support his ill parents. He worked in the treasury department of that company until 1892 when he resigned his position as assistant cashier in order to pursue a career in the arts. In 1893, Morris was a co-founder and co-editor of a new weekly newspaper, *The Citizen,* which included such authors as Owen Wister and Agnes Repplier on the board of editors. That year must have been a busy one as Morris also

Anna Wharton Morris and Harrison S. Morris
This undated photograph shows the couple in mid-life.
Courtesy of Princeton University

co-founded the Philobiblon Club of Philadelphia, an organization intended to "promote the arts pertaining to the production of books, the union of book-collectors and book lovers." Samuel Pennypacker, future governor, George W. Childs, newspaper publisher, and Provost William Pepper of Penn were listed as co-founders. Also in 1893, he was appointed the managing director of the prestigious Academy of Fine Arts in Philadelphia.

It is difficult to imagine - and surviving documentation sheds little light – how a twenty-year career in the coal business prepared him to step into such an important role in the world of art, although he was said to have maintained an active interest in the arts during his business career. Morris' first published volumes appeared in 1890 and 1891 when Lippincott published an art anthology and four volumes of poetry that he edited. Perhaps his success in publishing was the catalyst for a change finally to a career that he cherished all along. "A Mosaic," his 1890 work, was a collection of reproductions of pictures painted by members of the Artists' Fund Society of Philadelphia with accompanying text and Morris' poetry. *Publishers' Weekly* for December 1890 said it "ranks easily among the very best books of the season." They also referred to Morris as the "most warmly admired of our younger circle of poets." Morris went on to publish extensively, including novels, poetry, and art criticism for many publications. Morris also served as an editor of Lippincott's Magazine from 1898 to 1905 and was the art editor of Curtis' *Ladies Home Journal* from 1905 until his retirement.

In 1896, Morris married Anna Wharton, daughter of the great industrialist, Joseph Wharton. They had met at various literary functions in 1892. A devoted and life-long Quaker, Anna was self-conscious about her appearance as a youth and had confided in her diary that "I was seventeen years old the 15th last July. I am five feet ten inches in height and I weigh about 131 pounds. I am thin, and feel awkward." Though both married late, they seemed have been brought together by their shared literary and charitable interests, and tall Anna was fortunate to connect with thin-as-a-rail and even taller Morris who stood around six foot three.

Anna had purchased *Endsmeet Farm* in Cheltenham Township in 1882, probably with financial assistance from her father, and this became their first home upon her marriage. She was a frequent visitor to the farm during her single years, very much involved in her gardens as wells as the produce of the land. The 110 acre farm extended from the corner of Rices Mill Road and Church Road, along Rices Mill Road to the Limekiln Pike. The farm had previously been owned by Joseph S. Lovering, who owned the Sugar Refinery at 225 Church Street in South Philadelphia, and, not insignificantly, was Joseph Wharton's father-in-law. Lovering had purchased the farm in 1857 from Joseph's brother, Charles, who, in turn, had purchased it from his father, William Wharton: thus the farm was in the family a long time. In 1956, Cheltenham Township School district condemned the property and razed the old farmhouse in order to obtain the site for its new high school.

Morris and the Nearing Case

In 1915, Harrison S. Morris was involved in a pivotal case that foretold the future of higher education in the United States. Dr. Scott Nearing, a young professor in the new Wharton School at Penn, was an outspoken social activist and critic of government and business improprieties. Wealthy government and business supporters of the University objected to his frequent bombastic appearances in the press. Their protest to Dean Roswell C. McCrea resulted in Nearing's dismissal from the University, despite the fact that all parties agreed that Nearing was a gifted writer, orator, and teacher and never used his classroom "pulpit" to promulgate his socialist theories. Nearing protested to the board of trustees who called on Harrison S. Morris to illuminate Joseph Wharton's mission for his namesake school.

Morris was the executor of Wharton's estate (as well as his son-in-law) and he undertook to explain the Quaker values that inspired Wharton's gift: in particular, the importance of academic freedom as well as Wharton's desire to have his school in the forefront of teaching the "immorality" of "practical expediency" and the "necessity for punishing those who commit frauds, betray trusts." He made his defense of free speech and academic freedom clear. Despite Morris' intervention, the Board voted overwhelmingly to uphold the dismissal of Nearing. There were only two dissenting votes on the board: J. Bertram Lippincott and Wharton Barker.

The principled position of the Wyncote triumvirate of Barker, Lippincott, and Morris would eventually be upheld by later litigation in other cases that would cement the strong position of American higher education on the side of free speech. After leaving Penn and higher education, Nearing became a virtual hermit in Vermont and Maine, promoting a natural or "organic" lifestyle. Nearing went on in a later age to be a Vietnam War protester and, eighteen days after his hundredth birthday in 1983, he took his own life at his farm in Maine.

Endsmeet Farm of Anna Wharton Morris
Top: Viewed about the late 1940's just before its razing for the new Cheltenham High School. The view is from the area of today's front entrance of the school to the south.
Bottom: The farm pond. Rices Mill Road is on the left.
Courtesy of David J. Wolfe and John Neilson, Wyncote.

JOSEPH WHARTON

MARCH 3, 1907, 81 YEARS OLD

~~~~~~~~~~~~~~~~~~~~~~~~~~~~~~~~~~~~

Not years alone nor fortune make
    The gray beatitude of age;
Nor are the golden words he spake
    The glory of the Sage.

Unless the heart enrich the man
    And love transfigure gifts and gold,
The key is lost that keeps the plan
    And time but leaves him old.

You, from your eighty years and one,
    Look down on acres stacked with grain;
On acts of wisdom gently done;
    On honour without stain;

And all the seasons yet to be
    Can never make your spirit old,
For love has taught you liberty
    And truth has made you bold.

~~~~~~~~~~~~~~~~~~~~~~~~~~~~~~~~~~~~

From *Lyrics and Landscapes* by Harrison S. Morris
The Century Company, NewYork, 1908

Anna and Harrison traveled extensively. Harrison was appointed United States Commissioner for the International Exhibition of Art and History in Rome in 1911, and they observed the beginning of the World War while in Paris in 1914. Anna published several books of prose and numerous essays that appeared in such diverse publications as *The All Story Magazine, Lippincott's Monthly, Cosmopolitan Magazine* ("Her Money's Worth"), and *Women's Progress* ("A Career or a Husband"). After 1913, she became deeply involved in the prison reform movement and wrote extensively on that subject as well.

After Joseph Wharton suffered a stroke in 1908, Harrison Morris became increasingly involved in his businesses. Morris was already a part owner and treasurer of the Wharton Steel Company, later Bethlehem Steel, and became president of that company in 1909. He spent the rest of his active years caring for Wharton's extensive enterprises on behalf of the Wharton family.

Christine Chester Crowell (1887 - 1940)

Christine Chester was known to her neighbors as the daughter of the local minister, Rev. Carlos Chester. Rev. Chester was the founding pastor of the Calvary Presbyterian Church and he resided with his family in the church manse until leaving the pastorate. He and his family then moved to a rented house on Mather Avenue, then lived in the coachman's cottage on property owned by Mary Lippincott on Serpentine Lane. Rev. Chester was also an accomplished writer, having served as a newspaper editor before his service in Wyncote as well as the editor of a literary journal in Philadelphia during his time here. Christine graduated from the Chelten Hills School in 1897. In 1906, Christine married William Crowell, Jr., a young engineer who would achieve several patents for handling steam flow in 1919 and 1920, but otherwise find it difficult to support his family. An article he authored appeared in the prestigious magazine *Science* in 1911, discussing the scientific elements of healthful air-handling systems. Ironically, his article was immediately adjacent to another in that issue authored by a certain "William Kent." Christine herself became an author with the publication of *The Little House* in 1937. The book describes the difficult life of a young girl growing up in a suburban village and may well contain considerable autobiographical detail. The home of the title is believed to be the barn where Christine and her husband lived and she described her life there as well as her relationship with Miss Mary, Mary Lippincott, her patrician neighbor and mentor. A charming memoir by a neighbor recalls Christine's "red, gold, hair, straight as a poker. She could only wear it, because it was so fine, tightly pulled back in a bun; she hated it as a child and as a grown woman." (Spruill, 1990) Her hair and appearance also attracted the notice of family acquaintance, Mary Cassatt, who was inspired to paint her portrait.

Christine Chester may have led a complicated life. Her early marriage must have been noticeably problematic as Mary Lippincott supported the young family by providing their home: Christine and her husband never owned property in Wyncote and apparently struggled to make ends meet. Christine's husband, William the junior, was the son of William Crowell, artist Thomas Eakins' best friend from childhood. The elder William Crowell was also Eakins' brother-in-law after his marriage to Eakins' sister Frances. Eakins himself was engaged for eight years to Crowell's sister Kathrin, but the courtship appears to be forced on him by his father and he escaped marriage by Kathrin's death at the age of twenty-eight of meningitis. The elder Crowell was trained as an attorney, but declined to practice due to a "bad heart" and inexplicably turned to farming. He and his wife lived with Eakins for a while, but were disillusioned with his lifestyle that included painting his nude subjects while himself in the nude and roaming the house in an unclothed state. Among other indiscretions, Eakins was accused of having an incestuous affair with his sister Margaret, and later he was dismissed from the Pennsylvania Academy of the Arts, where he taught, for his controversial use of nudes. Both William and Frances became estranged from Eakins but William nonetheless served at Eakins' attorney during the time he was expelled from the Academy. Young Crowell was raised in poverty with his nine brothers and sisters on his parents' farm in Avondale, south of the city. Perhaps to alleviate their destitution and despite their trepidations

Christine Chester, 1897
Christine Chester is pictured in her graduation portrait
from the Chelten Hills School. She appears unusually
pensive and one wonders what concerns are on her
mind.
*Photo: Courtesy of the Old York Road Historical
Society*

about Eakins' character, William and Frances sent their daughter Ella, an aspiring sculptor, to live with Eakins and learn her craft. The parents gave specific warning to Eakins that he was not to require her to pose nude. Nonetheless, in 1895, Ella accused Eakins of forcing her to pose and sexually molesting her. Ella's mental state deteriorated and after spending some time in a mental institution, returned to her parents' farm and, in July of 1897, used a shotgun to commit suicide, an act that was witnessed by young William. Christine apparently led a quiet life as a wife and homemaker except for the publication of her book by Harcourt, Brace in New York.

In an unusual coincidence, there were two Christines in the Chester household. Another Christine, seven years younger than the author, was actually the daughter of Sarah Elizabeth Chester of Saratoga, New York. Under the name "Sallie Chester," Sarah identified herself on census forms as "authoress." Her first writing was published in *Harper's Magazine* in 1865 and she became a prolific author of children's books. In 1881, Sallie married a man named Logie, a person so obscure that history has not determined his first name. Marital problems of some kind were evident as both of Sallie's daughters, Christine and Leslie, were shortly sent to live with Sarah's brothers. Leslie was sent to Thomas Chester in Geneva, New York, and Christine was sent to live with Carlos Chester in Wyncote. Sallie died around 1900, about the time Rev. Carlos Chester was appointed at the Wyncote Church. Perhaps Rev. Carlos adopted the teenager by the time he moved to Wyncote, thus leading to confusion about her status and the two girls with the same name.

Ezra Pound (1885 – 1972)

Ezra Pound, a prolific poet and critic, was a major figure in the "Modernist" movement of the first half of the twentieth century. Although he was born in Hailey, Idaho Territory, his family moved east in 1887, landing in Wyncote in 1892 after brief stints in New York City, West Philadelphia, and several locations in Jenkintown. They lived on Fernbrook Avenue in the new village. Pound's father, Homer, was an active member of the community, member of the Wyncote Improvement Association, and an active member of the new Presbyterian Church where he taught Sunday school. One neighbor referred to them as a "highly respected family in our community." Another resident remembers Ezra, or "Ray" as he was known, as "sort of dashing youth with blond, bushy hair, wearing rather odd cowboy clothes and always a broad sombrero hat." (Eckman, 1957) Pound attended school first at the Heacock School where he was a classmate and good friend of Edward Heacock, who died later while on a Canadian expedition. In 1894, Pound saved Heacock's dog from a flash flood in the Tookany Creek and then had himself to be rescued by Heacock and his other companion, Tommy Cochran. He then attended Cheltenham Academy where he was considered "an unusually brilliant student, although quite eccentric" and enrolled at Penn for two years, but transferred to Hamilton College in Clinton, New York, to finish his studies in writing. After graduating, he obtained a teaching post at Wabash College but was removed from his post after only four months for allowing a stranded actress to sleep overnight in his room.

What constitutes his first published piece was printed on November 7, 1896, in the *Times Chronicle,* nearby Jenkintown's newspaper that also covered Wyncote. The pithy two-liner from the eleven year old "E. L. Pound" commented on the recent defeat of William Jennings Bryan. A cynic might say that the brand new newspaper was desperate for material. While in college, he wrote a more substantial piece, a poem that appeared in the November 8, 1902, issue of the same newspaper. It was entitled "Ezra on the Strike" and one verse in particular might strike us as eerily modern, even as it displays Pound's burgeoning tendency to mangle standard English:

No use talkin', he's the man - &
One of the best that ever ran,
For didn't I turn Republican
One o' the furst?

Pound moved to Europe and met an American violinist, Olga Rudge from Youngstown, Ohio, who became his lifelong mistress despite his marriage to Dorothy Shakespear. In a classic "small world" coincidence, Rudge was a friend of Esther and Priscilla Heacock: they were related and met through the marriage of cousins. As a writer, Pound's work "has had a difficult reception," in one analyst's dazzling understatement. (Menard, 2008)   Whatever accomplishments he may have attained as a poet were overshadowed by his affection for Mussolini in World War II (Pound was introduced to him by Rudge), his anti-Semitism, and his treasonous statements against the United States during the War. His bigoted tendencies were posited in a review of several books on Pound in a 1988 *New York Review of Books* article to be the result of exposure to those ideas in the community in which he was raised: a so-called "suburban prejudice." Pound himself claimed this was the case, using the phrase in a letter to Allen Ginsburg in 1967. After post-war confinement to St. Elizabeth's mental hospital in Washington, D.C. as punishment for his treason, Pound visited his old house on Fernbrook in 1958 before returning to Italy where he died and was buried in Venice in 1972.

Ray Thompson (1905 – 1982)

Ray Thompson was a Philadelphia native, a 1924 graduate of Northeast High School, and a journalism student at Temple University. He had been drawing cartoons since childhood and, after leaving Temple, decided to try his hand selling cartoons to publications such as Curtis' *Saturday Evening Post, Ladies' Home Journal,* and *Colliers,* among others, where he was favorably received. He was a pioneer in the field of cartoon advertising and was successful in many national ad campaigns, including the Atlantic Refining Company, the N.W. Ayer Advertising Agency, Kellogg's Cereals, Sun Oil Company, and many more. Thompson also authored many well-known comic strips (many on a ghost writing basis) for newspaper syndicates, including "The Shadow," "Roy Powers, Eagle Scout," and "Myra North, Special Nurse." Although not a glamorous post insuring name recognition, his work for Fleer Dubble Bubble Gum resulted in 750 comic strips that wrapped each chunk of gum. Later in his career, at his studio in Wyncote, he turned to painting in his spare time, depicting various

"Wyncote Park" by Ray Thompson
Watercolor, 1957., original 9 7/8" x 14 ½."
Courtesy of his son, Dr. H. Roy Thompson, Oreland, PA

local scenes in his favorite medium, watercolors, along with oils and pastels. He produced over one hundred works. Ray Thompson died in 1982 at the age of 77.

Elliott Lester (1894 – 1951)

Elliott Lester, a native Philadelphian, began his career as a professor at Temple University in Philadelphia. His first play, *The Mud Turtle,* was a Broadway success in 1925-26, running for fifty-two performances. As a result, in 1926, he left the teaching profession for full-time literary pursuits. His first success supported his move to the rustic countryside of Wyncote where he built his house on Serpentine Lane on property previously owned by Sharpless. His experience on Broadway led to film-making and he contributed to the transition from silent films to talkies. One film adaptation of his play "Two Seconds" featured a young Edward G. Robinson in the role of a convicted murderer facing the last moments of his life as he is led to execution. Lester's son, Richard, also entered the film industry and launched the career of Peter Sellers, produced the first Beatles movie for the Beatles' American introduction, as well as other renowned movies such as "Petulia." Richard Lester still works in his adopted country of England.

Horace Mather Lippincott (1877 – 1967)

Horace Mather Lippincott was a descendant of an early Cheltenham settler, Joseph Mather. His mother, Cynthia Shoemaker Mather was the great-granddaughter of Thomas Mather, the first resident of *Shadyside* at the corner of Washington Lane and Church Road. In 1871, she married Robert Cook Lippincott, a wholesale lumber merchant of Philadelphia. Horace was born in 1877 in Germantown and the family moved to *Shadyside* shortly thereafter. He received a degree from Penn in 1897 where he played cricket and served the alumni association for many years. His occupation was listed in *Who's Who* as a "Manufacturer," being first associated with the engineering firm of Leighton Lee and then serving as president of Soco Lumber and

Mining Company and then the Sand-Lime Brick Company. He is most remembered, however, as an historian and author. As a birthright Quaker, Lippincott made extensive studies in the history of the Society of Friends, including a history of the Abington Meeting. Other publications include *Early Philadelphia* in 1917 that studied the early history of the city, the history of Penn, a history of the Mather family of Cheltenham, a history of George Washington in the Philadelphia years and his relationship with the University of Pennsylvania, and a history of Chestnut Hill. His writings are a major source of information about Cheltenham and Wyncote.

Although a devout Quaker which required a pacifist position, he joined other influential Quakers in supporting the United States prosecution of the Great War. In 1918, he signed a petition entitled "Some Particular Advices for Friends & A Statement of Loyalty for Others." In part it read: "There are certain fundamental principles of right and humanity which every man must feel called up to defend, even to the extent of forcible resistance if long continued intolerable conditions caused by morally defunct people are to be ended before the world is enslaved."

He remembers growing up in Wyncote fondly:

. . . the last load of hay coming up the lane in the twilight and tired men walking beside the eager horses wanting to be home; cutting the ice and riding the sledges; the anemones and columbine on a wooded bank in Rock Lane; the terror of a near-by pond filled with snakes; the distant notes of a flute player on moonlit summer nights, and fishing with Grandfather in the 'old swimming hole' on the Tacony Creek at Church Road below Juliana's Cave. (Lippincott, 1938)

Unidentified Scene
This view is from the 1900 marketing brochure of the Jenkintown
Syndicate, which promoted Martin Luther Kohler's homes in Jenkintown
and Wyncote.   It captures the time of transition between the former
farmland of the area – seen on the right - and the new manicured estates -
seen on the left. Traffic was not yet a problem: the solitary vehicle travels
on an uncrowded dirt road.
Courtesy of Nancy Wood, Wyncote

EPILOGUE

This version and portion of the story of Wyncote ends about the turn of the twentieth century. There is much history after that to be sure – and we are still making history today, but the physical history of the village as we know and experience it was substantially completed by about 1900. It is a good place to stop: the history from that point on is a task for another book or another author.

I received tremendous satisfaction from researching and writing this story, although I asked myself many times "why bother." The answer is complex. When I started, I knew something of the history of this community of course, but this exercise corrected some misconceptions, uncovered many new facts, and engendered deeper appreciation for the quality of this community and the people that made it. Much of that satisfaction is of the trivial kind, such as figuring out why Maple Avenue is so inexplicably crooked between Webster and Fernbrook Avenues, or learning of the personal stories – call it gossip – of the luminaries that made up the first citizenry. I enjoyed learning of the life of the extended Wharton and Wanamaker families and the lifestyles and relationships that created such wealth and fame. To paraphrase President Eisenhower's term, they formed influential family "interlocking directorates" with their home base right here in Wyncote. I have to admit that I longed to find a diary of someone like Mary Wanamaker or Sarah Wharton Barker to gain insights to the more private life of a mother and homemaker in that era. It seems quite clear that the more visible accomplishments of their husbands would not have been possible without their domestic toil and dedication, conducted in the anonymity and obscurity that the age imposed on women. Time and time again, I was reminded that these were real people, with the same problems of illness, career, and family joy and tragedy that we face today. One can gain inspiration and even guidance from making that connection.

Another reward was the reminder that we shouldn't indulge too deeply in the tendency to pine for the "good old days." The past era is easily idealized when we wish we could meet our famous neighbor, say, the adventurous Col. John I. Rogers to discuss the new Phillies, or see the village while it still had its uncrowded country flavor. The photograph that begins this chapter raises such reverie. But who would really want to trade the amenities we enjoy now for the conditions that existed then? The Tookany Creek, a pristine path of water during the colonial era, became an open sewer by the time the village was created. All wildlife that depended on the stream were killed, and the smell was the source of lawsuits such as John Wanamaker's. Diseases that we don't even think about today were constant complications in daily life just a century ago. Malaria and typhoid struck down young and old and closed schools, neighborhoods, and church services, particularly in the summer. Frank Hellerman was reported "very low" with typhoid on August 24, 1896, and died within the week. Who, like Chelten Hills crossing watchman William Mack, after being hit by a train, would give up a five-minute ride to Abington Hospital today for the privilege of living then. Serious injury meant that you would be loaded on the next train and delivered to the Jewish Hospital at Broad Street and Olney Avenue, the closest medical facility. He died of his injuries on the train on a fine June day in 1893.

The railroad had an enormous impact on the development of the community. Instituted to bring commerce to the feet of Philadelphia businessmen, the railroad instead changed history by bringing those distinctively industrious and civic-minded capitalists out to a pristine countryside to build a new way of living. Mostly Quaker at first, they brought with them strict and honorable values that established a high standard of living for all who came and would come later. They were followed by members of the two Protestant denominations that were so influential in the business world and the life of the community.

Within that homogenous and upright culture lies a final important lesson. Studying that history can act like a mirror on our own cultural and societal attributes and assist us in evaluating them. The men of the late eighteenth century prided themselves on being enlightened citizens, generous to visitors and outsiders and models of probity in their behavior. And, they were. But studying their lives, we are all too aware of flaws in the tapestry of their lives. By today's standards, the flaws appear as blinders on their vision of social equity.

Women who ventured outside of domestic duties, such as Mary Elizabeth Hallock Greenewalt, were restricted or challenged: the powers in control thought a woman could not have possibly invented the electrical devices for which she received a patent. And if she was an inventor, she should not have been one. The restrictions extended to public behavior as well as when the *Times Chronicle*, in 1898, roundly criticized two young female residents for being seen on horseback on a Sunday morning. And, of course, Christopher Morley wrote eloquently of the foibles of the good citizens of Wyncote using his euphemism of Marathon.

While an 1894 *Wyncote Outlines* welcomed all visitors of the Beechwood Inn to services in the local churches, a darker side to the culture indicated that the "welcome" was not unconditional.

There was, after all, the practice of Probationary Hill where potential residents had to prove they met the requirements of some unwritten code to qualify for residency. But even worse treatment befell members of outside cultures in a very class-conscious society. The Italians that flocked to the village as stonemasons, quarry workers, and road building crews were not welcome. The *Times Chronicle* cried that "just no more Italians" should be allowed in. By June of 1897, all were evicted from Wyncote and forced to move to Edge Hill and Glenside. A Chinese man opened the Celestial laundry in the Wyncote business district in August of 1897. Although the service was welcome, the newspaper opined that it would have been preferable if such an ethnic establishment were to "occupy a shanty on a back street," out of prominent view. And Jews were simply disqualified as guests at Beechwood Hotel in 1891. It is interesting to note that people of color did not meet such overt discrimination in the village. Several authors attribute this outcome to the abolitionist heritage of the Quaker founders which was much more tolerant of blacks than society at large. Consequently people of African-American heritage lived and worked in the area from the beginning. Dorcas lived with the Heacocks and was the cook at the Chelten Hills School while John Burgess tended the Brannan farm and lived in the small tenant house by the creek on Rices Mill Road. Both had children who attended the Chelten Hills School. Summarizing this whole issue was the controversy over a 1988 *New York Review of Books* article by Denis Donoghue that blamed Ezra Pound's rampant bigotry and anti-Semitism on a supposed "suburban prejudice" which he gained while being raised in Wyncote. Pound made the accusation even more plausible by himself claiming this was the case, but most would argue that Donoghue's article puts too much spin on the issue.

The study of history can perhaps help put such issues into perspective in our own society, but there is no doubt that the more diverse nature of today's Wyncote community contributes to the goal of a more egalitarian society. The substantial homes, the sound government, the superior schools, the unregimented array of streets that makes this different from a modern development, even the at-once sub-urban and sub-arboreal forest of trees, many planted by Wharton Barker, that we cherish in the summer but rue when the leaves fall in the autumn, are distinctive traits. These community elements are direct products of the erudite care that the founders exercised in the formulation of the village many years ago. E. Digby Baltzell summarized the point exquisitely when he noted that their virtures were worthy of emulation by everyone: "honor, hard work, respect, authority." I, for one, am very happy to be part of this continuing story.

Thomas J. Wieckowski
Wyncote, Pennsylvania
May 2009

BIBLIOGRAPHY

Abel, G. Gilbert. " At Home with John Wanamaker," *Old York Road Historical Society Bulletin, Vol. VII (1943)*.

American Bee Journal. "Biographical: Mr. Wm. A. Selser and Family." Chicago, IL: November 2, 1899.

Atlas of Cheltenham, Abington, and Springfield. Philadelphia, PA: A. H. Mueller & Co., 1897.

Atlas of Properties Along the North Penn Railroad. Philadelphia, PA: G. M. Hopkins, 1886.

Balch, William Ralston. *State Celebrities.* January 3, 1882. [Unattributed newspaper clipping.] Wharton Barker Papers, Scrapbook #2, Box 26. The Library of Congress, Washington, DC.

Baltzell, E. Digby. *Philadelphia Gentlemen, The Making of a National Upper Class.* New Brunswick, NJ: Transaction Publishers, 1995.

Barker, Wharton. Letters, Wharton Barker Papers, Box 1. The Library of Congress, Washington, DC.

Barnes, J. H., and Sevon, W. D. *The Geological Story of Pennsylvania (3rd ed.)* Harrisburg, PA: Pennsylvania Geological Survey, 4th ser., Educational Series 4, 2002.

Bates, Jr., Frederick H. "Martin Luther Kohler: Publicity-Shy Developer." *Old York Road Historical Society Bulletin.* Volume L (1990).

Bauermeister, Carl Leopold. Revolution in America: Confidential letters and journals, 1776-1784. Translated by Bernhard A. Uhlendorf. New Brunswick, NJ: Rutgers University Press, 1957. Baurmeister, Carl Leopold. "Letters of Major Baurmeister During the Philadelphia Campaign, 1777-1778," *Pennsylvania Magazine of History and Biography*, LX, 42-43 (January, 1936).

Bean, Theodore W. *History of Montgomery County Pennsylvania.* Philadelphia, PA: Everts & Peck, 1884.

Biographical Directory of the United States Congress: 1774-1989. Washington, DC: Government Printing Office, 1989.

Brown, John Crosby. *One Hundred Years of Merchant Banking"* New York, NY: Privately Printed, 1909.

Brown, John K. *The Baldwin Locomotive Works.* Baltimore, MD: The Johns Hopkins Press, 1995.

Buck, William J. *A History of Montgomery County, Pennsylvania* Philadelphia, PA: 1884.

Buck, William J. "A Visit to Cheltenham," *Norristown Register*, November 10, 1857.

Carson, Anne Conover. *Olga Rudge and Ezra Pound: What Thou Lovest Well.* New Haven, CT: Yale University Press, 2001.

Carter, Jane Levis. *The Down River People.* Edgemont Township, PA: 1976.

Cawley, James and Margaret. *Along the Old York Road.* New Brunswick, New Jersey: Rutgers University, 1965.

"Chelten Hills." *The North American,* Philadelphia, PA: June 3, 1888.

"Cheltenham Township Tax Ledger." 1885, 1886, 1887, 1888, 1890. Historical Society of Montgomery County, Norristown, PA.

Chorley, Richard J. *History of the Study of Landforms: Or The Development of Geomorphology: The Life and Work of William Morris Davis.* London, England: Routledge Publications, 1973.

City of Philadelphia Leading. Merchants and Manufacturers. Philadelphia, PA: Historical Publishing Company, 1886.
Collins, Nelson A.. "Paintings by Russell and Xanthus Smith." *Old York Road Historical Society Bulletin*, Jenkintown, PA. Volume XVIII (1954).

Cook, Fred J. *Forgotten Heroes of the American Revolution.* New York, NY: William Morrow and Company, 1959.

Costain, Thomas B. *The Chords of Steel*. Garden City, NJ: Doubleday & Co., 1960.

Crowell, Christine Chester. *The Little House*. New York, NY: Harcourt Brace, 1937.

Cullinan, Gerald Cullinan *The United States Postal Service*. New York, NY: Praeger Publishers, 1968.

Curry, Josephine. "Beechwood: Chronicle of a Summer Inn," *Old York Road Historical Society Bulletin*, Vol. LII (1992).

Cushing, Marshall. *The Story of Our Post Office*. Boston, MA: A. M. Thayer & Co., 1893.

Dann, John C., ed. *The Revolution Remembered. Eyewitness Accounts of the War for Independence*. Chicago, IL: The University of Chicago Press, 1980.

Day, Sherman. *Historical Collections of the State of Pennsylvania*. Philadelphia, PA: George W. Gorton, 1843.

Donehoo, George P. *Pennsylvania: A History*. New York, NY: Lewis Historical Publishing Company, 1926.

Donoghue, Denis. "Pound's Book of Beasts," *New York Review of Books,* Vol 35, Number 9 (June 2, 1988).

Dunn, Richard S. "William Penn and the Selling of Pennsylvania, 1681-1685."
Proceedings of the American Philosophical Society, Vol 127, No. 5 (1983).

Dutton, L. R. "Jenkintown's Public Utilities." *The Jenkins Town Lyceum*. Jenkintown, PA: The Jenkins Town Lyceum, 1938.

Eberlein, Harold Donaldson and Horace Mather Lippincott. *The Colonial Homes of Philadelphia*. Philadelphia, PA: J.B. Lippincott, 1912.

Eckman, Hensel. Letter to Esther Heacock, March 3, 1957. Ezra Pound Collection, University of Tulsa.

Eckman, Hensel. *Edward Rockhill Heacock: A Reminiscence*. Privately published. 1964. [Gatter Collection, Annenberg Rare Book Collection, Van Pelt Library, University of Pennsylvania]

Edson, Edith McLane. "A James Peale Puzzle: Captain Allen McLane's Encounter with British Dragoons." *Pennsylvania Magazine of History and Biography* 75, no.4 (October 2001).

Evans, Frank B. "Wharton Barker and the Republican National Convention of 1880." *The Pennsylvania Journal,* Pennsylvania Historical Association (January 1960).

Fact Sheet – Former Wyncote Manufactured Gas Plant. Philadelphia, PA: PECO. April, 2007.

Faris, John Thomson. *Old Roads Out of Philadelphia.* Philadelphia, PA: J.B. Lippincott, 1917.

Foust, Doreen. "Wyncote, Pennsylvania: The history, development, architecture and preservation of a Victorian Philadelphia suburb." Unpublished dissertation. Philadelphia, PA: The University of Pennsylvania Library, 1985.

Foust, Doreen L. "Wyncote's Historic District," *Old York Road Historical Society Bulletin,* Vol. XLVII (1987).

Gallagher, Donald A. and Abram Clemmer. "Edge Hill, 1777." *Old York Road Historical Society Bulletin,* XVII (1953).

Gifford, Edward S., Jr. *The American Revolution in the Delaware Valley.* Philadelphia, PA: Pennsylvania Society of the Sons of the Revolution, 1976.

Goodwin, Bruce K. *Guidebook to the Geology of the Philadelphia Area.* Harrisburg, PA: Pennsylvania Geological Survey, 1964

Gospill, James. *Gopsill's Philadelphia Directory For 1885.* Philadelphia, PA: James Gopsill's Sons, 1885.

Hale, C. R. *Guide on the North Pennsylvania Rail Road between Phila. And Fort Washington.* Philadelphia, PA: Ringwalt & Co., 1859.

Hallowell, Anna Davis. *James and Lucretia Mott. Life and Letters.* Boston, MA: Houghton, Mifflin, and Company, 1884.

Hare, Jay V. *History of the North Pennsylvania Railroad.* Philadelphia, PA: Reading Company, 1944.

Hare, Jay V. "The Coming of the North Pennsylvania Railroad." *Old York Road Historical Society Bulletin.* Vol. IV (1940).

Haydock, William Kent. "The Kent Family of Chelten Hills/Wyncote." *Old York Road Historical Society Bulletin,* Jenkintown, PA. Vol. XLV (1985).

Heacock, Annie. *Boarding and Day School at Chelten Hills.* 1899. [Archives of the Old York Road Historical Society]

Heacock, Joseph Jr. *Personal Diary,* 1871. Heacock Papers, Friends Library at Swarthmore College.

Heacock, Senator Joseph. "Eulogy," Harrisburg, PA: *Proceedings of the Senate of Pennsylvania in Commemoration of Hon. Thomas B. Harper, Late a Senato."* Tuesday, March 7, 1911.

Heacock, Priscilla. "Chelten Hills School." Paper read before the Jenkins Town Lyceum, 1942. [Archives of the Old York Road Historical Society]

Heckewelder, Hohn and Peter S. Du Ponceau. "Names Which the Lenni Lenape or Delaware Indians, Who Once Inhabited This Country, Had Given." *Transactions of the American Philosophical Society,* New Series Vol. 4 (1834).

Heinemann, Heinz. *Before Memory Fades: A History of the Early Days of Calvary Presbyterian Church.* Wyncote, PA: Calvary Presbyterian Church, 1991.

Heinemann, Heinz. "Wyncote Elementary School," 2008. [Private essay on Mr. Heinemann's reflections of school and home in the early 1930's] Archives of the Old York Road Historical Society.

Holme, Thomas. "Pennsylvania - A Mapp of Ye Improved Part of Pensilvania in America, Divided in Countyes, Townships and Lotts. Surveyed by Tho: Holme." London: George Willdey, 1687.

Hotchkin, Rev. S. F. *The York Road Old and New.* Philadelphia, PA : Binder and Kelly Publisher, 1892.

Jowett, Garth S. and Victoria O'Donnell. *Propaganda and Persuasion.* Thousand Oaks, CA: Sage Publications 2006.
Kalfus, Ken. *Christopher Morley's Philadelphia.* New York, NY: Fordham University Press, 1990.

Kalm, Peter. *Travels into North America,* London, England: T. Lowndes, 1773.

Kohler, M.L. *Jenkintown.* Philadelphia, PA: 1900

Lippincott, Horace Mather. "Chelten Hills." *The Jenkins Town Lyceum.* Jenkintown, PA: The Jenkins Town Lyceum, 1938.

Lippincott, Horace Mather. "Chelten Hills School," *Old York Road Historical Society Bulletin,* Vol. VII (1943).

Lippincott, Horace Mather. *Early Philadelphia: Its People, Life, and Progress.* Philadlephia, PA: J.B. Lippincott Company, 1917.

Lippincott, Horace Mather. "The Old York Road." *The Old York Road Historical Society Bulletin*, Jenkintown, PA, Vol. 1 (October 1937).

Lippincott, Horace Mather. *The Mather Family of Cheltenham, Pennsylvania.* Philadelhia, PA: Lewis J. Levick, 1910.

Lippincott, Horace Mather. "Presidents Visit Us." *Old York Road Historical Society Bulletin*, Vol. XIII (1949).

McIlhenney, Senator Francis. Eulogy in "Proceedings of the Senate of Pennsylvania in Commemoration of Hon. Thomas B. Harper, Late a Senator." Harrisburg, PA: Tuesday March 7, 1911.

McLane, Allan. Journal. Dover, DE: Allan McLane Papers, Archives of the State of Delaware, 1779.

McVeigh, Wayne. Letter from Wayne McVeigh to Wharton Barker, March 18, 1881. Wharton Barker Papers, Box 1. The Library of Congress.

Miller, Edward. "Reports of Edward Miller, chief engineer, to the president and directors of the North Pennsylvania Railroad Company," Philadelphia, PA: The North Pennsylvania Railroad Company, 1854. (The Hagley Museum and Library, Wilmington, Delaware)

Mintz, Stephen. *The History of Private Life.* http://www.digitalhistory.uh.edu/historyonline/private_life.cfm. September, 2008.

Minutes of the Wyncote Civic Association. Elkins Park, PA: Archives of the Cheltenham Township Historical Commission.

Minutes of the Wyncote Men's Club 1906 - 1936. Elkins Park, PA: Archives of the Cheltenham Township Historical Commission.

Mitchell, Silas Weir. *Hugh Wynne: Free Quaker.* New York, NY: The Century Company, 1896.

Mitchell, S. Weir. S. Weir Mitchell Collection, Diary, Box 15, Series 5. College of Physicians of Philadelphia Library. Philadelphia, PA: 1895.

Morgan, Ralph. "Cheltenham Township in History." *The Jenkins Town Lyceum.*
Jenkintown, PA: The Jenkins Town Lyceum 1938.

Morgan, Ralph. Letter to Charles Mebus.. Jenkintown, PA: The Old Road Historical Society Archives, February 24, 1933

Morley, Christopher. *Mince Pie.* New York, NY: George C. Doran Company, 1920.

Morris, Harrison S. *Lyrics and Landscapes* New York, NY: The Century Company, 1908.

Mott, Lucretia. Letter from Lucretia Mott to Martha Coffin Wright, 5 September 1855. [Mott Collection, Friends Historical Library, Swarthmore College].

Myers, Albert Cook, ed. *Narratives of Early Pennsylvania, West New Jersey, and Delaware, 1630 – 1707.* New York, NY: Charles Scribner's Sons, 1912.

Nash, Gary B. *First City: Philadelphia and the Forging of Historical Memory.* Philadelphia, PA: University of Pennsylvania Press, 2001.

North Pennsylvania Rail Road Company. *An Act of Incorporation of the North Pennsylvania Railroad Company, and the supplements thereto: with the general railroad law of Pennsylvania.* Philadelphia, PA: 1853. [Hagley Museum and Library]

North Pennsylvania Rail Road Company. *Annual Reports of the Board of Directors of the NPRR: 1853 to 1870.* Philadelphia, PA: Crissy & Markeley Printers, 1870.

Parry, Elwood C. *Diary.* Wyncote, PA: 1889. [Cheltenham Township Historical Commission]

Parry, Jr., Ellwood C. "Where Did the Nineties Come From?" Address at 75th Anniversary of Calvary Church of Wyncote, November 2, 1967. Jenkintown, PA: Archives of the Old York Road Historical Society, 1967.

Parry, Jr., Ellwood C. "Treason in Abington," *Old York Road Historical Society Bulletin,* Vol. XXVIII (1967).

Pebble, Jim. Private e-mail to Thomas Wieckowski, January 28, 2003.

Penn, William. "Some Account of the Province of Pennsylvania," London, 1681. http://www.swarthmore.edu/SocSci/bdorsey1/41docs/38-pen.html

Platt, Frederick. "Horace Trumbauer in Wyncote." *Old York Road Historical Society Bulletin*, Vol. XLV (1985).

Report of the Commissioner of Agriculture. Washington, D.C.: Government Printing Office, 1868.

Report of the Transactions of the Pennsylvania State Agricultural Society. Harrisburg, PA: B. Singerly, Printer, 1871.

Robert's, Ellwood. *Robert's Biographical Annals, 1904.* Montgomery County, PA: Vol. II – Part 17: <www.rootsweb.com/usgenweb/pa/montgomery/roberts/roberts 217.html>

Root, A. I. *The ABC and XYZ of Bee Culture.* Medina, OH: The A. I. Root Company, 1919.

Rothschild, Elaine W. *A History of Cheltenham Township.* Elkins Park, PA: Cheltenham Township Historical Commission, 1976.

Scharf, John Thomas. *History of Philadelphia, 1609-1884.* Philadelphia, PA: L.H. Everts & Co., 1884.

Scharnberger, Christopher K. Earthquake *Hazard in Pennsylvania*. Harrisburg, PA: Millersville University, Pennsylvania Geologic Survey, 2003.

Scheele, Carl H. *A Short History of the Mail Service*. Washington, DC: Smithsonian Institution Press, 1970.

Schenick, Helene, and Michael Parrington. *Workshop of the World*. Philadelphia, PA: Oliver Evans Press, 1990.

Schmidtetter, Blanche. "A History of the Old York Road." *The Jenkins Town Lyceum*. Jenkintown, PA: The Jenkins Town Lyceum, 1938.

Scott, Alexander W. *History and Development of the School District of Cheltenham Township*. Elkins Park, PA: Cheltenham Township, 1983.

Scott, Donald. *Camp William Penn*. Charleston, SC: Arcadia Press, 2008.

Shaeckleton, Robert. *The Book Of Philadelphia*. Philadelphia: PA: The Penn Publishing Company, 1918.

Sinkler, Charles. "Traditions Concerning the Old York Road," *Old York Road Historical Society Bulletin*, Jenkintown, PA. Volume V (1941).

Smellie, ed., Alexander. *The Journal of John Woolman*. London: Andrew Melrose, Publisher, 1898.

Smith, Charles Harper. "The Battle of the Billet Reviewed." *Old York Road Historical Society Bulletin,* Vol. IX (1945).

Spruill, Dorothy. *A Memoir of Christine Chester Crowell*. Unpublished manuscript, 1990.

Spruill, Dorothy. *President's Message,* Woman's Club of Wyncote. Fall, 2008.

Spruill, Dorothy. "The Wyncote Civic Association," *The Wall Paper*.[Newsletter of the Cheltenham Township Historical Commission] Volume II Number II (Autumn 1989).

Stock, Noel. *Ezra Pound's Pennsylvania*, Toledo, OH: Friends of the University of Toledo Libraries, 1976.

Thompson, Charles Willis. "The Truth About Nearing's Case: Both Sides of the Controversy That Has Raised a Storm at the University of Pennsylvania." *New York Times Magazine* (18 July 1915).

Trego, Charles B. *Geography of Pennsylvania*. Philadelphia, PA: Edward C. Biddle, 1843.

Twining, Thomas. *Travels in America One Hundred Years Ago*. New York, NY: Harper & Brothers, 1893.

Van Diver, Bradford B. *Roadside Geology of Pennsylvania*. Missoula, MT: Mountain Press Publishing Company, 1990.

Wainwright, Nicholas B. *History of the Philadelphia Electric Company*. Philadelphia, PA: Philadelphia Electric Company, 1961.

Wallace, Paul A. *Indian Paths of Pennsylvania*. Harrisburg, PA: Pennsylvania Historical & Museum Commission, 1993.

Walzer, John F. "Colonial Philadelphia and Its Backcountry." *Winterthur Portfolio*, Vol 7. (1972).

Watson, John Fanning Watson. *Annals of Philadelphia and Pennsylvania*. Vol. II. Philadelphia, PA: Elijah Thomas, 1857. [Note that Willis P. Hazard did the illustrations for the book 1881 version of this book.]

Weigley,Russell F. ed. *Philadelphia: A 300 Year History*. New York, NY:
W.W. Norton & Company, 1982.

Weslager, C.A. *Dutch Explorers, Traders and Settlers in the Delaware Valley, 1609-1664*. Philadelphia, PA: University of Pennsylvania Press, 1961.

Yates, W. Ross. *Joseph Wharton: Quaker, Industrial Pioneer*. Bethlehem, PA: Lehigh University Press, 1987.

Zoller, Alfred F. "Bells, Whistles, Smoke and Flames: The History of Enterprise Fire Company of Hatboro." Hatboro, PA: 1990. <http:// www.efc.com/hisotry.htm>

Zulker, William Allen. *John Wanamaker: King of Merchants*. Wayne, PA: Eaglecrest Press, 1993.

Index